# DOORS TO LIFE

## The Stories of Gustav Jeeninga

by
Gustav Jeeninga

Anderson University Press
Anderson, Indiana  U.S.A.

Copyright 2002, by Anderson University Press

ISBN No.:  0-9646682-2-X

Published by Anderson University Press
Anderson University, 1100 East Fifth Street
Anderson, Indiana 46012  U.S.A.

Printed in the United States of America.

Project editor, Barry L. Callen.
Cover design by Kerry Shaw.
Interior layout and design by Randal Dillinger.
Editorial assistance by Arlene C. Callen.
Cover photo, "Maulbronn Monastery - 1997" by Lisa J. Franco. Used by
permission.

An ancient Hebrew coin is used as backgound for each of the chapter numbers. For detail on the coin, see chapter 29.

**For information**, write to the Editor, Dr. Barry L. Callen, c/o Anderson
University, 1100 East Fifth Street, Anderson, Indiana 46012. Email:
blcallen@anderson.edu. For additional titles available from Anderson
University Press, consult the Anderson University website at www.ander-
son.edu/aupress.

**For ordering**, inventory and sales are handled through Warner Press,
Anderson, Indiana. To order this or other Anderson University Press
books, contact Warner Press, specifying that you wish to order a product
of Anderson University Press (Warner Press inventory numbers are found
on the Anderson University Press website). Warner Press contact information: Phone: 1-800-741-7721. Fax: 1-800-347-6411. Email:
wporders@ warnerpress.org.

# DEDICATION

These stories are dedicated to my loving wife
Aletta, who comforted me when I failed,
who taught me humility when I was honored,
and who made our marriage a success.

# APPRECIATION

I extend special thanks to a few of the many special friends
who encouraged me and helped me write these stories.

Paul Austin
Barry L. Callen
Jeannette Freyburger
Joann Hill
Robert Lowndes
Tellis Martin
Charles and Bertha Perrill
Russ Sasscer
Marjorie Shuman
Ruth and Sam Smith
Chuck Zeigler

Charlotte Zeigler who convinced me
to write these stories for family and
friends to read, then typed many
of the original manuscripts.

# TABLE OF CONTENTS

## IV. LIFE IN ANDERSON

## V. EXPLORING THE ANCIENT PAST

## VI. LOOKING TO THE FUTURE

# FOREWORD

ANDERSON UNIVERSITY HAS BEEN BLESSED by many faculty members who have served the campus for several decades each, making the difference that only a longterm commitment can create. Rarely, however, has a teacher left footprints that point the way for future generations as have those of Gustav Jeeninga. Some of his prints lead to various classrooms, some to the Museum of Bible and Near Eastern Studies that he founded on the Anderson campus, while others lead in numerous directions worldwide. Now through this book we are enabled to view his whole life path as he tells of having walked through many doors that led him to life.

This is no mere autobiography—a kind of chronology that many of us might write. Rather, it is a series of graphic stories, many illumined by Gus' own superb photography, each illustrating how a life should be lived—daring, passionate, open to God. These truly are amazing and sometimes almost unbelievable stories. For instance, to share with him the May-June 1945 trek from the Nazi slave-labor experiences of Eastern Europe home to Holland is unforgettable reading. To sense the pathos and meet the people along his path, first home from war, then on to higher education in America, and then to ancient sites in the Middle East and Latin America, is to be instructed and immensely encouraged along one's own path.

I have long been an admirer of Dr. Gustav Jeeninga, particularly for what he could bring to students through his gifted instruction—so special in style and technique that a unique classroom in Decker Hall on the Anderson campus had to be designed to enable his teaching. As his Dean and later President, I appointed him to his teaching post and shared his vision. Later we became next-door neighbors, a personal privilege.

Dr. Jeeninga, "Gus," states that "so many doors have opened to me" and that "Anderson University challenged me to give of my best, look very carefully, and reach for the stars." Praise be! Through these stories, he testifies and reassures us that when we allow the Bible to illumine and guide our daily walk, powerful things will happen. Thank you, Gus, for continuing to teach us all!


Robert A. Nicholson
President Emeritus, Anderson University.
Colleague and Appreciative Friend,
Spring 2002

# FOREWORD

MENTION THE NAME "GUSTAV JEENINGA" in certain circles and hearts are warmed as memorable relationships are recalled by former students, faculty colleagues, and sharers in archaeological digs. There is a host of friends and associates from across the years at Anderson University and places far beyond. This is to be expected because Dr. Jeeninga has been one of the most distinctive, lovable, and productive scholars and teachers among the many who have served at Anderson University.

Gustav Jeeninga and I have been friends across more than forty years. We first met in 1962. He was an Associate Professor in the Department of Bible at Anderson College when I arrived on campus that year to speak during Religious Emphasis Week. We met after the first chapel service in which I spoke. He approached me, chuckling over something comical that had happened early in that service. As President Robert H. Reardon was introducing me, giving details about my life and work, a *faux pas* occurred as Reardon closed his introduction with the words, "I now present to you, Raymond Massey." As I stood and walked toward the pulpit, there was a mild rumble of laughter in the packed auditorium. Both students and faculty had politely reacted to President Reardon's embarrassing mistake in calling the name of *Raymond* Massey, the well-known star of stage and screen, rather than *James*, my first name. I knew that all eyes were on me, wondering *if* or *how* I might handle the mistake before I went on with speaking. Knowing President Reardon as I did, I was comfortable with what I felt would be appropriate on my part. I gave a mild smile and in an unhurried pace I said to the faculty and students, "I observe that your president is much more familiar with the world of the theatre than with the world of the church!" The previous mild rumble of laughter in the pews became a relieving big laugh throughout the crowd. Reardon accepted my levity with the grace I expected, aware as I was that the chapel crowd had enjoyed seeing him momentarily red-faced. Gustav Jeeninga, who loved humor, had especially enjoyed that moment and he voiced his appreciation to me for the way I had humorously handled the matter. I never forgot the spirit of his comment and the way he responded to my additional speaking across that week.

Seven years later I was back on campus as a fellow faculty member with Jeeninga, teaching courses in Bible and religious studies. As Gus and I explored ways to share with greater appeal the information of our required courses in Bible, he suggested, and I readily agreed, that we team teach. This inventive approach proved so popular that we continued it, and across each school year students rushed to find seats in our class. It was an enviable joy we had across those years to see new students line up seeking our signatures to be admitted once our class enrollment quota was filled!

In this autobiography Gustav Jeeninga has reported on this team teaching and on so much more from his life and labors. It is a reporting done with his characteristic gusto, openness, honesty, and humor. This book honors God who opened the eyes of its writer on "doors to life." I am confident that it will benefit many others whose hearts earnestly seek faith, hope, and meaning.

James Earl Massey
Dean and Professor Emeritus,
Anderson University and School of Theology,
Colleague and Appreciative Friend,
Spring 2002

# INTRODUCTION

*"The sayings of the wise are like goads, and like nails firmly fixed*
*are the collected sayings that are given by one shepherd. Of anything*
*beyond these, my child, beware. Of making many books there is no*
*end, and much study is a weariness of the flesh."*
*(Ecclesiastes 12:11-12)*

THE IMPULSE FOR WRITING THIS BOOK had its origin in story telling around dinner tables. For many years a group of close friends, many of them colleagues at Anderson University, would eat out together with my wife Aletta and me. Most of the time the conversation centered around social, religious, and political issues as they occurred on our campus or on the national or international scene. Because many members of our group had traveled widely, the conversation subjects always were interesting and enlightening, sometimes entertaining and even tragic.

Again and again my friends would tell me, after I had told some of my life's stories, that I should write them down. They even suggested that I should write a book. I hesitated, thinking that the material might not be significant enough for a wider audience. I was cautioned by Ecclesiastes 12:11-12. In later retirement years at Penney Farms in Florida, I had numerous occasions to repeat my stories with a range of new friends, again people who were rich in experiences from around the world. From them came the same book suggestion. Finally, I began the venture of writing, what my wife Aletta called "Gus' Confessions." At first my thought was that I would prepare a few personal reflections for a small group of family and close friends. Then in 2001 my friend Barry Callen, Editor of the newly founded Anderson University Press, journeyed to my retirement home and helped me gain a larger vision. The result is now this volume. Life has opened to me in many marvelous ways and I am ready to tell the world about it.

The hope in my sharing these stories is that they will convey intrinsic value beyond merely the details of my own life. These stories reveal the intellectual and religious conflicts I have faced and the ways in which I have handled new problems that often crossed my path. They include images of childhood, faith, and fear—especially fear during the violent World War II period. Some of these stories provide dramatic glimpses of human beings caught in terrifying circumstances. I lived through it all and survived. Some of the stories reflect the strong religious influence that my parents had on my whole outlook on life, as illustrated in the stories "Almost a New Lifestyle" and "Murder on My Mind." My subsequent migration from the Netherlands to the United States in 1947 launched many meaningful developments in my life's journey beyond the tragedy of war. Numerous opportunities and challenges emerged in the following decades, most bringing joy, some pain, all a little more wisdom. Therefore, the title of this book, *Doors To Life*, is quite fitting. Many doors have opened to enrich my life.

My first years (1924-1927) were spent in South Limburg, the Netherlands. It was there where my cradle stood. My father worked as a coal miner, deep under ground, and later became a merchant and Christian pastor. At the age of three, my family moved to IJmuiden, a city some twenty miles west of Amsterdam. IJmuiden was founded in 1876 when the North Sea canal was dug. This canal connected Amsterdam with the North Sea and so opened up my hometown to the world. The city's modern locks could accommodate what then were the largest ocean liners and battleships plowing the waters of the world.

At the start of World War II, at six o'clock in the morning of the 10th of May, 1940, I personally witnessed the first German bombs falling on my hometown. This was my introduction to the five-year-long period of occupation and control of our lives by the German Army. At the time of the German invasion, I was sixteen years old. From 1943-45 I was a German slave laborer. I was shipped off to work as a bread baker in Berlin-Blankenfelde. When the Russian army captured Berlin in 1945, I began the terrible task of finding my way home. I have recounted these awful days in the story "My Long Journey Home," memories drawn from a diary I kept along the way.

In May of 1947, at the age of twenty-three, I arrived in the United States as an immigrant. In Chicago I worked as a baker for my uncles. Then in the fall 1947 I enrolled as a freshman at Anderson College (University) to study for the Christian ministry. It was a college of the Church of God, my religious heritage. In 1951 I graduated and started graduate studies at Union Theological Seminary in New York City. After having completed one year of studies at Union, I decided to make a trip around the world, taking one whole year to do it. This journey I hoped would broaden my understanding globally. To pay for this great adventure, I worked for my Uncle Ernest Werner in Chicago from 1951 to 1952. Then from 1952 until 1953 I globetrotted by airplane, hitch-hiking, bus, taxi, and on foot to various destinations worldwide.

While on my world trip I married Aletta van der Breggen, a Dutch surgical nurse whom I had known as a church member in my father's congregation in Haarlem, the Netherlands. The wedding took place before a judge in the city of Haarlem on September 2, 1953. Later, on June 20, 1954, a church wedding was arranged in Park Place Church of God in Anderson, Indiana, with Dr. Charles E. Brown officiating.

After I returned to Chicago from my world trip, I felt a strong desire to become a teacher of Bible and biblical archaeology. Therefore, in 1954 I enrolled at the Oriental Institute on the campus of the University of Chicago. In 1957 I transferred to Northern Baptist Theological Seminary in Chicago, where I earned the B.D. degree and then a Th. D. in June, 1960. In the fall of 1960 I began my career as a Bible teacher at Anderson College. In the years that followed I participated in six major archaeological excavations in Jordan, Cyprus, and Israel.

Retirement came in 1989 and in 1992 Aletta and I moved to Penney Retirement Community (Penney Farms) in Florida. Aletta, who was a loving wife and strong supporter of my career for 47 years, passed away on November 10, 2000. I have continued living at Penney Farms and have stayed active there in various volunteer activities. It was there that I wrote these stories of my life, guided by the editorial assistance of my longtime friend and colleague Barry L. Callen, Editor of Anderson University Press.

I would be amiss not to highlight the significant role that Anderson University has played in my life's development. While I was a student there a half-century ago, the institution opened numerous doors to my inquisitive mind. My first view ever through a powerful microscope, watching the life cycle of amoeba and hydra, shook my self-confidence. Up to that moment I would have put down my life to defend my conviction that in that glass of water there was nothing but pure $H_2O$. In a small way I quickly became a scientist. From that day on I have found it difficult to be sure of most things. The thought always arises, "If I only had the right powerful microscope available I would be able to see the facts and the issues more clearly." While a young man, Anderson University challenged me to give of my best and reach for the stars.

In 1960, nine years after my graduation, I returned to my alma mater and for twenty-nine years taught on the Anderson campus in the areas of Bible, Near Eastern studies, and archaeology of the Near East and Latin America. Eventually I became founding Director of a museum on campus dedicated to Near

Eastern studies and Chair of the Department of Religious Studies. Whatever my achievements during those years, however, they were due in a large measure to the inspiration, support, friendship, and encouragement I received from the students who attended my classes and from my colleagues with whom I interacted and the administrators who supported my tenure and, most of all, my dreams.

I therefore offer these written accounts in the hope that the reader will experience some delight and even find some kinship with my adventures. They are but an expression of the experiences of us all. So many doors have opened to me. May, through the reading of these stories, a new door toward life swing open for you. Life is a trail of stories, tales full of joy, tragedy, and meaning—especially when illumined by faith. Whether I succeed in providing you with a joyful and meaningful reading experience I may never know, but not knowing is also a part of life.

Gustav Jeeninga
Penney Farms, Florida
Spring 2002

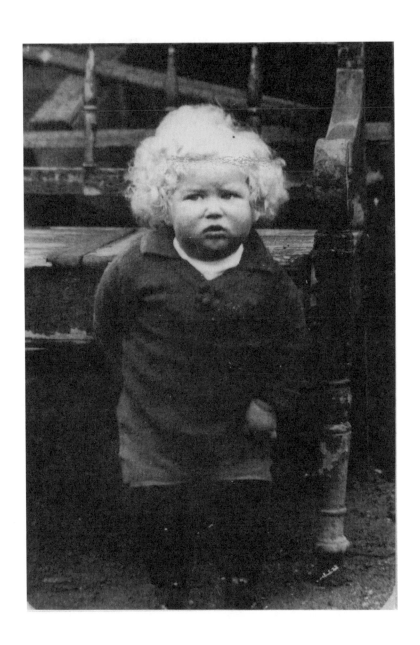

# PERSONAL ORIGINS
## 1924 ~ 1937

# LIFE'S BEGINNING
# AND SCARS

I WAS BORN ON NOVEMBER 18, 1924, in Treebeek, in the province of Limburg, the Netherlands. My parents were Fedde Jeeninga and Thea Flohr Werner Jeeninga. Mine was a good family, but

Gustav Jeeninga at age two, hiding the right arm with the split elbow.

some scars came to me soon in life. At first the hot water bottle felt wonderful because the crib was cold. It was winter and the Netherlands was covered by snow and ice. To protect me at three years old, my mother had heated a warm water bottle to place in my crib to keep me warm. After she had pushed the cork stopper tight, she tenderly placed the bottle alongside of my lower hip and soon everyone in the house was at rest.

About midnight my parents were awakened by my agonizing cry and came to my bed to see what ailed me. Since they did not see or notice any special problem they tried to shush me to sleep. As they slipped back to their bedroom, I continued to cry softly for a long time. Not until the morning, after my mother lifted me up from the crib while I screamed loudly, did she discover, to her dismay, that I had been crying all night long because the hot water bottle cork had fallen out and the boiling hot water had severely burned my right buttock.

The burn scar never disappeared and the spot has remained especially sensitive to pain. When I was a teenager, the scar finally brought me one benefit. My older brother Emil and my younger brother Fritz and I would often get in trouble with people in the neighborhood because of our antics. The victims of our tricks would complain to our parents about our misbehavior. This often resulted in a disciplinary action by our father who would find it necessary to whip us with a 1/4" bamboo rod.

After one of these disciplinary episodes, I discovered that when my father struck me on the buttock with the large scar, it hurt me much more than when he struck the other buttock. One day I explained to my dad about the sensitivity of my scarred buttock and pleaded with him not to beat me on that scar. After that conversation my father never again struck me with the rod on the sensitive side. I did, however, have two other problems.

When I was two years old, my parents took me to my grandparents in Recklinghausen Süd, Germany, where I stayed for one week. When my grandmother gave me my bath, she noticed that a small protrusion near my navel, which she knew had been there since my birth, had grown large enough to be the size of a large cherry. Grandmother urged my parents to take me to the hospital in Holland for a diagnosis, which they did. The doctor explained to my parents that it was necessary for them to operate immediately because the growth on my belly was a serious hernia that had reached a critical stage. The operation was successful, but left me with an enormous and ugly scar. Soon after came my elbow problem.

My sister Geertje, six years old, and my older brother Emil, five years old, were pushing and pulling each other in a fight for dominance. They lost control and crashed to the floor. I was three years old and playing with my toys on the floor. They landed on top of me and my right elbow hit the edge of the threshold, splitting it badly. The crushing blow brought tears and a loud crying. My parents rushed me to the hospital. It was Christmas eve. The nurses who received me said tenderly, "Here is our Christmas angel." I was a stubby little boy with a full head of white curly hair and a round baby face. The nurses saw in me one of the celestial stone-carved angels singing and flying around the organs and the altars of many of Europe's cathedrals. Carefully, the nurses laid me in a bed, but there I lay, untreated for three days with a high fever and an infected elbow because the physicians had gone home to celebrate Christmas! Not until the doctors had operated on the elbow did the healing process begin and the Christmas patient receive proper care. The split elbow remained and never again functioned normally. The arm could not be straightened and caused pain increasingly as the years advanced.

"For the Lord does not see as mortals see;
they look on the outward appearance,
but the Lord looks on the heart."
(1 Samuel 16:7b)

# BICYCLING TO FIND
# MY ROOTS

AT THE AGE OF SIXTEEN I started on my dream trip, a journey in search of my father's birthplace. I hoped to see even the house where he first saw the light of day. My bicycle was in good shape for a long trip. The tires had been checked for leaks, wear and tear, and the steering column and the wheels had been greased. The last thing I had done was to give the bicycle a splendid polish, for I was proud of my "fiets" (bicycle) which took me everywhere and never had left me stranded. My destination was the province of Friesland in the northern part of the Netherlands. I was to vacation with my "tante" (aunt) Geertje and my "oom" (uncle) Jeen. At the age of sixteen, this journey was a real challenge. I had never been on such a long bicycle trip by myself.

Gustav Jeeninga at age 16, with bicycle and friend.

The adventure started in IJmuiden, my hometown, some thirty kilometers west of Amsterdam. I biked the first twenty kilometers through the "polders" (diked-in grasslands). I saw Kievits (Lapwings) circling overhead. Often I had been in the polders in early spring to look for Kievit eggs. There was a Dutch tradition that whoever brought to the Queen of Holland the first Kievit egg in spring would receive a gift from the Queen. This special opportunity had escaped me every year I had tried. At about 10:00 a.m. I arrived in Amsterdam. At the harbour I bought passage on a ferry to cross the Zuider Zee. From Amsterdam the boat took me to the town of Lemmer on the west coast of Friesland, some forty kilometers away. From Lemmer there would be another thirty kilometers or so before I reached my relatives' house, located very close to the "Lange Rak" (Long River). They lived on the other side of the river near Uilesprong. The only way to get to the other side of this waterway was by ferry. This ferry (*Foetveer*) was a flat, wide boat pulled across the canal by means of a wooden handle connected to a steel cable.

Because very few people traveled in this hinterland, it was necessary to use a primitive bell hanging on a pole at the water's edge. The bell consisted of a part of an old iron machine hung from a chain, which was struck with an iron bar that produced a deep, but hard clinking sound. I struck the bell hard and waited. Soon a man with a short white beard appeared and looked me over briefly. I told him that I was visiting with my oom and tante Akkerman. He nodded lightly, but said nothing, and I stepped on board, taking my bicycle with me. When we reached the other side, my aunt and uncle were waiting for me and took me to their house a short distance down the dike. Because it was suppertime, tante Geertje fed me a typical Friesian vegetable soup. It was fantastic, but that was partly because I was starving. I had not eaten or drunk anything all day. In those years I was somewhat bashful around strangers. I had no experience of eating in a restaurant, so I avoided them. Also, in this part of Friesland it would be nearly impossible to find a restaurant. This was the "outback" of Friesland.

Soon after supper I told tante and oom that I was very tired from the long and arduous bicycle trip and would like to retire. I had been looking around the house and noted that it was very small and there were no bedrooms. Therefore I asked, "Tante, where do I sleep?" Tante said, "Come follow me." She took me to the kitchen, which also served as the entrance to the house, and pointed to a ladder which reached to an opening in the ceiling and into the attic. Tante said, "Guus" (my Dutch name), oom Jeen has fixed for you a nice straw mattress up there. There are some blankets there also. You will be quite comfortable. If you need to go to the bathroom, the kitchen door will be unlocked and the outhouse is to the left, some twenty feet away. I stiffly climbed up the ladder and in no time sleep took over. The last question I pondered was, where do tante and oom sleep? I learned the next morning.

Breakfast out of the way, I asked oom Jeen, "Oom, how do I find the "Lytsehuske" (Friesian for "little house") where my father was born? Oom Jeen put his hand on my shoulder and said, "Let's go outside, Guus, and I will show it to you. We walked to the road near the ferry. Then, using his crooked cane, Oom Jeen pointed to a house far off across the grasslands. "Look Guus," he said, "look towards the horizon and you can see it." I looked and saw a small structure surrounded by

Fedde Jeeninga (1895-1965).

polders. My heart was beating fast and I was anticipating what effect my visit to that insignificant looking structure would have on my understanding of my roots. Only when I arrived at the little house did I see how small and simple it really was. On one end of the structure there was a short chimney that extended about two feet above the red tiled roof. There were two small windows, one with a crack in it, on the north side of the house. Here also

Fedde Jeeninga's birthplace.

was the location of a door. A small window provided light to the attic. It was in this house that my father was born.

However, we must take one step back into history to anchor father's beginnings. Before father was born, the family lived on a stationary houseboat, floating on a "sloot" (ditch). The houseboat was very old and leaking, so much so that it became necessary to pull the houseboat onto land. There was no money to pay for a major repair. So, using the wood from the houseboat, my grandfather and some friends constructed a very simple house with a brick exterior. Soon after the family had moved in, my father was born and his mother died. It fell to tante Geertje, the oldest child and only girl, to run the household. Grandfather, and in later years the three sons, all worked as farm hands in the region. All these thoughts were going through my mind as I remember them from father's childhood stories. Now looking at the house and its environment more closely, I noted a small storage shed and nearby a nearly collapsed outhouse. The surroundings made a sad and forsaken impression. One could imagine a few chickens, goats, and sheep that during snowy and freezing days would have found some protection in the small trees and bushes nearby. In every direction the landscape was purely Friesian, polders everywhere. Among the animals in the polders were rabbits, geese, and varieties of ducks. Hunting in father's day was by license only.

Early the next day I went down to the kitchen. Since there was no running water in the house, I pumped water into a metal bowl and washed up. Tante Geertje put a typical Dutch breakfast on the table consisting of hot tea, open-faced sandwiches with Gouda or Edam cheese, chocolade-hagel, my breakfast favorite, and a slice of Friese Gemberkoek (Friesian gingerbread). It was during breakfast that I discovered where tante and oom had slept. I noticed on one side of the living room, which also served as dining room, etc., two large cupboard doors. The doors were standing slightly open. I was astonished to see that it was not a cupboard behind the doors but a closet bed for two. I had never seen anything like it and it baffled me that people would crawl into a closet, close the doors and go to sleep. Of course, I kept quiet about my thoughts.

Several days later I was bicycling back home to IJmuiden. I was feeling quite satisfied with the results of my search for family roots in Friesland. I had seen the "sloot" where at one time my grandparents houseboat was slowly sinking. I had been able to see and photograph the house were my father was born, and I had walked in the countryside where my father had grown up. It had been a marvelous pilgrimage. The fact that tante Geertje had told me, "Guus, remember, nothing has changed much here during the last fifty years or more," made this research for roots an unforgettable experience. *Zoals het klokje thuis tikt, tikt het nergens.* "Home sweet home."

## ADDENDUM

In 1967 Aletta (my wife) and I travelled to Friesland, the Netherlands, in the hope of obtaining some information about my father's origin. We went to the office of Civil Registration of the municipality of Opsterland, near the town of Terwispel where father was born. The gentleman behind the window asked, "How can I help you, sir?" I introduced myself and explained that I was trying to find some information about Fedde Jeeninga, my father. The official tilted his head slightly and said, with feeling in his voice, "Please accept my condolences. I learned just yesterday of the tragic news of how your father was knocked down from his bicycle by a drunken driver and subsequently died in the hospital from his wounds." Before the clerk could continue, I interrupted him and said. "Thank you for your sympathy, but the Fedde Jeeninga you are referring to was not my father. My father lived in the U.S.A. for many years and died two years ago from a terminal illness." We all thought it to be very interesting that the name Fedde Jeeninga was still being passed on in the descendents of the original Jeeninga ancestry. The clerk then brought the civil registration volume and permitted me to take a photograph of the page where my father's birth was registered. The birth date was March 24, 1894.

# SOURCES OF MY FAITH

MANY TIMES I HAVE HEARD, "As the king does, so do his people." The best example I have of how a Christian life ought to be lived is what I have seen in my parents. Through word and deed, they shaped my understanding of what it means to be and live as a Christian. The Bible was read daily at the dinner table and was the basis for short devotions after each major meal. In my boyhood home I learned to memorize Bible verses and I acquired much common wisdom. I learned to recite wisdom sayings. Over the years these sayings molded my understanding of the world around me and influenced my outlook on life. Here are a few examples of Dutch proverbs (with English translation).

> "Al is de leugen noch so snel, de waarheid achter-haalt haar wel." *(Honesty is the best policy.)*
>
> "Hoge boomen vangen veel wind." *(Tall trees catch the most wind.)*
>
> "Beter vijf vogels in de hand, dan tien in de lucht." *(Better five birds in hand then ten in the air.)*
>
> "Hoogmoed komt voor de val." *(Pride comes before the fall.)*
>
> "Na regen komt zonneschijn." *(After rain comes sunshine.)*

Besides common wisdom, proverbs, and my parents as prime examples, I was strongly influenced by the teachings of the Ten Commandments. My parents were brilliant life lights. They showed me the road ahead even when everything looked black. They emphasized the importance of a life of service to God and how to follow Jesus, and always to live by God's Word, the Holy Bible.

Fedde and Thea (Flohr Werner) Jeeninga.

My parents left me a copy of their personal testimonies of what was most important to them in this life. I share these testimonies with you in all their simplicity, but they are expressions of a profound faith in God and in the living Jesus Christ. These testimonies were the last thoughts my parents left in order to show me the abundant life. My personal testimony is that they succeeded. I have translated my father's words from the original Dutch.

## TESTIMONY OF FEDDE JEENINGA
## (MY FATHER)

I was born on March 24, 1894, in the province of Friesland, The Netherlands. My parents were members of the Reformed church and the family was brought up in that faith with some zeal, which was especially due to the devout life of my mother. I was made to go to church and Sunday School regularly. I emphasize "made to go" because I did not like to go. I went to church against my will. Nevertheless, this Christian upbringing had its advantage. I strongly believed that the Bible was the Word of God. If someone would have talked about the Bible in a mocking way, I would have fought to defend it.

Above all, I had a Christian mother. From what my older sister told me, my mother was saved as a young girl and had the experience of the working of the Holy Spirit. In her youth, the Holy Spirit had convinced my mother to discontinue her friendship with a girl who lived deeply in sin. My mother told the girl about her experience and broke up the association with her. In 1902, when I was eight years old, my mother passed away after several years of serious illness. She had not been afraid to die. Relatives had called an old Christian friend of hers who asked her, "Are you going to heaven, Albertje?" She answered him, pointing her finger upward to heaven, and nodded "yes." Then she passed away a few minutes later. She died in peace, having lived a true Christian life.

At times, my brothers and I had been very bad youngsters. At such times, my mother would kneel down with us and pray earnestly for our salvation, which hurt us more than having received a physical punishment. After my mother had died, our family began to break up. Several years later, my sister and two brothers went to Germany. There they lived a worldly life, drinking, dancing, gambling, and many theaters were included in their rounds, but the prayers of a pious mother had not been in vain.

My married sister, while in Germany, gave birth to a son who shortly after his birth became critically ill and died. The midwife who assisted her asked if she had called a doctor. My sister answered, "What can a doctor do for such a small child?" The midwife thought that my sister was just like two people she knew, namely, brother and sister Strunze who attended the Church of God in Recklinghause, Germany. After the midwife came home that evening, she contacted the Strunzes and told them that she had met two Hollanders and thought that they were of the same faith as the Strunzes and also believed in divine healing. She also told them about the sick child who had died. The Strunzes attended the Church of God services regularly and through them my sister came into contact with the Church of God.

Sometime later my sister and two older brothers were all saved at a convention of the Church of God in Essen, Germany. At this time, I was still in Holland. When I went to visit my father one day, he told me of having received a letter from my brothers. He gave me the letter to read. I was very surprised. The previous letters we had received had never been very interesting, but this one was quite different. They wrote about their conversion, the love and grace of God, and the life hereafter. They also wrote a few words of warning to my father and me. We also should be converted and mend our ways. After I had finished reading this letter, my father asked me what I thought of it. "Well," I answered, "if it is true what they write, I guess it is a wonderful thing." I was to learn about this personally sooner than I had expected.

In 1913, I too went to Germany. I distinctly remember that I was to stay with my brother John. When we retired the first evening I was there, my brother took me by the arm and said, "That is no way to retire for the night. First we will pray together." He put me down on my knees where I heard him pray for my salvation. Many thoughts were going through my mind. I had to admit that John had changed. On Sundays my brother and sister came together to talk about the Bible, sing a few songs and pray. As I was listening to them on one of those Sundays, I realized that before their conversion there would have been beer and cards on the table instead of a Bible and a songbook. Now they were singing, "Praise the Lord Who Bought Me." I started going with them to the services. The Lord started to influence my heart. I learned of sin, righteousness, and judgment.

At the end of one particular service in the congregation of Recklinghause, while everyone had knelt down to pray, I got up and went outside. Although we lived right over the church meeting place, I stood leaning against the wall outside and cried bitterly. I felt myself so cursed and lost in the eyes of God, believing that there was no one to help or save me. Still, someone had seen me go out and came to look for me. He took me back inside and we knelt down. The brothers and sisters prayed earnestly for me and talked to me. I became convinced that the Lord had forgiven my sin and I got up and gave a testimony of what God had done for me. In my heart there was a longing to go back to Holland to talk to my old friends and relatives about this wonderful thing which had happened to me. It was not very long afterwards that my brother John and I decided to go to Holland. I had quite a few things to straighten out there. I had done many wrongs there because my father was never home except on weekends and mother had passed away. I had been on my own.

When I arrived at my birthplace in Friesland, the people soon heard what had happened and what I was doing. They stopped me in the street to find out for themselves what they had been told. They found it hard to believe because they had known me so well. I had a wonderful opportunity to testify. After I had settled everything, I went back to Germany in good spirits and happy to be in the right with God and man.

## TESTIMONY OF THEA FLOHR WERNER JEENINGA (MY MOTHER)

My mother's testimony was written about one year before her death on June 6, 1971. Mother was born in Germany, brought up in Danzig, and married my father in Recklinghause, Germany. They met in the Church of God congregation in Recklinghause and soon moved to Limburg, The Netherlands. My mother spoke German well. After her marriage she learned Dutch and during her advanced years learned English while living in the U.S.A.

This is my testimony. I start with Psalms 103:1-4. I was born August 15, 1895. My parents attended the Baptist Church. I was in Sunday School since I was four years old. It was on a

Monday evening in January, 1907. It was revival time. I cannot recall the sermon but I never forget what happened that night. I was under great conviction, and felt like running out and far away, but the pastor said that everyone who wished to serve the Lord should stand. So I was quick on my feet and went forward. I cried very hard.

My Sunday School teacher knelt next to me and asked me some questions, but I had no answer, only tears. She asked me why I was crying. "Oh," I said, "I am a sinner and want to live for the Lord." She said, "Do you believe the Lord will forgive you?" "Yes," I said. She said, "Ask Jesus if he will forgive you."

I could not find the words, but after the teacher prayed for me I felt more free and asked the Lord to come into my heart, and I promised to live for Him. The teacher asked me again if I believed the Lord accepted me, and when I answered positively, a wonderful peace came over me and I thanked the Lord. I was so happy that I was jumping up and down on the way home, and singing a wonderful song. "What happiness it is to be saved through Jesus' blood," I sang. Indeed, "Jesus is mine."

# THE PASTOR'S
# GROCERY STORE

DECIDING TO LEAVE TREEBEEK, a Dutch mining town, was not easy for my parents. My father had a steady job working underground, but by 1927 his health was suffering immensely. My parents therefore had come to an agreement. The family would move. Father had secured a job in IJmuiden, a town some twenty miles West of Amsterdam. A large truck was rented with a driver. The whole family and all our belongings were stacked in the back and we left Treebeek early one morning for the all-day journey to IJmuiden. At that time I was three years old.

The economic times were bad in those years, and soon father was out of his job in the new town. My parents discussed how they might survive financially. Half a block away from our home on Eikenstraat 24 was a floundering notion shop that was soon to close its doors. My parents decided that they would venture going into business there. Mother emptied out the front living room of our house and began to sell dry goods. Soon our immediate neighbors began to frequent our "store" and there developed a small income that helped the family survive. Father filled two suitcases with men's shirts, socks, underwear, etc. Riding his transport bicycle, he peddled from door to door selling his merchandise.

In 1932 an important break came for my parents when the store down the street closed its business and moved out of the building. With some financial support supplied by several wholesalers, my parents moved into that store and soon opened their neighborhood grocery shop. The family moved into the back part

Jeeninga's grocery store, IJmuiden, Holland, 1935. Fedde and Thea Jeeninga (back row) with their family (front, left to right): Guus, Aunt Louise, Oppie, Emil, Geertje, and Fritz.

of the building. Even as a youngster, the business success my parents came to enjoy influenced my desire to earn my own money. When I was about eight years old, I asked my father how I could earn some money for myself. "Well son," he answered, "you will have to work for it. You must find out what the people need and offer it for sale to them." He said that he had a practical idea. Soon winter would arrive and there were many old people who needed small quantities of cut wood for starting their stoves. In the shed behind the house we had plenty of empty wooden boxes. "You may have them," he said. "Cut them into small kindling sizes and sell them by the bucket or sack."

"That sounds like a wonderful idea," I said, "but how do I get customers?"

"Guus, that is no problem. You must go from door to door. Ring the bell, introduce yourself, and tell them that you have kindling wood for sale for starting a fire in the stove. Tell them it costs five cents for the bucket full or ten cents for a sack." When I sold my first bucket of kindling wood, I thought I was soon going to be a millionaire. Of course, I learned many lessons, but the undertaking was a real success.

Soon the family grocery business prospered and we had customers spread throughout the town. When each one of us children reached fourteen years of age, we would get more deeply involved making grocery deliveries on our bicycles to faraway customers. When I reached fourteen I decided to visit the distant customers to help them make up their shopping lists. I would read off a list to help them think of what they needed. Then I made the delivery on my father's transportation bicycle that had mounted in front of it a large wicker basket with a closing lid. The basket could hold three good-sized grocery orders, but with that many groceries it was difficult to manage the bicycle.

Through all the years that my parents worked so hard to provide for their six children, they also were totally dedicated to the spread of their Christian faith. Father served a small Church of God congregation of about forty members. He was not paid for his services, but instead he and mother paid the rent for the place where the congregation met.

My mother was born into a Church of God family in Recklinghause, Germany, on August 15, 1895. Her father built a four-story house there in the year 1902, and also provided a meeting room for the fledging congregation on the second floor. It was while my father was working in a German coal mine near Recklinghause that he became acquainted with the Gustav Werner family and the Church of God congregation. During one of the religious services, father found his way to the altar and dedicated his life to Jesus Christ. Not too long afterwards, father met a young woman in the congregation. She was Thea Flohr, who was related to the Werner family. They fell in love with each other and were married in Recklinghause on February 14, 1921.

The Jeeninga grocery store survived the Second World War

and the German occupation. Because three of the six children had migrated to the U.S.A., my parents decided to follow them and reunite the family. The grocery store was sold, and in a few years it closed its doors forever. The store was remodeled into a residential home. Thus, the Jeeninga family store faded into history. However, many memories remain and the family went on, now in the "new world."

# BAKING AND MORALITY

THE BAKING PROFESSION is an occupation that you either love or hate. It is a vocation that requires daily artistic talent. The baker might encounter unusual and sometimes even critical moral and ethical situations. I started to work in a *banketbakkerij* (confectioner's shop) in 1938 as an apprentice—and I loved it. This was fortunate for me.

During World War II, I was forced into German slave labor and was shipped to Berlin, Germany, where Dutch men were made to work in the factories. I managed to persuade the German woman in charge of assigning the men to place me in a bakery. So I worked as a bread baker in Blankenfelde, a suburb of Berlin, from 1943 to 1945. In the bakery it was my responsibility each Friday morning to make buttercrust white bread. Early in the morning a mass of bread dough lay on a workbench waiting for me. I had to divide the dough into individual pieces to be scaled at twelve ounces each, and then knead them into single loaves. For weighing each lump of dough, I used an old-fashioned scale. For chopping up the dough I used a special baker's tool. It was a 5"x 4" stainless steel blade, simply referred to as a "cutter." It had one end rolled down half an inch to form a rounded handle.

The procedure for cutting the dough went like this. I used my right hand (being right handed) to hold the cutter. With my left hand I grasped about a handful of the dough and pulled it toward me. Then with two or three swift strokes I plunged the cutter into the dough till a lump was freed from the heap. The lump was placed on the scale to see how much it weighed. If there was too much, some was removed, if too little, a bit was added. Always I aimed at cutting the dough lump as closely as possible to the precise weight. This did not happen often, but there were times that I succeeded. "Practice makes the master." That's what my father had taught me.

One day something happened that made me stop playing the cutting game. We were working late because of a bombing attack early in the morning. After the sirens blasted a "clear" message, I returned to my workbench. I was determined to catch up on time lost. Confident that I had mastered cutting the dough into pieces rapidly and correctly to weight, I faced the task with determination. Taking the cutter in my right hand, I reached for the dough with my left hand. With slightly spread fingers, I grasped a lump of the dough and pulled it toward me. At the same time I raised my right hand, firmly holding the sharp cutting knife, and brought it quickly down to cut the lump free from the large pile of bread dough. However, in a fraction of a second a mysterious sensation rushed through my sense of touch. At the speed of light or faster, a message flashed through my conscience. It said, "Hold the knife, hold it right there. Don't cut!" My left hand had felt something strange hidden in the dough. There was an object in the lump other than bread dough.

I quickly withdrew my hands. For a brief and intense moment, I stared at the pile of dough and at the lump in particular. "What is going on here? Is this a joke?" "What do I do?" A voice whispered to me, "Forget it! You are late with your work. Don't investigate! Hurry up! Whatever it is, let a Kraut eat it. What do you care!" However, another sentiment filled my mind that posed the question, "Would you want a hungry child to suffer because the loaf about to be eaten was contaminated?" I hesitated. Coming to a final decision, I carefully cut off the lump. With apprehension I slowly broke the lump open. My suspicion that there was something foreign inside the lump was correct. I now could feel it. What could it be? Inch by inch the obscure object began to emerge. It was darkish and to the touch soft and pliable just like the dough. Bit by bit I glimpsed a small, glistening entity that I took for a shining glass bead. I mused, "Interesting." Then I saw another bead just like it. "Fascinating," I whispered. Then I spotted several sprigs and tried to guess what they were. But there was more. Two small "sticks" became visible, soon followed by two more, almost identical. At last, after removing the last clusters of dough, a three-inch long piece of "rope" revealed itself. I saw the trees, but not yet the forest.

Putting all these small items together, the puzzle of what was in the lump was solved. The mysterious entity in the dough was a dead mouse. How fortunate it was that I had found it before baking the loaf with the mouse in it. It would have been a stomach-twisting sensation worse than feeling seasick for the person cutting the loaf of bread and finding a complete, well-baked mouse in it. I had been tempted to leave the mouse where it was. However, my final act was to follow an important lesson my parents had taught me, namely, whatever you want people to do to you, do that to them (Matt. 7:12).

# DE VLIEGENDE HOLLANDER

DAGBLAD VERSPREID DOOR DE GEALLIEERDE LUCHTMACHT No. 130. MAANDAG 23 APRIL 1945

# RUSSEN VECHTEN IN BERLIJN

### Neurenberg en Dessau veroverd — Amerikanen in Tsjecho-Slowakije-Fransch n omsingelen Zwarte Woud en bereiken Zwitsersche grens

*Londen, 23 April.*—De Russen zijn doorgedrongen in Berlijn. Op Maandag 16 April begonnen zij aan het groote, lang-voorbereide offensief over de Oder en de Neisse. Hoewel de Duitschers sterke strijdkrachten hadden samengetrokken tusschen deze rivieren en de Duitsche hoofdstad, konden zij den Russischen stormwals niet tot staan brengen. De legers van Zhoekow en Koniew vorderden gestadig. De Duitschers leden bloedige verliezen. Berlijn werd omsingeld aan de Noord-, Oost- en Zuidzijde. Zaterdagmiddag vielen de eerste Russische granaten bij den *Potsdammer-Platz*. Tevens werd Berlijn voortdurend vanuit de lucht gebombardeerd door Britten, Amerikanen en Russen.

#### In de Duitsche hoofdstad

Het Londensche station, aan wie wij de oproep, heeft, wel, de Duitsche hoofdstad onder artillerievuur te nemen. Zij kwelen niet groot enthousiasme van hun taak. Vanaf Zaterdagmiddag viel een regen van Russische granaten in Berlijn neer.

Brandende huizen stutten in elkaar. In de treinen van de ondergrondsche en van de S-Bahn klonk het geteimmer van gewonden die naar de hospitalen werden vervoerd. Goebbels hield een dreigende rede waarin hij aankondigde, dat iedere maatregelen zouden worden genomen tegen elk huis dat de witte vlag uitstak. De verwarring neemt hand over hand toe. Er wordt veel gepiundeerd. "Brandend, sidderend, twijfelend, scheidend en plunderend gaat," aldus A. den Doolaard voor Radio-Oranje, "de hoofdstad van het duizendjarig plunderrijk zijn ondergang tegemoet."

#### Andere sectoren

Aan enkele andere sectoren van het front in Duitschland wordt nog hevig gevochten, o.a. bij Bremen en Hamburg. Bij de Elbe veroverden de Amerikanen Dessau. De afstand tusschen Amerikanen en Russen was Zondag ingekrompen tot nog slechts enkele tientallen kilometers. Zaterdag j.l. drongen troepen van Patton voor het eerst over de Tsjecho-Slowaaksche grens. Zij namen Asch.

Neurenberg viel op Hitlers 56-sten verjaardag.

In enkele plaatsen in het bevrijde gedeelte des lands hebben de Duitschers bloedigen wraak genomen op de burgerbevolking, die al bij het passeeren van de eerste Geallieerde patrouille verheugd de vlaggen uitstak.

**Weest voorzichtig!**

Wacht niet met alle openbare uitingen van dankbaarheid om de verlossing tot de Geallieerde hoofdmacht U heeft bereikt, en de bevrijding definitief is.

Het Zwarte Woud is omsingeld door Fransche troepen, die de Boven-Donau forceerden en anteren de Zwitsersche grens bereikten bij Schaffhausen.

*Ver over de twee millioen leden van het Herrenvolk hebben zich aan het Westelijk Front overgegeven aan de Geallieerde legers. In groote kampen worden zij geïnterneerd, vóór het transport naar het achterland begint.*

Het front bij Berlijn, op Zondag 22 April (Times.)

## Geallieerden aan de Grebbelinie

### Duitschers houden stand bij Delfzijl

*Londen, 23 April.*—Bij Delfzijl hebben de Duitschers hun tegenstand voortgezet. Poolsche troepen zijn de haven nu tot op 5 km. genaderd. Canadeesche en Britsche troepen staan nu bij de Grebbelinie. De Canadeezen hebben Nijkerk en Hoevelaken bevrijd en bereikten ten Noorden van Amersfoort het inundatiegebied van de Eem. Ede is veroverd door de 49ste Britsche divisie. Deze heeft "Nederlandsche" SS-troepen tegenover zich.

#### De inundaties

J.l. Dinsdagavond hebben de Duitschers aaten gebliazen in de dijken rond den Wieringermeerpolder. De polder liep onder water met het water uit het IJselmeer. Sindsdien echter hebben de Duitschers ook zout water naar binnengebracht. Zout water stroomt nu ook het Noordzeekanaal binnen, doordat de Duitschers bij vloed de sluizen bij IJmuiden open zetten.

Ook de inundatiegebieden bij de Waterlinie zijn door de Duitschers uitgebreid. Hier willen de Duitschers een Geallieerden stoot in de richting van Noord- en Zuid-Holland zooveel mogelijk vertragen.

#### In bevrijd gebied

Berichten van oorlogscorrespondenten hebben een beeld gegeven van de mate waarin de steden in Gelderland, Friesland en Groningen van den strijd hebben geleden.

In Arnhem zijn bijna alle groote gebouwen verwoest, o.a. het Palcis van Justitie, de Groote Kerk en het Stadhuis. De stad is door de Duitschers volkomen leeggeplunderd. In Apeldoorn daarentegen is betrekkelijk weinig schade aangericht. Er vielen niet veel slachtoffers. Het Palcis Het Loo is gespaard, maar heeft ook weinig schade geleden.

Zwolle is weinig beschadigd.

In Meppel is de telefooncentrale opgeblazen, in het station is beschadigd. De stad heeft weinig geleden. Steenwijk is onbeschadigd. In Heerenveen hebben enkele huizen schade opgeloopen. Leeuwarden en Dokkum hebben weinig geleden.

In Groningen is veel schade aangericht in het centrum, maar ook daar was de bevolking uitgelaten van vreugde, eindelijk verlost te zijn uit den nacht der bezetting.

Het front bij Berlijn, op Zondag 22 April (Times.)

XH113

# A WAR ODYSSEY
## 1938 ~ 1945

# THE HOUSE ON THE CANAL

*"For everything there is a season, and a time for every matter under heaven." (Ecclesiastes 3:1)*

THE THREE-STORY HOUSE on the canal in Haarlem, the Netherlands, was built around 1800. It has a long and interesting history and I became a part of it in the middle of the twentieth century. Hidden within its sturdy walls is an interesting but also very sad story. When Adolf Hitler's army occupied Holland in 1940, a physician, Guus (August) van der Breggen, practiced his medical profession in this house and lived there with his wife Diena, his two daughters, Aletta (22 years old), Noor (20 years old), and his son Lex (19 years old). Besides being known as an excellent physician in Haarlem, Doctor van der Breggen served the community in various capacities, such as a volunteer fireman. No one in the van der Breggen home anticipated the dark clouds of war and oppression that suddenly fell on the house on the canal.

Aletta (Jeeninga) van der Breggen and her parents, Diena and Guus.

On the tenth day of May, 1940, the Dutch population was

awakened early in the morning by swarms of German planes bombing strategic centers across the country. Aletta and Noor, who were nurses in a hospital in the Hague, were soon busy taking care of both Dutch and German wounded soldiers who were brought there. Doctor van der Breggen was doing the same in the hospital in Haarlem. The Second World War had drawn neutral Holland into its deadly web.

Around the dinner table in the house on the canal there was daily conversation about the dangers of the Nazi occupation of Holland. Dr. van der Breggen pointed out that there were among the Dutch people those who were pro-Nazi and secretly but actively favored and helped the Germans. The doctor said, "One of my patients, Mr. Bakker, was furious with me when I did not treat his wife, who had come too late for her appointment. To my amazement he warned me by saying, "If you again refuse to see my wife, even if she is late, you will bear the consequences!" Then Mr. Bakker turned the lapel of his jacket and on the inside of it was a pin with a Swastika on it. "I am a friend of the Germans," he announced to the startled doctor, "and you had better remember that!"

The Germans became more oppressive in response to Dutch opposition. The Dutch people were forced to hand in their radios. The Germans collected all the copper vessels people had in their homes for use as war materials. Blankets and clothing were to be taken to certain centers. People were forced to give them up and received receipts for them. If the Germans came to your house and you could not produce these receipts, arrest was immediate. Then the Germans began to take away Dutch young men to work in German factories. Many of them refused to go and chose to go underground (we called it "dive under"). If caught, they were shot on the spot. Also, those who did go underground would not receive ration stamps and thus were unable to buy food. How could they get help to survive? Fortunately, there often were dedicated relatives or friends who were willing to hide them and provide for these "diving under" persons.

To no one's surprise, one day Doctor van der Breggen informed his family that he was bringing four Dutch policemen to the house on the canal to hide them from the Germans. They had refused to work in Germany and also were members of a group of Dutch freedom fighters. A hiding place was found between the ceiling of the veranda and the roof of the house. The men brought a radio with them and picked up news from England about the progress of the war. They would forward this news to an underground printing press that published a small newspaper. This paper was distributed among sympathizers of the resistance movement. Of course, these activities were always open to the danger of detection. The consequences of being involved included imprisonment or being put in front of a firing squad.

Ella Rodenburg and daughter Eline, Rotterdam, 2001.

The house on the canal had a secret that very few people knew. The German occupiers of Holland, 1940-1945, never found out about it. What was the secret and how did I learn about it? It was not until September 3rd, 2001, when I flew back to the Netherlands from my retirement home in Florida to visit family and friends whom I had not seen for over fifteen years. My wife Aletta (van der Breggen) had recently died. Arriving in Amsterdam, I was warmly greeted by Aletta's niece, Ella Rodenburg, and her fourteen-year-old daughter Eline. In a little more than one hour by car we arrived at Ella's house in Rotterdam. This home would be my headquarters during my stay in Europe.

The next few days I experienced the true nature of Dutch hospitality. Knowing of my interest in Dutch history and archaeology, Ella and Eline gave me a very thoughtful gift, a recent edition of a book that described and illustrated the archaeological history of the Netherlands.

Ella's father, Piet Rodenburg, guided me through an exhibit called "Tracing the Past" (*Opgespoord Verleden*). This archaeological display interprets the ancient history of the Netherlands based on the various archaeological excavations across the country. I was pleased to learn that the oldest dugout canoe found thus far in the world was found in 1955 in Pesse, in the province of Drenthe. The canoe has been dated to 6500 B.C. and was made from a 16-foot-long log of a linden tree. The discovery dates well before the time of the famous Sumerian civilization in Mesopotamia, ca. 4000 B.C. These facts supply new ideas concerning the history of the low lands. This archaeological key is opening many new doors to the ancient past. But a more recent past, the 1940s, was also of great interest to me.

One of my major objectives in this 2001 visit to Holland was to take a few photographs of Aletta's family home on the canal in Haarlem. These photographs were needed for this book of mine and also to complete a family photo album I was putting together. It would be helpful to obtain a few pictures from the outside and the inside of the house. Maybe I could even find out more regarding the secret hidden in the ancestral house.

At Heemstede, a small town just south of Haarlem, I boarded with my friends Cees and Lies Peper. They provided me shelter for several nights while I explored Haarlem. One morning I took Bus #1 which soon put me right in the middle of the city of Haarlem, Aletta's hometown. I left the bus in front of the Vroom-en-Dreesman Department store. In my youth this is where I had often enjoyed a cup of tea with a delicious pastry. I walked north for about four blocks and reached New Canal Street where I turned right. Walking along the canal a short two blocks, I looked

The van der Breggen House on the Canal, Haarlem, Holland.

across the water and recognized Aletta's home. The house appeared to be in excellent condition. It had been painted recently and renovated. The three-storied dwelling was part of a row of old mansions built against each other.

Many years ago I had been in this house. Warm and pleasant memories stirred within me. What was the great secret of the abode? Might I have the opportunity to go through the front door and actually enter the house again? But how? I did not know the present residents. Because the weather was beautiful, I was able to take several good outdoor pictures of the dwelling. I continued my walk, then crossed the bridge down the street a short distance away and walked back along the canal to the house. Now I stood right opposite it. I had a perfect location for a close-up photo of the building. This is my lucky day, I thought.

While I was putting a new film in the camera, a lady on her bicycle stopped in front of the house and parked her bicycle against it. When she saw me taking a photo of the house she said something to me, but I did not understand what she said. This was not because I did not understand Dutch. I have never forgotten my Dutch. Later I discovered that the lady who spoke to me was Irish and spoke Dutch with an accent. I walked over to the woman and introduced myself. Then I asked her, "Do you live in this house?" She replied in the affirmative. I then continued, "My wife, Aletta van der Breggen, was brought up in this house. Her father was a physician. The family lived here for many years until after the Second World War."

"It is so nice to meet you, Mr. Jeeninga," she replied. "I have heard about the family and I am very interested in the history of the house." Then she asked, "Would you like to come into the house and see it on the inside?"

I was jubilant. What an unexpected open door to learn more about secrets in the van der Breggen residence. "I would love to," I said expectantly. Mrs. Blaauw led the way and brought me into the livingroom. I remembered that from there it was possible to see the veranda. It had been between the ceiling of the veranda and the roof that four Dutch policemen would hide in case of a search of the house by German soldiers. These policemen had refused to work for the Nazis and had to "dive under" (go underground). The van der Breggen family had opened their house to these men and allowed them to survive the war. Aletta had told me about their hiding place. Now that the house had been renovated, it was difficult to recognize the original situation.

After tea and cookies, we all went into the garden behind the house. Mr. Blaauw had joined us by this time. It was here in this garden that the van der Breggens had cut down a tree that was over 100 years old. During the last year of the five years of war (1940-1945), coal was not available. The people had no heat to stay warm and no fuel with which to cook. With the help of friends, the tree came down and provided the family with enough fuel to last through the final year of the war. Of course, the wood was used very sparingly. Now I was anxious to learn any details related to the secret of the residence. I asked Mrs. Blaauw if I might take a look at the basement. "The basement?" she asked perplexed. "Why do you want to see the cellar? It is small and junky. There is a water reservoir and a coal bin. This bin we now use for storage only."

I replied, "I take it then that you do not know about the secret of the house?"

"No, I don't know what you are talking about. But of course you may see the cellar. Can you tell me why you want to go down there?"

"Yes, I would be pleased to tell you about that," I answered. Then I told her the following account.

Soon after the German Nazi army had occupied Holland on May 10, 1940, they demanded that every Dutch family surrender all objects of copper and bronze to the authorities. These metals were needed to produce artillery shells. Those families who did not deliver their copper or bronze objects by a certain date would have their homes searched, with possible dire consequences. Doctor van der Breggen was not about to give up the family copper and bronze heirlooms from Indonesia to be melted down for German weapons. Only a few unimportant vases were given to the Germans. But what should the doctor do with the precious family collection?

About this time the family had planned a vacation in Denmark. A few days after they had arrived, Doctor van der Breggen said that he had to return to Haarlem for business reasons. No one in the family thought that strange because that had happened during other vacations. After all, a doctor is on call day and night, vacation or not. No one knew that the father had returned to Haarlem for a very special mission. At the house in Haarlem a friend of the doctor was waiting for him. The man was a mason by trade. Together, in the heat of the summer, they went to the basement of the family house on the canal and broke open a section of the wall. Then they excavated behind this wall a large cavity. In this open space they placed a safe. The secret and very hidden place had come into being. In this safe the family copper and bronze vessels, the silver, gold jewelery, and other valuables were placed. But there were also some other precious items put in the hidden recess—a second secret.

Doctor van der Breggen had many friends in town. Among them was a Rabbi who was probably a patient as well as a personal friend. The Rabbi was deeply concerned about how to protect the sacred objects of the local synagogue. These included the candelabras and the holy books like the Torah scrolls. The Rabbi was at a loss. The Nazis surely would come to confiscate them. Doctor van der Breggen was also concerned. He had never faced such a situation before. What should they do? He told the Rabbi, "I have a few ideas. Give me the books of your personal collection. I have friends in the city library. We will catalogue your books in a special way so that they become a part of the library collection. After the war is over, it will be easy for you to retrieve them. As for the synagogue paraphernalia and the Torah scrolls, I will find a special hiding place for them. In two weeks deliver all these items to my house and I will take care of them. I cannot tell you where I will hide them.

As soon as the family and synagogue treasures were placed in the safe, the brick wall was rebuilt. The walls of the cellar were covered with large white tiles. No one would suspect that a major construction had occurred in this cellar. No one would ever guess that behind those innocent-looking tiles were some very real treasures.

"Why don't we remove the tiles and locate the safe?" Mrs. Blaauw wanted to know. I retorted, "There is nothing behind those tiles today."

"Did the Germans find the safe then?" asked Mrs. Blaauw.

My answer was, "I will tell you the rest of the mystery of the two secrets." With a flair, I recounted that only Aletta had been told by her father what he had done underneath the house. Her father had shown Aletta the location of the hidden treasures. After

Partial map of Holland, highlighting the hometowns of Gustav Jeeninga (IJmuiden) and Aletta van der Breggen Jeeninga (Haarlem).

Germany was defeated, the Rabbi's son, who had survived the war and now was the Rabbi of the Haarlem synagogue, contacted the van der Breggen family. He inquired about when he might retrieve the synagogue's sacred articles that Doctor van der Breggen had hidden. Aletta now revealed the location. With the help of two workmen, the tiles were removed and the bricks pulled out. The safe was still in place. Doctor van der Breggen's plans for hiding these treasures had succeeded. The Germans never discovered the family treasures or the Jewish sacred utensils.

I found it difficult to leave the basement. So many thoughts went through my mind. I clearly sensed that I was in touch with a very sensitive moment of history. This was a special time in the life of my family. Although now herself dead, was Aletta somehow standing near me? My mind went back again to the dangers that had been faced so bravely in the 1940s.

During the war years, the possibility of the Germans raiding the house on the canal was very real. Then one day it happened. There was a knock at the door. Several German soldiers stood at the entrance. The house alarm had reached the people in hiding and they had disappeared into the hiding place. The housemaid went to the front door as slowly as possible. When she opened the door the soldiers rushed by her and searched the house thoroughly from top to bottom, but without finding anyone. The danger had passed—temporarily, at least.

In this same period, Mr. Bakker, who earlier had warned Doctor van der Breggen of his pro-Nazi connection, went to the Germans and told them that this doctor was an enemy and might himself be connected directly to the resistance movement. Then one day, unexpectedly, two German officers rang the bell at the house on the canal. "Is Dr. van der Breggen in?" they wanted to know. The doctor came out of his office and asked the officers in German, "What can I do for you? Is one of you sick?" "No sir, we are here to take you to the Police Headquarters." "But for what?" the doctor inquired. "I have done nothing." The only reply was, "We have our reasons. You must come with us."

Mrs. van der Breggen and Aletta were in the hallway. They were speechless and very worried. Mrs. van der Breggen asked the Germans, "Do we need to pack some things for the doctor. Some clothing maybe?"

"No, not now," the officers answered. "Maybe later. First there will be a hearing." As the doctor walked away he said very confidently, "Don't worry, I will be back soon." But tragically, that never happened. This was a black day for the family. After a short while the doctor was transferred to Dauchau in Germany, the most dreaded of the concentration camps. A plan by the freedom fighters to free the doctor during his transportation was rejected by Dr. van der Breggen. To put ten or even more other people and families at risk was something he could not approve.

While in the concentration camp the doctor practiced medicine in the hospital barracks. At the end of 1944 the doctor died of an unknown illness. After the war a priest visited the van der Breggen family and reported that he had been sitting at the doctor's bed when he passed away.

"Your husband," the priest said to Mrs. van der Breggen, "did a lot of good for the sick in the barracks. He surely was a wonderful man."

Immediately after the war, Mr. Bakker, who had caused so much pain and suffering to those who struggled against the Germans, was himself arrested and imprisoned.

# ALMOST A NEW LIFESTYLE

NOT IN ONE HUNDRED YEARS would I have thought of revealing this story. For me the episode I am now disclosing was one of the turning points in my formative years. From 1943 to 1945 I was a Nazi slave laborer and lived in a small space in the three-storied house of my German boss, Herr Liebing in Berlin, Blankenfelde, Germany. I could not have imagined how profoundly those two years would affect my soul and innermost being.

For the first eighteen years of my life my parents influenced my religious convictions and molded my ethical and moral standards. How would these early guiding principles meet or fail to meet the challenges of my life in an environment shaped by a cruel war? This war disrupted my social and spiritual lives and filled them with destruction and death. Added to all this confusion was a world of ideas permeated and controlled by Nazi socio-political philosophy. I found it most difficult to find answers to the scores of questions that bombarded my mind. One thing is certain. I have never been able to forget one of the numerous episodes that took control of my youthful years and placed me in an unusual and critical circumstance. That firsthand story is shared here.

My roommates in that small place above Herr Liebing's bakery were Ivan, Theodor, and Leo (their Russian and Polish last names have slipped from my memory). More important is that they were prisoners of war like myself and also worked in the bakery of Herr Liebing, a member of the Nazi party. Ivan, so he told me, lived in the isolated steppe of deep Russia when he was drafted into the Russian army. As long as I knew him, he drank large amounts of vodka and, when available, also the strong German liquor "schnaps." He lived a secret life. Because we rarely associated, he had little or no influence on me. Of course, we could hardly converse. His German was nil and so was my Russian. In spite of these hindrances, we did at times get ideas across, as I discovered on one funny occasion.

At lunchtime each day Ivan was the first to go to the kitchen to eat. Then when he returned to work it was my turn. Usually, before I went down to the kitchen, I would ask Ivan, "*Was gibts, Ivan?*" ("What do we have for lunch?"). On this one occasion Ivan could not think of the German word for "fish," but he did know the word for water. Therefore, he said, "*Wasser. . .und. . .,*" then using one hand, he moved it horizontally forward while he wiggled his hand, suggesting a swimming motion. Obviously he was trying to tell me I was going to get water and fish for lunch. In fact, when I sat down to eat, the cook placed in front of me a plate filled with water and in the middle of the plate lay a whole herring, including its head and tail.

My second and older roommate was Theodor who had been a village school teacher in the Ukraine. Theodor smoked a pipe constantly. I often wondered where his mind was when he sat at his bedside and smoked his smelly pipe in total silence. In a way Theodor and Ivan were in my room but not in my life. It was quite another story with Leo, my third roommate. Possibly because he spoke German well enough for us to socialize, I joined him on one of his risky pursuits.

For a short period Leo, a Polish slave laborer, had lived in a nearby worker's camp. Herr Liebing had received permission from the Camp Commander to have Leo live with us in our room above the bakery. It was Leo's prompting, and my response to it, that brought me into a dangerous moral predicament. I was nineteen years old and still innocent. Not that I was ignorant or dead to the physical drives of youth, but because of my strong religious upbringing I had thus far escaped falling into the trap of living an immoral life. Often I recalled the words of the Preacher in the

Book of Proverbs who wrote, "My son, pay attention to my wisdom that you may preserve discretion.... For the lips of an immoral woman drip honey.... But in the end she is bitter as wormwood... (Proverbs 5:11- 6).

Clearly, Leo was a man of the world, so to say. At his early age of twenty, I only learned much later, he was already a Casanova. Every Saturday afternoon he would leave Blankenfelde to go to Alexander Platz, the downtown of Berlin. He would not return until late Sunday evening from his long weekend escapade. One day, out of curiosity, I asked him, "Leo, where do you go on weekends and what do you do?" "I'll tell you, Gus, and also invite you to go with me." "But where do we go and what do we do?" I inquired. "OK, we go downtown and meet my girlfriend and her friend. They are two Polish girls. We meet on Saturday afternoon and go to the movies."

I responded, "That sounds like a pleasant evening. I suppose that after the movie we will dine out at some local restaurant. Right?" "No," he said, "but it will be much better than that. After the movie the girls will take us to their apartment and prepare a delicious meal for us." I said, "Afterwards we play games or cards I suppose? That surely makes for a cozy evening. I think I would enjoy that." Then I asked, "Where do we spend the night? You never sleep here in your own bed on the weekends when you are away." "That is no problem at all," announced Leo. "Each one of the girls has her own bedroom. I sleep with my girlfriend. It is just wonderful and so exciting. Of course, you will sleep with the other girl. Isn't that a wonderful setup?"

At that point I was thrown into confusion. I could not do that. I heard Leo continuing. "Gus, you must come with me next weekend. The girl is very lovely. I am sure she will like you." "No way, I cannot do that," I insisted. "Don't count on me," I tried to say convincingly. The weeks came and went and Leo kept after me to come with him. He would elaborate on the intimate time he had with his girlfriend. Week after week I was under crafty pressure by Leo. With his powerful ability to persuade, I gradually became enticed by his proposals. Cunningly, Leo had achieved his goal. He had won me over. Yes, I would join him and the two girls. The day arrived when I finally said to him, "Leo, OK, I'll go with you next weekend. Count me in." Nevertheless, my mind was not at ease with this fateful decision and with starting a new lifestyle.

The following Saturday afternoon, Leo and I took the U. Bahn (subway) to Alexander Platz. I was all dressed, wearing a recently and neatly-pressed dark brown suit. I was self-confident and knew I was looking sharp. We met the two Polish friends just outside the exit of the subway. After a short and simple, somewhat unpolished introduction, "This is Micah and this is Ilse," we agreed on where we would watch a movie. Leo's girlfriend, Micah, walked on Leo's left, Ilse was on his right and I walked on the right outside. I felt isolated. That fact turned out to be significant in the consequent developments.

There was something not right about this arrangement. I was self-conscious and anxious. A lively conversation was going on between the three of them in Polish. I was totally ignored. I wondered what they were discussing. The fact that I did not know Polish had no doubt something to do with my misgivings. Furthermore, several questions were running through my mind, such as: "Do you know what you are doing? Do you think it is OK and smart to get involved sexually with a girl you do not know or love? How would father and mother feel about your action? Have you thought through where this new lifestyle might ultimately take you? And what about your Christian principles and commitments?"

Strolling down Friedrich Strasse to find the theater, I was depressed and felt caught in a baited trap. How could I tell Leo and the girls that I was going to break the date? One thought kept going through my mind, "What ever you do, get out of this snare. Right now." Suddenly it came to me like a flash. "Make a U-turn. Turn around and walk away from it." That is just what I did.

Without saying a word or saying goodbye, I turned around and walked in the opposite direction and soon was lost in the crowd. I quickly walked to the subway and scooted home. On Monday morning I had to face an angry Leo. I apologized to him for how I had walked out on him and his friends. I did not attempt to explain the reasons, but only said that I was not able to handle a situation like this.

Years have rolled on since that unwise date. Many a time I have thought back on that critical decision I made. I have thanked God for the right values implanted in my subconscious by my dear and dedicated Christian parents. I am now more than convinced that if I had gone through with that partnership in that Polish girl's apartment, it would have forever stained my spirit and mind, and no doubt would have altered my destiny. My abrupt walking away was a sudden ending and a new beginning.

*"In all your ways acknowledge Him,*
*and He will make straight your paths."*
*(Proverbs 3:6)*

# HUMBLED BY
# MAN AND MOUSE

BEING A DUTCH SLAVE LABORER under the Nazis brought many dangerous and embarrassing moments to my life. Here are two, one precipitated by a man and the other by a mouse.

On a Sunday afternoon in November 1944, I was walking towards the Brandenburger Tor (Gate) in the city of Berlin, Germany. It was rather cold and I was wearing a dark blue skiing outfit with a typical German black cap to keep me warm. I had put my hands deep into my pockets. Germans walking down the street and seeing me in this black outfit could have thought that I was a German youth, except that I did not wear any of the customary German insignias—like the long, sheathknife (a kind of bayonet), an important symbol of Hitler's youthful fighters.

A short distance ahead of me rose the beautiful Brandenburger Gate that I so much wanted to see. In the quietness of the afternoon, I suddenly heard a loud voice coming from behind me, shouting in German, "*Nim deine Hände aus deiner Tasche!*" ("Take your hands out of your pockets!"). German soldiers were forbidden to put their hands in their pockets because Hitler's soldiers must always be ready to fight. I turned around to see who had said that and to whom. I did not see anybody but a tall German army officer in full military regalia walking a short distance behind me, but I did not see anyone to whom the officer was shouting the command. Therefore, I continued my walk. Again I heard the officer's command, "Take you hands out of your pockets!" I walked on, minding my own business. By now the officer had caught up with me. Suddenly, I received a hard kick in the buttock administered by his leather boot. It nearly threw me to the ground. I whirled around and asked him why he had kicked me. I also said to him, "I am not a German and I am not in the German army. I am a Hollander in Germany as a forced laborer. He looked perplexed and briefly apologized, then quickly walked on. I at least had the satisfaction of knowing that his act to embarrass me had turned on him and he was embarrassed by his blunder. Solomon once said: "When pride comes, then comes shame" (Proverbs 11:2).

Later, after the Russian armies had captured the city of Berlin at the end of World War II in 1945, it was not clear that food would be available for anyone. So I decided to store a supply of food and hide it. After hiding in a corner of a dark cellar a sack of flour, two hundred pounds of it, I forced six loaves of bread into an old, unused chimney. Then I decided to add to my food survival supplies even more flour to ensure that whatever might happen to my hidden provisions, one of the hiding places would survive the onslaught upon the city.

In my search for a container to put the flour in, I found a large and strong carton box that I filled with flour. While I decided where to hide the box, already I could hear clearly the explosions of bombs in the distance and the crackling of machine guns coming closer. I raced back up to the second floor, for time was running out. I then broke up some of the floorboards and placed the well-stuffed carton box between the beams and nailed the floorboards back into place—with the hidden treasure secure under the floor I was convinced no one would look there and I would have something to eat in the future.

During the next few days the city of Berlin fell to the Russians. Three weeks after that historic event I ran out of daily provisions. With great confidence, I climbed back up the stairs to the upper floor of the building to reclaim the flour that I had hidden under the floor sometime ago. Feeling satisfied for planning so wisely earlier, I pulled on the floorboards. They started to creak and then gave way as I twisted an iron bar between them. Finally the box containing the flour became visible. I removed and opened the box. I was astounded because the box was completely empty. But how could that be? Who had removed my flour? Was this a nasty joke? Then I saw a small hole in the side of the box and the droppings of mice. To my chagrin, the flour had been eaten by mice!

*"I returned and saw under the sun that*
*The race is not to the swift,*
*Nor bread to the wise, ...*
*Nor riches to men of understanding,*
*But time and chance happen to them all."*
*(Eccl. 9:1, Possibility Thinkers Bible)*

# MURDER ON MY MIND

DURING THE EARLY YEARS OF MY LIFE the possibility of my planning to kill another human being never entered my mind. Looking back on those years, I think I was an average kid who sometimes exploded in anger. Beyond those short moments of showing a temper, however, I was quite gentle.

Because my father was a staunch conscientious objector and a pacifist, I grew up with a strong conviction that the use of force should be opposed. Of course, I had not thought through this issue for myself in real life. I merely copied my father's religious stance in such matters. How would I deal with these issues when as an adult I met them head on? Here is a true story that helps answer the question.

I remember the thoughts that went through my mind years ago: "How, where, and when shall I do it?" I had decided to kill that "Rot-moff Friedrich" (a Dutch expression degrading Germans). At first I was shocked when I realized that I had decided to use force to kill Friedrich, but my anger against this particular German was intense and irreversible. What had happened to bring me to this most acute decision?

For some time I had been working as a Dutch slave laborer in a bakery in the city of Berlin. According to my diary entry of July 10, 1943, the Allied military forces had landed in southern Italy. A few days after this significant turn in World War II, other bakers and I had taken a break for lunch. I was sitting on a sack of flour, chewing away on two slices of Berliner Landbrot (German bread) and a slice of bacon between them and I was truly enjoying it. The bread-truck driver, Friedrich, a middle aged German, was standing nearby waiting for a load of bread to come out of the ovens. The next minutes of our lunch were destined to become moments of drama.

Someone, I do not remember who, walked into the bakery and announced, "I just heard over the radio that the American Allied forces have landed in southern Italy and are marching towards Rome." Then, with a twinkle in his eyes, he added, "But the German armies had a successful withdrawal." That was wonderful news for us prisoners of war and slave laborers. Spontaneously, I shouted, "Hurrah! Wonderful! That is great news!" A large fist landed on my mouth with a vicious blow, causing one of my lips to split as my teeth were forced into the flesh. I spit blood while a sharp pain raced through my head. That fist came from Friedrich, the German truck driver, who obviously did not share my joy and exuberance over the successful invasion.

In retrospect, it was rather stupid of me to openly rejoice in the German defeat in front of Germans. I should have controlled myself, knowing that I was in Berlin, the capital of "The Third Reich." In fact, I was in the "Lion's mouth." Still, my mouth hurt and my ego was deeply offended, so much so that my self-control was swept away. I was enraged, wrathful, and eager for revenge. There was an ominous silence in the shop while everyone was waiting for what was going to happen next. Before anyone could say a word or interfere, I jumped up from the flour sack I was sitting on and said in a hoarse and angry voice to Friedrich, *"Du Deutches Schwein, tue das nochmal und Ich werde Dich dein Kopf zerbrechen"* ("You German pig, try to hit me again and I will break your skull").

The reaction came immediately. Friedrich, my senior by at least twenty years, walked towards me with a determined gait and hate in his eyes. A battle for more blood was in the offing. I was very tense in anticipation. My mind searched for a quick idea. Then I suddenly remembered that my younger brother and I, at the ages of fifteen and sixteen, had practiced the art of Judo on each other. We never reached a high level of expertise, but I recalled one law of Judo defense, which was both easy to execute and almost always successful. I decided to use that skill and got into position to perform the move as my enemy moved towards me.

Everyone around us stood motionless and watched in anticipation. What would happen next? As soon as Friedrich stood in front of me, I stepped forward and with both hands seized his left and right lapels, while at the same time I pulled Friedrich towards me. I threw myself backwards toward the floor, pulling the German with me. When I fell on the floor, I bent my knees and thrust both of my feet into his stomach. Immediately I straightened out my legs and shoved Friedrich's body over my head and away from me. He landed against a brick wall and fell on the floor. Before he could recover and stand up, I stood over him, holding a wooden stool in my hands and said, "Try to get up and I'll crush your skull." He did not say a word or move a muscle. One of the workers, I think it was Otto, a Yugoslavian prisoner of war who was standing nearest to me, quietly took my arm and said, "That is enough, Gustav. Let's break it up." Still shaking, I left the bakery and went up to my room on the second floor above the shop. There I sat on my bed trying to figure out what had happened, what I had done and said, and what might be the consequences of my actions.

After a short while I heard footsteps coming up the staircase leading to my room. The door opened gently and Ivan, a Russian who was one of my two roommates and also a prisoner of war, stepped in and said, "Gustav, the boss, his wife, and Friedrich are standing at the telephone and are talking about calling the Gestapo (the German secret police). What are you going to do now?" I asked myself, "Yes, what shall I do?" Then I asked Ivan, "Will you please go down and find out if they actually have called the Gestapo and let me know immediately? If they have, I plan to escape through the window, down the roof of the house, and run for my life. With luck I may reach the Swiss border and find a safe haven. Fifteen minutes later, while I waited in fear, Ivan returned and reported, "They talked for a short while, and argued back and forth, but they did not call the Gestapo. I do not know why, but it looks as if you are in the clear, at least for now. I was happy with the turn of events but remained curious about the reasons for their not calling the feared German police.

In the days following the fight, tranquility returned to the workplace. However, my mind was far from being at peace. My ego was deeply bruised and I was still extremely angry with Friedrich. In fact, my anger and hate were so deep that I decided to kill him. The how, when, and where were on my mind for the next weeks. During this tense period, I had befriended Tom, a Hollander, who was working for a butcher in Berlin. He too was a slave laborer. Every so often we swapped his meats or sausages for my Berliner Landbrot. I learned from Tom that he had a source where he could obtain a gun for me. From that day on I began to plan seriously to shoot and kill Friedrich as a payback for his brutal fist punch to my mouth.

Finally the day arrived. Tom delivered to me the deadly weapon. He slipped it into my pocket secretly, I paid him, and he left quickly. I returned to my room to view the firearm. The first odd thing I noticed was that Tom had not supplied me with any bullets for what appeared to be a standard pistol. Most likely the bullets were in the clip. I studied the pistol from various angles. It was a strange weapon. I found the clip for the ammunition, but it was located on the top of the gun and not in the handle—and there were no bullets. It would be impossible for a bullet to be fired with the clip on the top of the gun and in a horizontal position. Gradually it became clear to me that this gun was a starter pistol, the kind used in sports events to get games started. The clip was for caps that were not fired, but only produced a loud "bang." I was frustrated because now I could not complete my careful plan of revenge against Friedrich.

The upshot of this fiasco was that I never carried out the

murder that had been on my mind for so many weeks. This turn of events was to my advantage, as I only realized later. The chances that I would not have been detected as the murderer of Friedrich were worse than slim. I now realize that if I had succeeded with my plot, I most likely would have been captured and put in front of a firing squad. If I had gotten away with the murder, I would have been living in the shadow of the life of a criminal. Looking back years later, I am thankful for the hand of God in my life during these most critical and frightful days.

*"And Jesus said, 'You shall not murder.'"*
*(Matthew 19:18)*

*"All who hate a brother or sister are murders, and you know that murderers do not have eternal life abiding in them."*
*(1 John 3:15)*

# A BIRTHDAY GIFT FOR ADOLF HITLER

NO DOUBT YOU HAVE WISHED TO EXPERIENCE, at least once in your lifetime, a really exciting event. You may even have longed for an incident to happen in your life that could be classified as a "once-in-a-lifetime" happening, an experience that only a few hundred people can claim to have been involved in. Such an incident would be worthy of telling over and over again.

Having gone through just such a dramatic, yes, almost fatal episode, I would like to tell you about it. That significant event occurred in Berlin, Germany, while I was a Dutch slave laborer for Nazi Germany. The critical day was April 20,1945. The drama unfolded and reached its climax in Berlin-Blankenfelde, a suburb of Berlin, which was under siege and soon to be overrun by Soviet military forces.

During the final days of the Third Reich, the German Führer, Adolf Hitler, was in hiding in the cramped conditions of his bunker (*Führerbunker*) some fifty feet below the city. This underground shelter, near the Berliner Zoo, was about fifteen miles from where I was working in Herr Heinrich Liebing's bakery. This put me in the bull's eye, Hitler's bunker being the target of the Allied forces. In his underground shelter, the Führer was following the progress of the war. He was also planning to celebrate his next birthday, and no doubt sensed that it was to be his last.

According to western historians, Hitler had planned to leave Berlin on April 20, his fifty-sixth birthday, for Oberzatzberg (Eaglesnest), and from there direct the last stand of the German

Third Reich. From the German general, Karl Koller, we learn that Hitler's birthday, celebrated in the bunker on April 20, passed quietly. However, it was not as quiet over Berlin on that festive day as the German general would want us to believe. Of course, being some fifty feet underground would make it difficult to know what was going on above the ground.

On Hitler's birthday, at about 10:00 a.m., I found myself stripped to the waist and sweating profusely. I was removing some seventy-five loaves of bread from oven No. 3, an old-fashioned, coal heated, brick type of baking oven. Suddenly, I heard machine gun fire in the distance. This sound was slightly different from the clatter of machine guns with which I was familiar. Where did this sound come from?

Abruptly, Günther, a young man from the neighborhood, came running into the workshop, shouting, "American fighter aircraft are strafing the streets of Blankenfelde with salvos of heavy machine gun fire. The gunners are shooting at anyone in sight. Several people already are wounded and two are dead!" I was shocked at this news and asked Günther to tell me more. With a shaky voice, he described his ordeal. He was returning home from work and was crossing the street when suddenly he heard the sound of airplanes coming toward him. In the next few moments, projectiles were exploding everywhere, and he ran for cover.

I was troubled by Günther's story. American fighter planes had shot at him, a civilian! I asked him to explain to me how he knew that they were American airplanes and not Russian or British? "Why," I insisted, "would an American pilot rake civilians walking peacefully on the streets of the outskirts of Berlin?" "Günther," I said, "You know as well as I that there are no factories or military installations in Blankenfelde. All men of military age are on the front fighting for Hitler and their fatherland." "Whatever," said Günther, "but I just heard it announced on the Berlin Radio that American fighter aircraft are flying over Berlin. Today is the Führer's birthday. The Americans are helping the

Germans to celebrate Adolf Hitler's birthday!"

I knew Günther well. He was my closest friend. His love for Hitler was nil. At one time he had confided in me and told me this joke: "The Führer was flying over Berlin with his private pilot to see the damage the Allied bombing had done to his people and his beloved city of Berlin. Hitler said to his pilot, "I wish to do something nice for the German people. Do you have a good suggestion?" "Yes, mein Führer," said the pilot, "I suggest you jump out of the airplane, right now!"

Günther left the shop. I was anxious to learn more about this fearful happening. I was mulling over the question of how the Americans, who had condemned the Germans for bombing the open city of Rotterdam, could shoot to death civilians walking on a quiet street in Blankenfelde. I did not realize how soon I myself would become a target in this drama.

I had finished my day's work at 2:00 p.m. and left the bakery. I put on my steel helmet to protect my head from flying shrapnel. I walked slowly down the cobble-stones towards the center of Blankenfelde. We locals preferred to call it "the village." When I arrived at Haupt Strasse (Main Street), I took a left turn and started to cross the street. When I reached the middle of the road, I heard the thundering engines of fighter aircraft. I looked down the one-mile long Haupt Strasse and, to my amazement, saw seven airplanes, next to each other, roaring in my direction. There was no time to make a decision about what to do. The seven fighter planes flew just a few feet above the level of the housetops. I was in great danger, and I knew it.

For only a split second did I see flashes of fire coming out from the wings of the aircraft. Bullet-like projectiles were fired from the planes' machine guns. Instantly there were exploding projectiles all around me throwing deadly metal fragments in every direction. Running like a rabbit under fire from the hunter, I rushed to a house nearby where the front door stood wide open, and I threw myself into the hallway while jagged fragments of hot metal smashed into the door jam and ripped the wooden door into pieces.

As swiftly as the assault had struck Blankenfelde, the quietness of the village returned, but only superficially. In sorrow, the dead were removed and the wounded attended to. After the roar of the fighter planes dissipated in the distance, I got up from the hallway floor and realized that I was unhurt. I was angered by this experience. How should I react to this barbarity? I detested the American assault on civilians. This grisly deed, in my opinion, was inexcusable. I sensed that I had just gone through a pivotal moment in my life's understanding of what is right and what is wrong.

My adventure on Adolf Hitler's birthday on April 20,1945, was truly a once-in-a-lifetime event, experienced by relatively few people—thankfully! It had been a day filled with excitement, but also full of meaning. It was a day of maturing and gaining a new understanding of the human race on a new and broader moral and ethical scale. In wartime, even one's allies may harm their friends. If this frightening day in 1945 taught me anything, it was the truism of the saying, "War is hell."

*"To everything there is a season,*
*A time for every purpose under Heaven...*
*A time of war and a time of peace."*
*(Ecclesiastes, 3:1; 8b)*

# MY LONG JOURNEY HOME

FROM BLANKENFELDE TO DRIESEN TO IJMUIDEN.
The Private Diary of Gustav Jeeninga, Recorded
During His Treacherous 750-Mile Journey
Home from the War.

NEVER DID I DREAM that I would participate in butchering a cow, using a four-inch long pocketknife. But I did. During April 1945 the Russian army gained control of the city of Berlin. I was living in a suburb of Germany's capitol called Blankenfelde. With Germany defeated, I was no longer a slave laborer and was very ready to go home to Holland. But to get back to Holland turned out to be a hazardous odyssey, almost like Odysseus' wanderings of long ago. I now look back and can only repeat, "and the Lord went before them" (Exodus 13:21). Following are excerpts from my private diary detailing my long journey home from the terrors of war and slavery.

## MAY 10, 1945

Early in the morning a Russian policeman, with an interpreter, knocked on my door. The knock was ominous, as they usually were during the Nazi period. The Russian asked me, "Who are you and what are you doing here?" I explained with hesitation, "I am a Dutch slave laborer and wish to go back home to Holland." Then he looked at his watch and said, "You must leave here within one hour." "Where do I go to get transportation home?" I asked. "Well," he said, "walk east to the next major city and you will find a train there to take you home."

I was nonplussed. Why should I walk east? Holland lies west of Berlin. I had a suspicion that there were no trains and that no arrangements had been made for our repatriation. This increased my fear of a long march to work camps in Siberia. Two of my Blankenfelde friends, Otto Batic and Ivan Shwarska, were from Yugoslavia. I had worked with them for two years in the Liebing bakery. They also had been told to leave Blankenfelde within one hour. Otto, Ivan, and I decided to travel together. We left Blankenfelde and walked about two miles. Because it was late in the day, we looked around and found a barn to stay in for the night.

Three other Yugoslavian prisoners of war, Demetrius, Nicholas, and Peter, friends of Otto and Ivan, joined our group. At suppertime, Otto left "to get something to eat." However, no store of any kind was open and we wondered where Otto thought he might get supplies. It was getting dark when Otto returned. "What have you brought back for supper?" Ivan asked him "Where did you get that?" "Oh," answered Otto with an innocent look on his face, "A few days ago I walked by this farm and I heard the cackle of chickens. These are two of them." That evening we really enjoyed bite after bite of the meat of the last two chickens of an angry German farmer, our former slave master. More than once in the next few weeks Otto would prove to be very inventive, imaginative, and cool headed.

## MAY 11, 1945

The following morning several girls from Blankenfelde, girl friends of our Yugoslavian comrades, appeared, bringing some food and a small four-wheeled wagon to transport our luggage. I was convinced that this gift was the last expression of their passion for their lovers. Their romance was shortlived. A German ditty says it well. *In jedes Städchen ein anderes mädchen* ("in every city another girl").

# MAY 12, 1945

The next morning the lovers broke apart after long and emotional embraces and kisses. I had done the same the day before at the time I left Blankenfelde. While tears were drying in the heat of the May sun, our group of six headed east. Fortunately the road turned sharply to the left, and eye contact with the lingering sweethearts was abruptly ended. The next town and what lay ahead of us now took control of our minds.

A Dutch underground newspaper, *The Flying Dutchman*, Monday, April 23, 1945. The headline reads: "Russians Fighting in Berlin."

It was already ten in the morning, a sunny and warm day. Taking turns, we pulled and shoved our wagon forward down a hardened road. We were not alone on the highway. Russian army columns returning to Russia passed us in long lines of trucks. When one of these columns passed us, we shouted *"Dóroye útro!"* ("good morning"). One of the soldiers, sitting on top of a loaded truck with loot taken from Berlin, threw us one, then two, and then some more cigars—a total of eight. I do not know why, but I suspect that Otto and the others, who not only spoke Yugoslavian but Russian, had asked for "a smoke" and for food—cigars taste better after one has had a satisfying meal. Another Russian threw a one-pound package of butter toward us. We missed catching it.

The butter splashed on the asphalt. The generous or bored Russian threw a second and then a third package of butter. They all landed on the highway. Nevertheless, we shouted, "*Spasibo!*" ("thank you"). With care we scraped the butter from the pavement and used most of it in the next few days without any negative effects.

In the afternoon, another column of Russian trucks passed us. This time a disgruntled soldier, without a smile on his tired-looking face, and probably also because he did not know what to do with it, threw us a violin. I wondered if he ever considered that he might get some good money for it. The violin was handed to me because no one in our group knew how to play it. Also, there was no violin bow with the instrument. When I was seventeen I played the mandolin banjo in our town's band. I took the violin and played it as I would my banjo, using my fingers to pluck the four strings. I did produce some music while walking on the highway, but it was not anything like a high-quality melody.

In the evening after supper, I played the violin in the hope of entertaining my comrades with some soothing chamber music. A crow nearby was squawking. My friends thought that the crow and I harmonized well. I probably plucked too hard on the strings and the E-string snapped. I could no longer play the violin, to the delight of my comrades I am sure. It was not the best music that I had ever played. Many years had gone by since I had played the banjo. What should I now do with this bow-less and three-stringed violin? I followed the Russian example and threw the violin in the bushes along the road. Many times since, I have wondered if I threw away an original Stradivarius violin and with it a small fortune. I will never know.

Struggling for some ten kilometers down the road, we finally arrived near the town of Blumberg. We spotted an empty house. The inhabitants had fled in a hurry when the Russian army was about to overrun their town. The family members had left most of their furniture behind. I found a soft couch and claimed it as my bed for the night. Among the books the unfortunate family had left, I chose one that interested me. The book described Germany's social and economic development during the last fifty years before Hitler. Weeks later I finished reading the volume. I concluded that the book needed to be revised and an additional chapter should be added to bring the study up to date. This concluding chapter should point out that Hitler had been right when he yelled over the radio his prophetic promise, "In ten years you will not recognize Germany!" No truer words were ever spoken.

## May 13, 1945

After a short morning walk, a morsel of bread, and a cup of hot water, we started on a new adventure or new crisis. First, we visited the Headquarters of the Russian army, located in the center of Blumberg. Here we begged for food and asked about transportation to Yugoslavia and Holland. The Commander in charge suggested, with an optimistic tone in his voice, that we should walk to the next larger town where there was a train depot, a food distribution center, and transportation for repatriates like us. It was the reply we had heard before. A new saying became common in our group. We would say to each other in Russian, "*Pozhalysta doroga*" ("Please, take the road").

After having walked eight kilometers, we were fortunate to meet a truck driver who was willing to take us about twelve kilometers short of Landsberg. The road we traveled might be called "Death Valley," a terrible stretch of road meandering through the countryside. We passed through villages and hamlets. There was total silence, like the minutes before the pastor gives the final parting words at a gravesite. Did a monster tornado strike this region? Houses lay flat or were torn to bits. Barns and sheds had disappeared, only their foundations remaining. Mangled bodies of both humans and animals lay putrefying in the heat of the sun. Swollen corpses, lying on their backs, legs up in the air like blown up balloons, lay strewn out everywhere. The air was filled with the stench of rotting flesh. It did not help us much to cover our noses. The stench of death penetrated everything. This was truly a "Death Valley."

We moved along in total silence. I noticed the stare in the eyes of several comrades. Demitrius was fidgeting with his fingers, Ivan's hands were clinched into fists and pressed against his knees. Tension was in the air. Were they thinking thoughts similar to mine? What had happened at home in Yugoslavia and in Holland during the last weeks of the war? How had my parents, brother, and sisters survived the battles raging through Holland? I suffered silently as this panorama of a stinking battlefield passed before my eyes—a real Armageddon. Where we slept that night I cannot recall. It must have been under the stars.

In the morning we agreed that Otto, Ivan, and Demitrius would walk to Landsberg to inquire regarding the availability of food and transportation. It was not until late in the afternoon that they returned. The Commandant, they reported, was interested in our plight and assured us that there was plenty of food and good transportation waiting for us. Ivan asked, "Where must we go for help?" The Commander came up with the quick answer that we had heard before, *"Pozhalysta doroga."*

Since we left Blankenfelde, our concern about provisions had been of little concern. We started with some supplies when we left Berlin, but by this time our food stock had dwindled. Otto and I decided to try to catch some fish. The river Netze, fifty or more feet wide, was only a few hundred feet from where we were staying. I asked Otto, "Where do we find a fishing hook?" Pointing to a building near the river, Otto said, "Let's search that house. We may be lucky and find a safety pin." Luck was with us and we found a safety pin. "Let me shape this pin into a fish hook," Otto offered. By now I knew that Otto could do just about anything. I remembered him telling me that he had a love affair with one of the Blankenfelde beauties, but had no place to go to be alone with her. So, one night he removed a hanging lock from an entrance to a large barn in the country. He took the lock to the bakery workshop and fitted a key. He then replaced the lock on the barn door. Now he and his friend had a secret place to rendezvous. Similarly, Otto fashioned a fish hook from the safety pin. We also located a bundle of sewing thread for use as a fishing line. To dig up some worms was easy. We fished for more than one hour but the fish did not strike at our bait. There were no mosquitoes or insects around, which might explain why the fish did not bite. The fish were somewhere else.

## MAY 15, 1945

No one prepared the breakfast this morning. There was no food left to eat. When we passed through Landsberg, Peter and Nicholas stopped at the Russian Headquarters in the hope that they might get some rations. The Commander—I wondered if all Russian soldiers were called "Commander"—suggested what we now expected to hear, *"Pozhalysta doroga."* My mind was disturbed. I had been told that people who had walked east, under Russian direction, ultimately arrived in Siberia, or in some other wasteland. Because of this possibility, our group was contemplating a turn sharply southeast toward Yugoslavia. I agreed, planning to find my way back to Holland after we reached that destination. We continued our journey in the direction of Posen, a town in East Germany. After arriving there, depending on circumstances, we would map out our next significant move and direction. However, a few kilometers just ahead of us lay the hamlet of Driesden.

"Fortune" met us this day, a day filled with shifting contingencies. After pushing and pulling our loaded wagon for many miles, we hitched a ride on top of a horse-drawn cart that had caught up with us. Otto had succeeded in stopping the last wagon in the column and persuaded the driver to let us sit on top of his cart until we got to the next town. Otto's charm and diplomacy, and no doubt his linguistic ability, paid off. He struck up a conversation with the driver and asked, "Where are you going today?" The Russian explained, "This column is headed for the little town of Driesden. Near Driesden we have a staging area with hundreds of cows." Otto pressed on, "What are you doing with all that cattle?" "We have taken these cows from the Germans and are now driving them to Mother Russia."

Realizing a unique opportunity for a deal, Otto explained to the driver that we were out of food. "Can you help us?" Otto queried. He knew that many Russian soldiers loved to smoke. Cigarettes were a commodity highly prized, but difficult to obtain. Otto suggested casually that we might trade a cow for twenty-five packages of cigarettes (a total of 250 cigarettes). Otto and his new friend Basil worked out the details of the agreement. We would give the Russians twenty-five packages of cigarettes and we would butcher the cow and give him one-quarter of the beef. The rest of the cow would be ours. As a bonus, we would also receive twenty-five pounds of bread flour. In Dutch we would say, "We had fallen with our nose in the butter."

The next five or more kilometers we journeyed in high spirits and in a happy mood. Even though the violin was abandoned, we sang, told jokes, and laughed without restraint. Even the countryside had changed. We were surrounded by softly rolling hills. The hills dipped down deeply into water holes, swamps, small and larger blue lakes. Many of these lakes were surrounded by rich farmland. Spread between them lay multicolored meadows. Here and there stood farms that had escaped the ravages of the scorched earth policy. The May weather was balmy and the sky the dark blue of an Indigo Bunting. A variety of bird songs, including the lapwing, the meadow lark, and even the common starling and sparrow floated towards us from across the pasture. We heard the humming and the buzz of insects sounding to us like an orchestra tuning instruments before the great performance. I almost forgot where I was, why I was here, and where I was going. This was not Death Valley, at least not here.

The sun was inclining towards the far horizon. We arrived at a farmhouse not too far from Driesden. This was the area where the herd of cows was to be, including the cow we had bargained for. While we walked towards the meadow, we discussed how we were going to pull off the butchering task. Among the six of us there was no butcher. Demitrius was a baker and so was I, Otto was an airplane pilot, Nicholas and Peter were shopkeepers, and Ivan had been a doctor's assistant. He also served as our barber. Ivan was appointed the butcher because, we all agreed, he knew more about anatomy than any of us.

We entered the pasture. There were nearly a hundred Holstein cows. The herd was agitated, nervous, and shifty. I asked, "Why are they so agitated?" Peter, with an air of knowing what he was talking about, explained, "These animals have been herded down the road for many days, but many of them have not been milked. They are suffering pain as their udders swell. Other cows already have gone dry and no longer suffer that discomfort."

Otto and Demitrius entered the meadow. The Russian explained to Otto, "You see that cow over there?" He pointed to one of the larger ones. "That is the one I want you to catch." With some ambivalence in his voice, Otto replied, "*Spasibo*" ("thank you"). The fact that a specific animal was targeted made the capture of it more difficult. It would have been much easier to take just any one of the cows. Otto and Demitrius began to stalk the animal. The cow headed slowly in the opposite direction. When they gained on it, it increased its speed and changed direction. It was entertaining to watch the hunt. It was also obvious that the brute was not in the mood to be captured. Someone yelled, "Catch its tail!" and another one instructed, "Take it by the horns!" We all were amused and had a fit of laughter.

While watching Otto and Demitrius running after the bewildered cow, it was clear to us that they needed more help than just some shouted advice. Soon we all were in the pasture and chasing after what was to be our next meal. Six highly motivated and hungry men, like a family of hungry lions hunting down an antelope, encircled the confused animal and closed in on it. Unexpectedly, the cow stood still, watching our movements. What now? What do we do? Suddenly, the nervous beast ran, head down, straight forward. In harmony, as though we had practiced it many times over, we all ran up to the excited creature. Those closest to its tail took hold of it and did not let it go even though they had to run. Ivan succeeded in grabbing one of its horns. Someone else, I did not see who it was in the excitement, with a cry of victory, lunged forward and reached for one of the ears, but failed. He stumbled into the grass with a moan of disgust. In the next moment Peter was hanging on the other ear, and Nicholas was dangling from the muscular neck with a vice-like grip. The cow slowed down. Taking a few more steps, it stopped. Its body heaved violently and its nostrils flared. It no longer had the strength to run.

Slowly we pulled the cow towards the fence. What was our next step? How does one kill and butcher a cow? We discussed our options. "Shoot it?" I suggested. "But we do not have a gun," said Demitrius. "Well then, let us cut its throat," said Peter. He offered his three-inch long pocketknife. A muffled laughter ran through the circle. "I know what we might do," said someone. "We can strangle it to death." Ivan strongly objected and argued against it. He felt that it would cause the bovine to suffer too much. That was an interesting viewpoint coming from a doctor's assistant. At last we came to a general agreement. We needed a sledgehammer to kill the cow. This is the way it is often done in slaughterhouses. Using a metal tube with an explosive charge, a steel rod is driven into the cow's forehead. The cow is dead immediately. We decided to achieve the same results by use of a sledge hammer weighing eight pounds.

From a farmhouse nearby we "borrowed" a sledgehammer.

It was Ivan's job. While two of us held the cow by the horns and two by the tail, Ivan positioned himself to administer the deadly blow. He lifted the hammer and layed it back over his shoulder. He swung the tool forward with all his strength. The sledgehammer found its mark. We heard a muffled thud. Nothing happened. The cow stood steady on its four legs, like a five-hundred year old California cedar. Ivan repeated the strike. I watched the cow closely and noticed that its eyes rolled around and lost their luster. Still the dumb animal stood its ground. With the third blow, well placed and with added gusto, the sledge achieved its objective. The cow sank and dropped on its side without a sound. Immediately Ivan attempted to cut the animal's throat. This was very difficult to do with a three-inch long pocketknife. One wonders how Stone Age men butchered the buffalo. With a deep stab into the throat, Ivan hit a major artery and the blood came gushing out.

It took four of us to hold the cow in place so that Ivan could butcher it. We kept the animal on its back as four of us held on to its four legs. However, an unhappy development occurred. When Ivan was attempting to remove the stomach from the cow, the stomach broke, and the partly digested food, mainly grass, poured forth over the rest of the skeleton. Ivan suppressed a truly bad Yugoslavian curse. It was a smelly heap. We all took several steps back to avoid the horrid odor. Necessity drove us back to finish the job. In desperation Ivan shouted, "Bring buckets of water. Hurry up." The remains soon were washed clean. Ivan started to section out the cadaver as agreed upon earlier with Basil. Carefully, but quickly, Ivan removed the shank, heel of round rump, and sirloin tip. The Russian nodded his approval. We helped him load the meat on his wagon. In no time he disappeared over the hills as the shadows began to creep across the fields.

Ivan was all smiles. He realized that much of the fine beef was ours. It was getting late and he asked, "What do we do with all this fresh meat? We cannot keep it. In one or two days the meat will be spoiled." Demitrius, always offering a simple response, asked, "Why not first cook a good portion of it for tonight, and have a feast?" Peter added, with a smile of satisfaction on his sun-burned face, "Yes, then the rest of the meat we will eat tomorrow evening. "Otto, always with better ideas, pointed out that there was too much beef to eat and offered to find someone who might exchange some of the meat for non-perishable food. Everyone agreed.

Without another word, Otto was already walking to the farmhouse, and soon returned with a large iron cooking pot. Using large stones gathered up from the field, we constructed a primitive fireplace. Large chunks of chuck and porterhouse beef filled the caldron. When the water was boiling, we knew that in minutes the meat would be ready. Eating was on our mind. The sooner the better. We waited impatiently. I was fidgeting with my pocketknife, stripping away the bark from a stick, with no goal in mind. Nicholas was walking to the fence watching the cows, but he did not notice that they were no longer agitated. Were they aware that we would not be back to chase another one of them? The rest of the comrades were sitting around the caldron, just lingering. A few were playing with their still-empty cans or plates that they held ready in their hands. It was taking more time for the meat to be cooked than our stomachs could stand.

It was almost midnight. By the light of the smoldering embers, we finally ate quietly the chunks of delicious meat, until we were more than satisfied. One by one we drifted off into the darkness of the night. Our stomachs filled, we carefully searched for our chosen sleeping quarters. I cannot recall where I slept. I was exhausted, like a purple martin that had just finished crossing the Gulf of Mexico. All I wished for was to be in the arms of Morpheus.

*"When you lie down, you will not be afraid;*
*Yes, you will lie down and your sleep will be sweet."*
*(Proverbs 3:24)*

## May 16, 1945

Well rested, we faced a new day. The sun warmed the wet meadows and, as the dew lifted skyward, so did our mood. The extra beef we had left was soon exchanged for flour and butter. From the remaining meat another excellent and tasty feast was dished up. No longer did we worry about our next meal. But the joy of plenty of food was soon tempered.

For the next ten kilometers we again traveled through a valley of death. A "Battle of the Bulge" must have been fought in this region. Cattle lay rotting in the field and human bodies lay scattered around. Some human bodies were merely mush. Many unfortunate people had been crushed or squashed by the iron tracks of tanks and personnel carriers. The utter destruction of civilized life lay grossly displayed. Burned out frames of automobiles, motorcycles, houses, and barns dotted the countryside as if a fire-breathing monster had blown its flurry across the land. Among this devastation, as chance would have it, we located a building sufficiently intact to give us shelter from rain and wind.

## May 17, 1945

We had a wonderful night of sleep. We broke camp by ten o'clock in the morning. With the sun high in a clear sky, it turned out to be a delightful twenty kilometers walk to just outside the city of Driesen. It was decided that we would wait until the following morning to enter Driesen. Once again "fortune" guided us to a burned-down farmhouse with the barn intact. Here we made camp for the night. Fortunately, a side arm of the famous river "Netse" rushed by in front of the barn. Maybe its water was used to douse and save the barn from the fire. We all went for a swim. With a small piece of soap, only one piece available for everyone, we washed away the accumulated dust and dirt of the last few days. The spirit of the group was upbeat. There was much laughter and joking and lively conversation. The topic centered around going "home." Tomorrow we should be in Driesen. We had been told that a train was waiting for us and would whisk us to Yugoslavia and me to Holland. No one wished to question the veracity of what we had been told.

## MAY 18, 1945

Streams of sunlight broke through the slits of the creaking old barn and woke me at eight o'clock. After a quick *katte wasje* ("a cat wash") in the Netse and a superficial shave, I hiked one mile. When I returned everyone was up and around. The breakfast was ready. By 10:30 a.m. we had loaded our small wagon and headed in the direction of Driesen.

For the first time since we had left Blankenfelde, our small wagon broke down under the heavy load. The repair was easy and quick. After a healthy walk of eleven kilometers we entered Driesen. It turned out to be the hub for gathering up the prisoners of war and slave laborers of the Germans. The Russians directed me to the quarter where there were some ninety Hollanders. Each nationality was given its own quarter. I was assigned to a house which had been appropriated from a German family whom the Russians had evicted. The rooms had been cleared of all furniture (shipped to Russia?) and subdivided by boards on the floor into individual beds. The mattresses consisted of a layer of straw. For a pillow I used my rucksack.

Next we had to register. Then we had to see a doctor and were "deloused," even though I did not have any lice. We were told not to go outside the city of Driesen. At 7:00 p.m. everyone had to be indoors.

## MAY 19, 1945

In the afternoon I paid a visit to my Yugoslavian friends. I joined them in search of a small stove so that they could cook their meals. The Russians supplied us with bread flour and a sheep or goat. It was up to us to bake the bread and butcher the live animals. Searching through a few empty German homes, we chanced upon a small but functional furnace. With difficulty, two of the group raised the stove up on their shoulders. They walked away with the stove as if they were giving their younger brother a horse-ride. To me fell the honor of carrying the stovepipe. With shouts of encouragement, we transported the small but heavy stove up to the attic and placed it right under the skylight.

For the help I had given my Yugoslavian travel buddies, they invited me to join them for supper. I was convinced that they invited me because we all knew that soon we would part. The chance that we would see each other in the future was most unlikely. The weeks that we had shared together, the good, the bad, and the worst had welded an unbreakable friendship between us. The inevitable separation was a moment we all wished would just disappear. Even though the free supper made it possible for me to save a piece of bread for another time, it did not diminish a sickening vibration in my soul. I could not understand the "why" of this sensation. I dislike saying goodbye to my friends, especially when that goodbye has a finality to it. The sun was setting fast as I strolled back to my room. The darkness of the evening first softened into shadows. As I reached the door to the house I called "home," the night blackened out the faces of my friends, forever.

## MAY 20, 1945

During the day the news made the rounds that the Russian Administrator was looking for bakers. "Are there any bakers among you?" they asked. "If so, let them report immediately." Here was my opportunity to do something worthwhile, and no doubt something that would provide some benefits. I reported, "I am ready to start as soon as I am needed." When I presented myself, there were two other Hollanders there claiming to be bakers. The tensions that emerged are interesting to reflect on.

The Russians had set aside a bakery shop on Main Street. Not so pleasant was the fact that there was no running water in town and no electricity. The battle for Driesen had damaged the city badly. The oven was an old fashioned one. Coal was placed in the mouth of the oven and was kindled to burn white hot. Then the coals were removed and dumped into a large vat filled with water in front of the oven. Steam would swirl around the face of the oven man. If available, cold maltz beer would cool him off. Next, the oven was cleared of ashes using a large mop to swab the oven clean. The loaves were placed on a broad bread-plank and "shot" into the baking chamber.

One of the volunteer bakers, seeing what lay ahead of him, quietly disappeared. He probably never worked in a German bakery or on an old fashioned oven. The other volunteer baker, I will call him Cees (having forgotten his true name), and I discussed our first responsibility. We needed to develop a sourdough, a leaven consisting of dough in which fermentation is active. It was clear at once that we had different ideas about the procedure. The discussion soon turned into an argument and became seriously offensive. Both sides used words that I cannot repeat here. The upshot was that Cees called me "an. . ." and promptly walked off the job. I suddenly found myself solely in charge of producing bread for nearly a hundred Hollanders.

Immediately two problems faced me. Could I produce, as soon as possible, a leaven "start." All I knew was that the basic method called for mixing some flour, some warm water and salt, and leave it rest, usually overnight, but under a controlled temperature. From my arguments with Cees and my understanding of the principles involved, I proceeded to mix the leaven, putting it aside for the next day. My second problem was how to secure physical help. The lack of running water and electricity called for extra manpower. I asked for three men to help me. They were quickly recruited.

## MAY 21, 1945

At eight in the morning I rose easily because the sun was shining brightly into my room. It was going to be a sunny and warmish day. Weather conditions always have affected my mood. This day the pleasant weather put my optimistic nature in high gear. The gossip was that we would leave for Holland in eight or nine days. My upbeat mood was somewhat tempered when I heard several versions of the date of our exodus. By the end of the day none of these floating rumors had been clarified or confirmed. I had lost my interest in them. My optimistic high melted like an iceberg nearing the equator. Besides, more important matters began to whirl through my mind. How well had my sourdough leaven germinated? Would it be ready for use to produce a spongy bread?

The three recruits arrived at the bakery at 1:00 p.m. In several relays they walked about a quarter of a mile, each with a bucket and pumped water from a well. The archaic pump had to be primed by pouring water into the pump first. After quickly forcing the handle up and down, a spurt of water was forced up, and shortly thereafter the water was flowing abundantly. In the meantime, I had dumped the flour into the mixing trough. After the water and sourdough leaven were added, six willing but inexperienced hands began to mix the ingredients into a spongy mass. To work a breaddough into loaves is a baker's art and takes some experience. Therefore, my helpers, who were not bakers by trade, were allowed to leave.

By this time the oven had reached its needed temperature. I

took the bread-plank, a baker's tool with a four-foot long handle, and placed the loaves, one by one, into the oven. The first loaves went toward the back, the next loaves in front of them, and so on. The whole experience was a success. We had started at 1:00 p.m. and at six o'clock I delivered some fifty loaves of delicious bread to the authorities. My payment for my labor consisted in receiving an extra loaf of bread. For the next ten days I baked bread for the hundred Hollanders.

*"What gain have the workers from their toil?. . .*
*I have seen the business that God has given to everyone*
*to be busy with. . .it is God's gift that all should eat*
*and drink and take pleasure in all their toil."*
*(Eccl. 3:9-13)*

## MAY 22, 1945

Noise from the kitchen at six a.m. caused me to get up from my straw mattress. Our butcher (a Dutchman) was busy dismembering a sheep. I was happy to know that this day would be special. There would be meat on the table.

## MAY 23, 1945

The early morning weather discouraged me from going for my usual walk. It was cold and a strong wind was blowing down the street. To entertain us in-house, Tom Klaasen, an artist from Haarlem, was doing portrait sketches. I volunteered to sit quietly on a kitchen chair to provide the modern Rembrandt a subject. In only a few minutes, Tom completed a remarkable likeness of me. I have always regretted that I did not treasure this drawing and stow it away in my satchel.

## MAY 24, 1945

At eight a.m. I quickly splashed water on my face at the bank of a small tributary of the river Netze. I was not feeling well. Many individuals in our "house" suffered from dysentery. No medicine was available. I did not escape the debilitating illness. The emergency latrine we all used consisted of a long wooden beam that was fastened to several vertical poles. The poles were driven into the ground at the edge of a hastily dug trench. For several days the latrine was crowded with desperate patients. Our desire to go home increased with every run to the privy.

## MAY 25, 1945

In spite of the dysentery, the good news of the day raised our spirits. We were told, by way of the underground fast news, that shortly we would be leaving Driesen for Holland. However, I was more than rudely shaken when I was told that the transportation back to Holland would be by way of Odessa, the Black Sea, the Mediterranean Sea, France and Belgium. The fear of a possible Siberian detour for a few months or a lifetime filled my mind. The sobering news kept changing throughout the day. By nightfall the story about our departure had been blurred by the lack of light and insight.

## MAY 26, 1945

After baking bread in Driesen for the last time, I took a long walk. During the remainder of the day I did not hear any news about our departure or itinerary. The uncertainties had me on an emotional edge.

## MAY 27, 1945

Early in the morning I had a serious dysentary attack. This inconvenience did not prevent me from being hopeful about a whisper I heard affecting our going home. It was clear that it did not imply today or tomorrow, but soon.

## MAY 28 AND 29, 1945

All day long on May 28 talk was about leaving Driesen. But on May 29 no one still seemed to know anything for sure. Nevertheless, the word went around that the exodus from Driesen would begin tomorrow. Excitement was building again.

## MAY 30, 1945

At sunrise one could hear everywhere the Dutch greeting, *Goede Morgen*. Feverishly, everyone was packing. The day of departure was here, for sure. I was feeling fine. The dysentery had run its course and I was secure. By 2:00 p.m. we were marching in formation under the direction of several Russian soldiers to the Driesen railroad station. I was ecstatic. I had not been in such a happy mood for a long time. I looked forward to being on a regular train for a smooth, speedy, and uneventful ride to Amsterdam and home. So I thought.

Our Dutch unit was very unfortunate. We were assigned to three open freight cars. These railroad wagons had no roofs or seats. We climbed on board and each one staked out an area for himself. I found it impossible to sit on the floor of the freight car hemmed in by four sides. I could not see the world around me, only the sky above me, now getting darker for the day was ending.

I investigated my surroundings, as little as they were. At the back end of the freight car I located the flagman's platform with a three-step staircase on the right side of the car. I grasped immediately the value for me of this location. It was precisely what I was looking for. I picked up my satchel and sat on the top of the narrow stair. Now I had privacy and a view of the world.

At 9:00 p.m. the train vibrated and started to move slowly in an easterly direction. "Are we heading for Russia?" After four or five miles the train entered the main railroad station of the city of Ost Kreutz just across the Polish border. Here the train stopped. I wondered why. Still, I did not know our true itinerary and that bothered me to no end. After some thought and weighing my options, I came to a radical decision. As soon as I was convinced that the transport was heading deeper into Poland, I would jump off the train! "Why do you not try to get back to Holland on your own?" I heard myself asking. It would be worth a try; it certainly would be better than landing in a labor camp in Siberia.

The activity on the station's platform kept my mind occupied. Men, women, and children, some with heavy loads on their backs, were rushing by me in both directions. Who were they? Where were they going? Various scenarios crossed my mind. Unexpectedly, one of these hurried strangers stopped in front of where I was sitting. Without one word, or acknowledging my presence, he wedged himself between me and the backside of the freight car. I was flabbergasted.

Observing him for a while, I concluded that this man was a Russian soldier. He wore a well-used Russian army uniform. He sat very quietly and looked straight ahead of him. I looked him over more closely. There was something strange about this soldier. He carried no army rifle. He carried no side arms. He had no military insignias on his sleeves, his chest, or lapels. I speculated: Was he an escaped prisoner or a criminal? I was not happy to have him sit next to me. I had no idea what I should do.

Before I reached a conclusion, another episode called for my immediate attention. This trip was starting out with uncertain and perplexing surprises. My reflections were rudely interrupted when my eyes caught three teenagers running down the platform at full speed. Presently they passed directly in front of me and the stranger sitting next to me. One of the youngsters lost his bulky rucksack which fell on the platform only three feet from us. The unfortunate boy did not slow down one bit to pick up his rucksack, but raced on behind his two comrades. They were soon out of sight.

While this drama was in progress, the train had started to pull out. "Ivan," that is what I called the Russian soldier, sprang from the train in a flash. He grasped the abandoned rucksack and was back in his seat next to me, with the rucksack secured as quickly as a monkey snatches a banana out of your fingers at the zoo. Ivan placed the rucksack between us. My curiosity now turned from wanting to know who this stranger was to wanting to know what was in the rucksack. I debated within myself, "Who is the real owner of this rucksack?" If I would have been alone on the staircase, I probably would have picked up the unexpected treasure.

I continued my silent argument. "This Russian does not belong to our transport and therefore has no right to be on our train. I realized that my argument had no influence on who owned the rucksack. I had to think about a different approach. A course of action suggested itself to me, and I reacted immediately, but slowly. Nonchalantly, I picked up the rucksack and placed it on my knees. Ivan looked at me and I smiled mildly at him. Ivan did not move or say a word. I wondered why not? I proceeded to loosen the string on the top of the rucksack. I stuck my hand into it and felt something round. I pulled it out and saw that it was a large bag of cookies. Next I lifted out a nice piece of chocolate fudge. I placed each catch to my right. Again I put my hand into the rucksack and held a chunk of bacon in my hand. I guessed it weighed 250 grams. I was utterly amazed at what I was collecting.

However, the end of this treasure hunt was not yet in sight. Again I put my eager hand into the rucksack. Ivan remained silent and impassive. This time I found a ham sandwich. I now put

everything into my satchel on my right. Being extremely brave—
or just brazen, I plunged my hand back into the rucksack and
started to pull out a loaf of bread. Ivan, without a spoken word,
made it quite clear to me that I should leave the loaf of bread in
the rucksack. At the same time, he resolutely pulled the rucksack
away from me and held on to it. I am sure that he no longer trust-
ed me to leave him something. Of course, he was right. I had
developed a real love for the contents of the rucksack, not unlike
a gold digger entering a gold mine who does not come out until
he has all he can get.

The sharing of the rucksack's contents took place while the
train rolled on in a westerly direction. It was night and we made
ourselves as comfortable as possible, sitting on that small staircase
as the train swayed onward. When I awoke during the night ride,
I discovered that we were shoulder to shoulder, supporting each
other unawares. Having shared the riches from the rucksack, we
now shared the night.

## May 31, 1945

At 2:00 a.m. the train arrived in the city of Landsberg. Ivan
got up and left me without saying a word. He never had said
much. He took with him the rucksack with the loaf of bread, and
who knows what else. I shall never know.

The weather was nasty. It was bitter cold, and the intermit-
tent rain showers made life even more miserable. Confused, we
watched as our three freight cars were disconnected and taken to
a side track by themselves. No one explained to us what was going
on. The locomotive returned to the front of the remaining train
cars. We decided to abandon the sidelined freight cars and board
the remaining passenger cars. The compartments were already
overcrowded. The people stood in the aisles.

I searched for an empty spot. All choice locations were occupied. I noticed a corner where I could stand. After I had eagerly

made myself master of the coveted nook, I discovered the reason why this location was available. It was a smelly spot. It was right opposite the lavatory. The latrine was plugged up. Adding to my discomfort was the lack of glass in the windows around me. The windows had blown out long ago. The draft was wicked and the odor unbearable. The predicament was inescapable. It was not until 2:00 p.m. that the locomotive got up steam enough and left the station. I was depressed.

## June 1, 1945

During the night, in order to sleep, I was forced to lie down in the passenger passage. The attempt was mostly unsuccessful. After passengers had stepped on me several times, I spent the remainder of the night standing up, trying to stay awake. When the sun broke through the darkness of the night, I was ready to take some radical action to improve my miserable location. I was in desperate need of finding a place where I could sit or lie down in some comfort. I looked at the possibilities, but realized that they were as scarce as the availability of food. A strange idea struck me. Why not climb up to the roof of the train? Up there you can either sit down or lie down. I opened the exit door at the back of the train and looked around. Then I saw the iron handles for climbing to the roof. I proceeded slowly and climbed onto the roof.

Fabulous. I was alone, dangling my legs from the edge of the train. I sat comfortably with my back in the direction the train was moving. I had a wide view of the landscape. The benefits of sitting on the top of the train included getting fresh air, a comfortable breeze, space, and no competition. For a while I was enjoying the peace and comfort of this uncommon location. Then suddenly fear gripped my heart. I realized that my life could be in great danger. A question shot through my mind. What will happen when the train passes through a tunnel, or passes under a bridge? The likelihood that I would be knocked off was quite possible. At a speed of 35 to 50 mph, I knew my head would not survive such a bashing.

I twisted around and looked forward. Then I noticed small air pipes sticking up from the roof of the train. These pipes had cleared tunnels and bridges many times. If so, then I could clear them also. Lying flat on the roof, I could hold on to the airpipes and thus pass easily under tunnels and bridges. After this scare had passed, I kept my eye on what lay ahead. Later I was told that some repatriots never made it home because they had been knocked off the roof of the train.

For the last few days most everyone's food supply had been consumed. The anxiety that fills one's mind when one does not know if there will be a meal the next day is terrifying. I began to experience that panic. At this time, miraculously, a freight car was hooked up to the last passenger car. It was filled with potatoes! We were told that these potatoes were on their way to Berlin for the Russian military. The train stopped again. The locomotive needed some repair and left us sitting on the tracks in nowhere. Presently, a few daring and desperate fellows ran back to the potato wagon and helped themselves to hands full of potatoes. I quickly followed them without a qualm and did the same.

But what can you do with raw potatoes? Learning from others, I too searched along and off the railroad track for a container. At last I found an old rusty can. Alongside the railroad ran a small river. Here I washed the three potatoes I had "organized" —a term we used to say that we had secured a food supply. Then I scooped water into the can. Having collected some dry wood, I made a fire close to the train and waited for the potatoes to come to a boil. In happy anticipation, I watched the potatoes boiling. But why should I have expected that all would go well? I should have known better. Life sometimes is but a succession of uncontrollable vicissitudes.

Just about the time the water reached the boiling stage the

train shuddered, backed up a bit and then began to move forward. The train was leaving! There was no conductor to announce *Einsteigen, Bitte*. With difficulty, I picked up my hot can with half-done potatoes. I raced after the train to reach my "favorite" spot. Without salt or pepper or butter, I chewed away on my not-so-well-cooked potatoes.

Several hours later, as the darkness of another night fell around us, the train came to a halt again and the engine disappeared another time. An interesting scene developed up and down the railroad track as small cooking fires were ignited and campfires were lighting up the sky. Here and there small groups were singing, accompanied by guitars and mandolins. I was deeply moved. Many times I had sat around a campfire playing my banjo (mandolin banjo) while vacationing in Holland. But that was some years ago and a world away. This night, as usual, was uncomfortably cold. Sleeping was impossible with only one blanket over my shoulders. I did succeed in enjoying a few short snoozes.

## JUNE 2, 1945

At noon we still had not seen the locomotive. The day was long and dreary. Five of my comrades decided to walk to a farm-house visible in the far distance to beg for food. We carried our small rusted tin cans with us. We were well on our way when we heard the locomotive whistle in the distance. The engine had returned. We discussed what to do—go on to the farm or return without food to the train. Three decided to go on to the farm and take a chance of missing the transport train. Cees, my friend, and I decided to return. We arrived just in time. They were hooking up the engine and immediately pulled out.

We watched in sadness as our three friends ran back to the train, but to no avail. I have often wondered how they made it back to Holland on their own through communist-occupied East Germany. How did their odyssey end?

Our slow progress was due to the mechanical difficulties of the locomotive. We had a different or repaired engine nearly every other day. From our morning unofficial news source I learned that the train was about twenty miles from the city of Berlin. We had traveled a little more than 100 miles since we left Ost Kreutz. At present we were traveling at a snail's pace. It was easy to walk alongside the train, a good exercise, and keep up with it. At 4:00 p.m. the train stopped. The locomotive once again disappeared.

Having suffered through several sleepless nights, I found myself totally exhausted. It was a sunny and warm day. Spotting flowering bushes that provided shade, I sat down to rest. Soon I lay flat on my back and was counting locomotives. I had no idea how long I slept, but it was almost the cause of a nasty predicament. I was rudely awakened by a sharp kick in my side. A man stood next to me and asked, "Do you want to be on this train? Then you better hurry." I did not know who he was. Was he a German or a Russian? Never mind. Whoever he was, he saved my day. I have thanked him many times over. I jumped up. The train was already moving and picking up speed. The last passenger car was about to pass me. With a desperate leap, I threw myself at the last wagon and was able to pull myself up the steps of the doorway. There I sat a while to catch my breath. From here I climbed to the roof of the passenger train and crawled and partly walked to my car, more up front.

## JUNE 3, 1945

The day of June 3 was almost gone. We had passed through Strausberg. Now we were only five miles from Berlin. The train came to an abrupt stop. "Out! out! out!" the Russians were bellowing at us. Anyway, that is what it sounded like to us. They marched us one mile to a small city park. Here we were expected to stay for the night. "How many nights?" we asked. But no one seemed to know.

The journey thus far had not been a luxury cruise. The next nights were going to be even worse than my experience on the train. We were to sleep on the ground, under the open sky. There was no food and no promise of food to arrive soon. It was cold and windy. The blanket each person had been given was not of the best quality and hardly served its purpose. Wood was being collected and large fires soon lit up the surroundings. Moving as close to the fire as was safe and comfortable, we victims of circumstance prepared to survive through the first night of increased misery.

I had enough of camping and said to Cees, my friend on this journey, "Let us go to the village, knock at a door, and ask for shelter." "That is an idea worth trying out," said Cees as he gave me a broad smile. Looking somewhat sheepish, he queried, "Who does the asking?" I volunteered. The main street of the village had a few houses which showed promise. The one that had white window curtains encouraged us to try. At our first knock the door opened and a middle-aged woman asked us what we wanted. We explained that we were returning to Holland under Russian direction and were camped for the next two or three nights in the town's park. I asked, "Would you have a room and a bed for us two?"

The neatly dressed woman looked us over quickly with a keen eye and some concern. She asked us, softly, "*Sind Sie sauber?*" ("Are you clean?"). This concern was a natural fear. People traveling in large mixed groups, especially in war devastated territories, often shared the company of body lice. My response was quick and convincing. "Oh, yes ma'am, we are clean, don't you worry." And I meant it, but I was wrong as I discovered several days later.

Cees and I were happily surprised when the German woman invited us into her house. Our first try succeeded without a flaw. When we returned in the evening, the hostess served us a fine and nourishing meal. She showed us the bedroom with two beds. What an inviting sight, clean, white sheets, blankets, and a fluffy pillow. For the next three nights we thought we had landed in Utopia.

# JUNE 4, 1945

Cees and I slept until 9:00 a.m. We left the house to "organize," that is, go in search of food, each on his own. During the morning, while walking in the country, I met two young German women. I asked them, "Do you know where I could get some food?" They pointed to a farm. "Go to that farm house. That farmer is very generous." I knocked at the door. The farmer's wife opened the entrance, but just a little. She said, "What do you want?" "I am very hungry," I said. "Would you have something to eat for me?"

I felt rotten. Never in my life had I begged for food. This was humiliating. But hunger drove me to this level and disgrace. Then something happened. I was poorly prepared for it. It was unexpected and it made me fall even lower in my social behavior and graces. Instead of inviting me in or giving me a morsel of food, the woman said firmly, "No, I cannot help you." At the same time she slammed the door shut in my face. Well, almost. I acted against my father's teachings —he had told me when I was a brazen youngster, "Don't ever be so rude as to put your foot in the door if people do not wish to help you or listen to you." So, I had never forced my foot in someone's door. However, circumstances now called for an immediate action. Swifter than the farmlady could shut the door, my foot shot forward, even faster than a snake striking at a field mouse. My foot prevented the door from being shut. "Please, please ma'am," I pleaded, "Do not close the door. Just a few potatoes will do."

Nearly a minute passed. Then the pressure on my foot relaxed. The door inched open. The reluctant woman said, "Come in, follow me." We reached the large family kitchen. "Please, sit down there." While I ate the sandwich she put in front of me, she filled a brown paper bag with a few potatoes and a piece of dark brown bread. With my trophy I returned to the camp in the city park. I felt extremely fortunate. I had enough food for another day. I hoped that Cees had been as lucky as I.

Once more the Russian Commander called on me to bake bread for our Dutch transport. This solved my need for a few more days. The flour had arrived and had been delivered to the local bakery of Meister (Master) Heinrich Mansfeldt. His bakery was on Main Street. I was asked to assist Meister Mansfeldt. At 3:00 p.m. I walked into the baking shop. I wondered if the shop was in good working condition. For instance, would there be electricity and running water? Who would be helping to knead the dough? I was happy to find running water was available, but no electricity. Mixing the dough would have to be by hand—an exhausting task.

Meister Mansfeldt appeared to be a typical small-town baker, not unlike the one I had worked for in Blankenfelde. He was the "Meister" baker in town and he acted that way. Would this lead to a confrontation between us? It appeared from the beginning that from his point of view I was merely an apprentice or a neophyte. He showed me the flour, the mixing trough, and the oven. He indicated that I could start working. I put on my baker's apron and poured the water, the leaven, and the flour into the trough. Mansfeldt was watching me passively, I thought. With all the ingredients in the trough, I put both of my hands into the mix and began to work the dough. This was going to be hard work, a job that leads to much perspiration. Mansfeldt, I noticed, had not put on his apron. I wondered, "Is he going to stand there and not help me?" I had understood that I was to assist him. We both were responsible for producing the bread.

I decided on a calculated risk, so I asked him, "Meister Mansfeldt, are you not helping me with mixing the dough?" He looked at me absentmindedly and merely nodded "No." I decided to send him a clear message of what I thought of that. Pulling my hands out of the mix, I proceeded to scrape my arms and hands clean of the dough. Meister Mansfeldt was surprised and said to me, "Gustav, you are not finished yet. The dough is not mixed properly." I looked at him with a soft but sarcastic smile and responded, "I was asked by the Russian Commander to assist you, not to do the job by myself." The astonished Mansfeldt came quickly back with, "Don't go, Gustav. I will help you." Putting on his apron, we continued, side by side, mixing the dough. As the mix improved, so did our conversation. A more friendly atmosphere began to prevail.

From that point on Mansfeldt treated me as an accomplished baker, almost as an old friend. After the last loaf came out of the oven, he said, "Gustav, I am sure you would like to take a bath. My wife has filled the bathtub with hot water. You will find the tub in the garage. There is soap and also a towel. Then he added, surprisingly, "After you are finished, please come to the kitchen. We will have evening supper together. I greatly enjoyed the warm bath and the delicious supper. Before I left Mrs. Mansfeldt had packed me a nice breakfast. We parted with, *aufwiedersehen* ("see you again"). We had been asked to bake bread the following day also.

## JUNE 5, 1945

Rather late in the afternoon we were back at the bakery. Someone stopped by the shop and told me that we had to be ready to leave at any moment. Trucks to pick us up were on the way. I left Meister Mansfeldt to complete the work and hurried back to the city park. I did not want to miss the buses. But, as had been true so many times before, delays slowed down our departure. The night approached fast and it was icy cold. I did not dare return to the house to sleep in our comfortable and warm beds for fear of missing the transportation by truck to Magdeburg, some 100 miles away.

## June 6, 1945

About 2:00 a.m. the night turned colder. It also started to rain. After one hour the rain stopped. It was not until 10:00 a.m. that we boarded the overloaded buses. I found myself amidst a group of Belgians. The nearly 100-mile trip was a wild one. The roads had been damaged during the attack on Berlin. Bombs had blown craters and tanks had turned up the roads as though a giant Toro-Tiller had gone by. Skirting the southside of Berlin, we ultimately arrived at Magdeburg on the Elbe River. On the other side of the river was the American zone. It was now 7:00 p.m. We were happy to have arrived here. Only a few more steps across the bridge and we would be in the hands of the American forces. But first we needed to eat and spend one more night with the Russians. After standing in a long line for nearly two hours, I was handed a bowl of some kind of soup and a large piece of brown bread.

Dead tired and exhausted due to lack of sleep, I searched for a bivouac. The floor of the building assigned to us was of concrete. It was extremely dirty. By chance I found a discarded closet. Dismantling one of its doors, I used it as a mattress. It shielded me from the cold concrete floor. I congratulated myself for the ingenious thought. I do not remember anything that happened during the night. I just slept.

## June 7, 1945

At 6:00 a.m. I joined a small team of volunteers to go to the kitchen and pick up breakfast. We waited for the food for 700 comrades—French, Belgians, and Dutch, but we did not receive it until 10:00 a.m. During breakfast we were told to be ready to leave by noon. However, it was not until 5:00 p.m. that we were marching the last mile and a half to reach the Elbe River and the bridge that separated the Russians from the Americans. When the motley column of Hollanders finally approached the bridge over the Elbe, the new border between east and west, there fell a strange silence over the scene. I felt uneasy, even a bit scared. Would we really be free this day? Would the Russians truly let us march across the Elbe to freedom? Or would they aim their machine guns at our backs, as they would do later along the Berlin wall, and mow us down, just in sight of liberty? The heavy silence that surrounded me was broken only by our shoes meeting the iron roadbed of the bridge. The total hush convinced me that I was not the only one worried.

When the first individuals crossed the halfway mark on the bridge, the point where the Americans were in control, there rose a thunderous roar from the column. The multitude of Dutchmen surged forward. Then the column disintegrated and everyone ran to cross the border. Around me, including myself—I am somewhat emotional—I saw many who had tears in their eyes when we passed the American soldiers. These brave soldiers smiled at us. It was obvious that our arrival was anticipated. Everything was well organized. Trucks speeded us to our sleeping quarters. We were given a simple but nourishing meal. Fear was now replaced by freedom. Past worries faded away. Laughter filled the air and the future looked bright. No more waiting. Only a few more days of travel. Then, home sweet home, no more to roam.

## JUNE 8, 1945

From Magdeburg to the German-Dutch border was a distance of about 200 miles. By mid-morning we were informed that we should get ready to leave. We marched to the train station and were divided into groups of ten. Each group received a burlap sack with cans of Brazilian corned beef, bread, sweets, and packages of vegetables. Everything went "Hurry, hurry." I was among a group of ten that boarded a freight car. However, this freight car had a roof to protect us from the weather. All in all, this time I did not feel the panic I experienced when I boarded the Russian freight train when we had left Driesen some 300 miles back.

The train traveled about 50 miles per hour. The landscape we passed through was beautiful. Spring flowers covered the fields and meadows. I even recognized an occasional bird—the meadow lark, the marshhawk, and of course the most common European bird, the house sparrow. A few times I spotted one or more deer standing at the edge of a dark forest. What a pleasant sight! At times we traveled through areas where the damage of war was quite visible, but it no longer appeared as terrible and frightening now that we were in the land that had been liberated from Adolf Hitler's hands and his Nazi collaborators. Even the "tack, tack, tack" of the train's wheels on the railroad track sounded like music, even if it was monotonous.

My group of ten pulled together towards suppertime. The burlap sack was opened and the food portions were equally divided among us. Our eyes sparkled at the abundance of delicious canned meats. It had been a long time since we had had meat to eat. The last abundance of meat I had eaten was when my Yugoslavian friends and I had butchered that cow near Driesen on the Polish border. The eating feast began. Faster than we should have, we gulped down the corned beef, followed by vegetables and chunks of bread that were washed down with the help of canned drinks. Instead of keeping the sweets for a snack later in the evening, we devoured them so fast that one might think we feared the Russians were coming on board to steal our food.

During the night the train stopped at Osnabruck, a German city only 75 miles from the Dutch border. Here we were asked to get off the train. We were served a plate of hot soup and some German bread. Sadly enough, the soup was burned and it was an effort to swallow it. But that was not the worst of it. The situation was about to get even nastier.

Soon after we had left Osnabruck, a few among us began to complain about stomach cramps and pain. Others were moving towards the sliding doors of the freight car. It soon was necessary to slide the doors open. There was a row of sick men lying on their stomachs with their heads hanging outside the train. I was among the first victims of our gluttony and lack of self-control. The delicious and rich foods that we had so speedily consumed were causing us great discomfort. As time passed, nearly everyone had taken a turn at hanging his head outside and watching the railroad tracks fly by. Maybe we should not be judged too harshly. It could be that our upset stomachs were not due purely to our gluttony, but to their inability to hold the abundance of rich food.

## June 9, 1945

We arrived at the German-Dutch border near the city of Bendheim. We were now only 4.5 miles from the Dutch border. We thought that our lives from now on would be tranquil indeed. This was not to be the case.

Breakfast passed without difficulty. Then we were taken to a large sports stadium or high school gym. There we were told to undress and take a shower. Coming out of the shower, we had to stand while in the nude before a medic who searched our bodies. I was curious about how I would pass the test. I remembered that when we were at Magdeburg, I had felt a strong itching on several body parts. Suspecting that I had picked up a few Russian lice, I had hidden in some bushes. There I stripped and examined myself. To my horror, I found "Ivan-lice" that had invaded my privacy. My underwear was well occupied. My first defense was to get rid of my contaminated underwear. Then I found a bucket with water. I gave myself a thorough bath. During the days that followed I felt relief from those tiny parasites. How long would that last?

Nearing the examiner, I almost held my breath. Quickly and professionally, the officer examined my body. He looked at me, smiled, and said, "Marvelous, you are as clean as a whistle. You may proceed." I picked up my clothing and got dressed. On the way out, I passed an open door to a large room. There I saw several men from our group who were being shaven all over their bodies. Later I learned that they had been deloused. My trip and inspection in the woods had paid off well.

Climbing on the trucks that were waiting for us, we drove the last five miles to the German-Dutch border. Here we were directed to some apartment houses where we spent the night before crossing into the homeland.

## June 10, 1945

You would have thought that after our showers at Bendheim, we were clean. Then why did we again have to take showers? Unknown to all of us was the special reason for this final shower. Let me explain.

Having had a quick shower and knowing that I was clean, we marched in a single line, still in the nude, to an exit door. On either side of this door stood two officials and near them a few armed policemen. My curiosity kept climbing. What was going on here? It was clear to me that they were not looking for lice. If not, then for what? The line kept moving at a steady pace. I noticed that when a man reached the two officials, he was told to face them and lift up high both of his arms. "Up, high, straight!" he was told. Then his arms were inspected closely and with a sharp eye.

When the fifth person ahead of me reached the examiners, he raised his arms. They inspected him diligently. It took them somewhat longer than others they had inspected. My wish to know what was going on heightened. Then I saw his arms come down. The armed policeman stepped forward. I heard the click of metal. I could clearly see that they had handcuffed the man. He was arrested and led away. Why? My heart beat faster. Anxiously and uncomfortably, I waited my turn. I saw what had happened, but I still did not know why. Finally, I faced the examiners myself. At their command, I raised my arms with apprehension. What did they look for? Inspecting me briefly, the officer to my left, apparently in charge, touched my left shoulder lightly and said, "Don't you worry. All is well. Welcome home." The man must have sensed my fear.

Still I wanted to know what they had been looking for under my arms. While getting dressed, I heard others discussing that same question. I asked the person next to me about it. He explained, "The examiners were inspecting everyone to see whether or not we had a tattoo under our arms. It was the tattoo of the German elite military unit referred to as the "SS." If that symbol was under your arm, you were immediately arrested. A number of Dutch boys and men had joined the German military. This news shocked me. The fifth person ahead of me; and the one who had been arrested had been the main leader of the group of Hollanders that had left Driesen. How did he do it? How did he hide his secret? No one apparently had suspected that he was a Dutch Nazi. Fortunately, he had been caught before he slipped back into Holland.

## JUNE 11 AND 12, 1945

Life was so much better back in Holland. Food and sleeping facilities were excellent. We were in Enschede, Holland, and were free to walk about the city at will. The watchword of these several days, however, was still "Wait, wait, wait."

## JUNE 13, 1945

Having been in the "wait, wait, wait" status, I could not imagine that June 13 was going to be my lucky day, and this despite the number 13. We were awakened at 2 a.m. and told to be ready to go on board a ship leaving from the city of Kampen, some 50 miles northwest from Enschede, to go to Amsterdam across the Zuider Zee, a 40-mile sea voyage.

The weather was stormy when we boarded the ship. It rained hard and a wicked wind was blowing across the Zuider Zee. When we reached open waters, the ship was tossed to and fro and up and down. Soon we had a great host of sea-sick people on board. I was not feeling too well. However, I once had been told that, to prevent becoming sick, one should find the center of the ship and sit there. Here the tossing of the ship would be less than elsewhere. I found a place near the center of the ship and this did the trick for me. I did not get sea-sick.

The closer I was coming to my home the more my worries intensified. How would I find my family? Was this going to be a wonderful reunion or a sad meeting? Would I find my family alive and well? Did our house still stand or had it been blown to bits by a bomb? I was tense. My fingernails were shorter than the day before.

As we progressed across the Zuider Zee the weather turned milder. I was watching for the coastline of North Holland. A dark line on the horizon slowly turned more distinct and the outline of a row of dwellings changed imperceptibly into a village and then into a city. "Amsterdam!" someone shouted. Most people stood quietly and said nothing. Were they feeling and thinking as I was? How at the same time do you express great joy and a feeling of fear? Amsterdam. What a wonderful sight. It was like a beacon of hope. It was the capital of the province of North Holland, and only about thirty miles from my hometown, IJmuiden. But how would I get home?

Just before leaving the ship we were instructed to follow our appointed leaders who were waiting for us on the quay. We walked a short distance and arrived at the Amsterdam Central Railroad Station. There we were served a sumptuous lunch. Of course, any decent meal was a feast for us compared to what had been our fare for the last months. Once again we were registered. We then were

Destruction of part of IJmuiden, the Jeeninga hometown.

given tickets to board buses waiting for us. The bus I entered was listed as going to the cities of Haarlem, IJmuiden, and Beverwijk. I found a seat at the window in the middle of the bus and relaxed. That is, up to a point. I was now confident that I would be home shortly. Only a few more miles and this treacherous odyssey of mine would end. The possibility that a deadly hazard was still threatening the happy completion of my long journey never entered my mind.

I looked around the bus. Many passengers were staring out the windows. Others looked straight ahead, expressionless. These people looked as though they were going to jail instead of home. But how can one be happy when facing an unknown future? Returning home for us was like taking a leap in the dark. With pictures of "Valleys of Death" still fresh on our minds, it was difficult to shout with joy. Once more the slogan for the day was "wait, wait, wait."

Having dropped off a number of passengers for Haarlem, the bus ran smoothly northward. Being the only one to go to IJmuiden, I was informed that I would be dropped off at the North Sea Canal ferry. From there I could walk the last five miles home.

I thought through my options. I now was in territory that was very well-known to me. Between the highway we were traveling and my home there were large estates surrounded by woods. As a youngster I had often climbed the fences of these private grounds. With my neighborhood friends, I had played there and climbed the large beech trees. Going through these woods would be a considerable shortcut to my house. I told the driver that I would like to get off now and not at the ferry. I said to him, "I will walk home from here." The driver tipped his cap in agreement and put on the brakes. Picking up my rucksack, I stepped out of the bus as happy as a bird leaving its cage.

In Holland, as elsewhere in Europe, bicycle paths run parallel to most highways. I walked on the bicycle path and set myself a fast pace. The highway and the bicycle path looked forsaken. However, a short distance ahead of me I saw an old and very short woman pushing a two-wheeled cart. The load appeared almost too heavy for her. Soon I caught up with the senior citizen. I thought, "Poor soul, you probably have been visiting farms to buy food for your household." I felt the urge to go and help her push the cart. But I could not do that. She might slow me down. I wanted to go home the fastest and shortest way possible.

When I was passing her, I glanced at Lady Methuselah. Surely, I did not know her. I picked up my pace. I still had to cross the woods. There were some miles still to go. Having barely passed her, I thought I heard her say something. Probably she was talking to herself, I reasoned. I heard her again, but now it was louder. I sharpened my ears a bit, but hurried on. When I heard her shouting again, the voice sounded familiar. I now heard her most distinctly and I slowed in my tracks. She shouted, "Guus, Guus, Guus!" I stopped immediately and waited in total amazement as the woman caught up with me. I looked at her more closely. Then I recognized the old, short, and very skinney woman as our neighbor, Mrs. van der Pile. I ran up to her. She left her cart and ran towards me. When we met we embraced and hugged and kissed.

For some time we could hardly speak.

Finally I asked her, "How is your family?" "All my sons are home now and are doing fine," Mrs. Pile replied. Then I asked her, "How are my parents, Oppie, Fritz and Hilda?" "Don't you worry," she said. "They are all just wonderful and there is a great surprise waiting for you at home."

"What is it? Please tell me right now," I urged her on. With a twinkle in her lively eyes and a naughty little twitch on her face, she told me. "Your brother Emil is also home!"

"Are you sure?" I blurted out, "Emil is alive and home?" I begged her to tell me more, but to do it quickly since I wanted to hurry on. I told her that I was going to take a shortcut through the woods. Mrs. Pile stopped and took me by the arm while she looked at me with fear in her eyes. Then she said emphatically, "Oh, no, you can't do that, I won't let you take that shortcut!"

"Why not?" I wanted to know.

Mrs. Pile, full with emotion, explained. "The Germans have placed landmines in all of those woods. Today no one with any sense goes there. If you do, you most likely will lose your life or at least a limb or two."

Listening to Mrs. Pile's warning terrified me. Instantly I was convinced to change my travel plan. In silence we continued our journey together. I could not get her warning out of my mind. I thought about the consequence of walking through those treacherous fields full of landmines. I could see the headlines in the local newspaper. "He was almost home, but then he lost two legs after walking into a field of landmines!" How enormously tragic that would have been.

Finally, only a few blocks of houses separated me from Rembrandt Street, our family grocery store, and my home. Anticipation of seeing our home nearly made me tremble. We turned the final corner and "home sweet home" came clearly in view. "I will pick up my rucksack later," I whispered, breathing heavily. I left Mrs. Pile and ran down the street toward our house,

Bicycle entrance (*poort*) to the Jeeninga home (right), IJmuiden.

faster than a horse runs when smelling his barn.

Between our neighbor's house and my home was a covered gateway. As I ran through the passageway I shouted, as loud as I was capable, the usual home-coming yell of my younger days. I was hoping my family would hear me. Unknown to me, the family was sitting around the livingroom center table. There was father, mother, Oppie, Fritz, and Hilda. One other person was present. Just by pure luck, Emil, my older brother, had received several days of furlough and was also there. He had survived the Omaha Beach landing and also had successfully come "home."

The first to hear my boyish yelling was my youngest sister, Hilda. She jumped up from the table and hollered, "Guus is home! Listen, he is in the "poort" (gateway). Who opened the door when I stumbled in? I don't remember. The air was filled with emotional electricity as I hugged one after the other, and finally all at once. My odyssey had come to a wonderful, unimaginable ending. All was well at home. Only one of my family members was not present that day. It was Trudee, the oldest daughter and oldest child in the family. But no one was worried for she was doing well, then living in faraway Chicago in the United States.

The Second World War was over and done with. My long and dangerous odyssey was completed. Worries were laid to rest. We all could start new lives and plan for the future. The many happenings we all had experienced turned out to have been "meaningful happenings." The best of all was "home sweet home" or, as the Dutch like to put it, *zoals het klokje thuis tikt, tikt het nergens* ("as the clock ticks at home, it ticks nowhere else").

*"I [God] am going to send an angel in front of you,*
*to guard you on the way and to bring you*
*to the place that I have prepared."*
*(Exodus 23:20)*

# TO THE NEW WORLD
## 1946 ~ 1959

# POST-WAR
# NEW BEGINNINGS

ON JUNE 13, 1945, I WALKED INTO OUR HOUSE in IJmuiden and found the family sitting around the living room table. All were overjoyed to see me back home alive and well. What a special day it was because I was also greeted by my older brother Emil whom I had not seen in over five years. Emil was on furlough from his army duties in the Dutch-Canadian Irene Brigade. He had survived landing his American tank on Omaha Beach; I had survived the Allied bombings of Berlin and the Russian conquest of the city; my parents, two sisters and one brother had made it through a time of near starvation. For us the Second World War had a happy ending that brought some exciting beginnings.

In the months that followed my return, I found work again in a pastry bakery. I joined my parents at church on Sundays, but inwardly rebelled against religion. The experiences of war with all their horror and evil had shaken my faith in God. Many a night I argued with my parents about the existence of God and the meaning and value of the Christian faith. After many months of reading, debating, and searching, I began to formulate a new and more mature base for my faith. Gradually I began to sense a call to follow in my father's footsteps and decided to enter the Christian ministry. This decision would turn out to be the force that laid the foundation of a lifelong involvement in Christian service and education.

Our church youth group in Haarlem-IJmuiden was led by a young lady named Aletta whom I had not known until I returned home after the war. I learned that her mother had been introduced to the Church of God congregation by the family maid, Jeanne Peper, who herself was a member of the Church of God congregation in Haarlem. Mrs. van der Breggen had brought Aletta into contact with the church and my father, the pastor, who guided her in the study of the Bible and spiritual matters. The foundation was being laid for the development of some very important future relationships.

Our youth group often met at the home of Aletta, often referred to as "the House on the Canal." One of the interesting things I noticed in the house was the great number of clocks. Doctor van der Breggen's hobby was collecting clocks and keeping them all going on time. Down the block from this home on the Barteljorisstbraat 19 was a well-known Haarlem watch shop owned by Casper ten Boom. The doctor had found a friend in Casper, for both were in love with clocks. In fact, several of the clocks in Guus van der Breggen's house had been bought at Casper's watch shop. However, the two families had something more serious in common than clocks or watches. Both families had been involved in the resistance movement, although they had no knowledge of each other's doings. The ten Boom's family activities became known world-wide when Corrie ten Boom told her family story of hiding Jews, the family's imprisonment, death, and survival in her famous book *The Hiding Place* (1971).

Aletta too knew the ten Boom family and had been in their watch shop. Before the war Aletta had bought a golden watch at that shop. She wore it proudly until it finally stopped forever in 1975. Then after the war Aletta and Corrie had several conversations, but these were never focused on the war years, but on what to do to improve the plight of so many unfortunate people. In spite of their similar circumstances, both their fathers having died in concentration camps, they did not look back, but concentrated on the future with hope.

During these first post-war years I too was looking forward to the future and it's possibilities. When I was a child, my Uncle

August (Gustav) Werner had told me on one of his visits to Holland that I should learn the baker's trade and come to America to work in his shop, "The Amber Bakery." Soon after I had returned home from Germany I wrote to my uncle in Chicago for the papers that would allow me to migrate to the U.S.A. On May 13, 1947, my parents, two sisters, a brother, and Aletta took me to Schiphol, the Amsterdam airport. When I walked to the wait-

The ten Boom watch shop, now a museum, Haarlem, Holland (2001).

ing airplane, the family and Aletta waved goodbye to me. I was aware of a feeling of sadness for leaving my family. I was certain that this also was the end of a budding friendship with Aletta.

In the Fall of 1947 I enrolled at Anderson College and began my ministerial training. Less than a year later, to my joy, Aletta came on a visit to Anderson, Indiana, as a houseguest of Dr. and Mrs. Charles E. Brown. It was then that our friendship intensified. But the evolving relationship was interrupted when Aletta returned to Holland to work for the Church of God Board of Missions on behalf of refugees of the war.

Nearly four years later in 1953 I left Chicago on a trip around the world for one year. It was a life's dream come true. My first stop was Holland. On Sunday morning I went to worship in the Church of God congregation in Haarlem. It was a wonderful morning to meet old friends, including Aletta and her mother. Before I left the United States I had made plans to attend the

European Convention of the Church of God that was to be held that year in Denmark. Unknown to Aletta and me, she and I both had been invited to serve as youth leaders during the convention. Because we were Dutch, the organizing committee placed both of us as guests in a Danish home. It was thought best to do so since Aletta spoke Danish as well as Dutch. We were surprised but enjoyed working as a team.

Before the convention ended, Aletta and I had agreed to a new beginning together. We were married on September 2, 1953, in the City Hall of Haarlem, with Aletta's sister Noor and her husband Hans as witnesses. I had my old friend Cor Kistemaker as my witness. Aletta's mother had arranged for a fancy dinner in one of the family's favorite restaurants near Haarlem.

By this time, the House on the Canal had been sold and turned into legal offices. I always regarded it as a good omen that I had known the family and had been in the House on the Canal numerous times when it was still occupied by the van der Breggen family. Therefore, I was delighted to hear that a few years ago the house was sold to a young couple with three children. The house now has been renovated into a family residence again. Fantastic. The House on the Canal has returned to its legacy, *zoals het klokje thuis tikt, tikt het nergens* ("the way the clock ticks at home, it ticks nowhere else").

# WINDOW # 47

EXCITEMENT! YES, I WAS VERY EXCITED INDEED. It was May, 1947, and I found myself standing at the departure gate at Schiphol, Amsterdam's airport. I was emigrating from the Netherlands to the U.S.A. I had not been at an airport or on an airplane ever before. In fact, I hardly knew anyone who had traveled by air. Now I was about to go on my first flight, not a mere hundred or so miles distance, but several thousands of miles across the Atlantic Ocean, in fact all the way to the New World, to North America. The final destination in America was none other than the renowned "gangster city," Chicago.

My neighborhood buddies were awestruck and some were even jealous. Everything about this trip to America was new to me, and that included my visit to the bank in Amsterdam where I had to pay my airfare, some 990 Dutch guilders, which was just about all the money I had in the bank.

There was definitely something about this journey that made it remarkable, one of a kind. Let me tell you of one incident that was of a most unusual nature and now is hard to believe ever really happened. But trust me, it is true. First, I will describe some details that led up to that near-fatal event.

When I entered the aircraft I was escorted to my seat by the steward. The seat was at the window that, as I learned later, was the emergency window. The seat was located just above the left wing of the plane. To my right sat a friendly but somewhat quiet gentleman who told me that he was from Canada. Maybe that was the reason he was so quiet—he did not speak Dutch and I could not speak English.

When the plane, a Constellation, taxied into position for

takeoff, my body tensed, no doubt because of my ignorance about the meaning of all the rumbling sounds around me. Added to this noise was the thundering roar of the plane's engines increasing their power just before we were to leave the ground. Finally, the Constellation began to roll forward with increasing speed. I found myself holding on to my seat with both hands. I was both experiencing fear and was enthralled by amazement that this huge, bulky vehicle, wonder of wonders, was leaving the earth! The moment of the take off was the highlight of my first introduction to air travel. The departure was successful and the flight continued smoothly. I relaxed in my seat and felt safe and at ease.

Hours later we landed in the city of Reykjavik, Iceland. One hour later we reboarded and continued the journey. I was looking forward to another exciting experience. This time I felt more at ease as the plane taxied into position, raced its engines, increased its speed, and roared into the sky. But I was unprepared for a totally new experience.

I do not know how high we were flying when it happened, but suddenly a large object fell into my lap. To my amazement and horror, I realized that it was the emergency window that had popped out of its position to my left. I looked outside as the clouds flew by; I could hear the air rushing by the vacant window frame while I wondered what to do and what would happen next. By now the steward, working in front of the cabin, was alerted, realized what had happened, and immediately was aware of the tremendous danger that I and the other passengers were in. He came racing down the aisle, took the window from my lap, and thrust it back into its frame. He held the window in place until he was certain that the aircraft had reached an altitude high enough to have the air pressure inside press and keep the window tight in place. I was saved and would make it to Chicago after all!

I often have reflected on this exciting, most uncommon, and truly frightening incident. I know that I might have been sucked out of my seat, a quick ending to my new and promising journey to America even before I had reached its shores. However, my first flight—and the many that would follow—was in my heavenly Father's hand.

*"I know that whatever God does,*
*It shall be forever.*
*Nothing can be added to it*
*and nothing taken from it."*
*(Ecclesiastes 3:14)*

# NOT YOU!

EXPERIENCE IS AN EXCELLENT TEACHER and I have learned much about life from it. Numerous times I have discovered that my being only five feet five inches in height and youthful looking for my age has been in my favor at times and turned to my disadvantage at other times.

On my trip around the world in 1952-1953, I found myself one day in the passenger waiting room at the Athens, Greece, airport. A little earlier I had handed over my passport to a custom's officer to be checked and was asked to wait until my name was called. Then I could pick up my passport and board the plane. The waiting room was filled with passengers waiting to be cleared and to board.

I was sitting close to the double swinging doors through which an airline clerk came into the room to call out passenger names. The room was beginning to empty out and I expected my name to be called shortly. The double door swung open again. The burly airline clerk, with a rough voice, came charging into the waiting room loudly shouting, "Mr. Jiemieha, Mr. Jiemieha." As the clerk passed me, he never slowed down. I was not certain whether or not the clerk was calling my name. Therefore, while he hurried past me, I asked him, "Are you calling for me?" The clerk, without giving me a glance, blurted out, "No, not you," and he walked on, shouting over and over again, "Mr. Jiemieha, Mr. Jiemieha." But no one responded to him. I decided that he was calling for me and I was quite irritated by his snub. I got up and walked through the swinging door and up to the customer's window and received my passport and permission to board the airplane. Then the nasty clerk returned, still looking for Mr.

Jiemieha. Then he saw me getting my passport. He now asked me if I were Mr. Jiemieha. I responded, "Well, yes, I am Mr. Jeeninga, but who are you?" Then I continued, "I have never been given such a rude response as you gave me. Please, tell me, what is your name? I think I will write a letter to the company and complain about your behavior."

The clerk tried hard to change the discussion by telling me that he had visited Chicago and loved America. He also wished me a wonderful flight back home. After I had gotten seated on the airplane, I mused about the many different personalities one meets on a trip around the world, and what influence one's age, height, and looks make on how some people might treat you.

*Solomon: "He who is devoid of wisdom,*
*despiseth his neighbor." (Proverbs 11:12)*

# FIRE! FIRE! FIRE!

LIVING DANGEROUSLY CAN BE THE RESULT of a conscious decision or it can be because of circumstances outside of one's control. In my story described below, I like to think that living dangerously came from certain conditions and not by my choice.

While on my world trip in 1952-1953, I stopped in Japan to visit friends and see the country. After a most wonderful vacation in that most unusual culture, I boarded a Pan-American Strato-cruiser to fly to Hawaii on my way back to the U.S.A. To my surprise, this enormously large two-deck airplane only carried twelve passengers. I mused about the destiny of this flight as I remembered the world-map hanging in the office of my travel agent in Chicago. Written on the top of this map was the line, "Destinations Unlimited." That line had excited me when planning my year-long journey around the globe. Now, while flying over the waters of the Pacific (i. e., supposedly "peaceful") Ocean, I did not include the possibility of a sinister development.

During the flight I moved from my passenger seat to the lounge on the deck below to relax, look out of the window, and enjoy watching the clouds and sea far below. At one point I was looking passively down the right wing when the spell was suddenly broken. I was startled when I saw thick plumes of smoke beginning to pour from the outer right engine. I was horrified when I saw flames beginning to leap out from all sides of the propellers. Then the engine suddenly stalled, the smoke dissipated, and the flames were gone. To my stunned mind, I saw another strange thing happening. From underneath the wing a short piece of pipe began slowly to lower from the wing until it reached at least two feet. I was dumbfounded and worried when I noticed a water-like substance coming out of the short pipe. The liquid almost immediately vaporized. What was happening?

With only three engines still running, the plane began a slow descent. Were we going to ditch into the Pacific? Rushing back toward my passenger seat, I ran into the steward and told him what I had seen. He assured me that the captain was aware of the emergency and had everything under control. I knew that that was just a general statement. Soon I learned that the liquid that poured out of the short nozzle under the wing was airplane fuel that was jettisoned to lighten the airplane for a landing on only three engines. The steward explained that the aircraft was going to stop over on Wake Island, located halfway between Tokyo and Honolulu. With this information, I slid back into my seat, still apprehensive about the outcome of this flight.

The arrival on Wake Island was smooth. It was a very flat, sandy island with only low vegetation. While the aircraft was being repaired, the small group of passengers was taken on a free sightseeing tour of the island. Evidence of World War II was very obvious everywhere, including Japanese burned-out tanks and other military vehicles. The best part of our visit to Wake Island came when we were taken to a motel and had a chance to get some rest. Up early the next morning and with the engine repaired, we flew off into the blue sky. Once more I moved to the observation deck while planning my upcoming visit to the Hawaiian Islands. All of a sudden my tranquil moment turned to astonishment as I watched flames and smoke pouring out of another engine on the right wing. I suppressed a bad word and rushed up to the main cabin to learn the bad news that the captain had shut down the burning motor and was dropping another load of petrol into the ocean. We banked sharply and returned to Wake Island.

After four hours of hard work, the engineers insisted that the repair was complete. The Strato-cruiser took to the sky with ease, but I wondered whether it was headed for an "unknown destiny." For the next hour calm returned among the passengers and crew and I was half asleep in my comfortable chair when I realized that I had awakened because of an obvious change in the roaring sound of the engines. I took a quick look out of the left window and, to my utter disbelief, was looking at engine number three on fire! I knew I was not dreaming or imagining it because I was rather close to that smoking and flaming motor. The blades slowed their rotating, the plane banked to the left, a little nozzle appeared, and the usual dumping began. The captain's voice came on the intercom and announced that we should shortly be landing on Wake Island. I always can claim that I have visited Wake Island three times.

When we boarded the fourth time since leaving Tokyo, the steward did not say much, but just smiled. My mind was on engine number four. I have often thought what might have happened to this flight if all three engines had started burning at the same time instead of in turn, hours apart? We soon arrived safely in Hololulu.

*"Do not boast about tomorrow, For you do not know*
*what a day may bring forth."*
*(Proverbs 27:1)*

127

# PIVOTAL ENCOUNTERS
# WITH DEAN RUSSELL OLT

WHEN I WAS ABOUT SIXTEEN YEARS OLD, I read these words: "Whoever walks with the wise becomes wise. . ." (Prov. 13:20). Most of my encounters with intellectuals and other wise persons were accidental. Some of these contacts had a momentum of their own, and often were catalysts to subsequent developments. This was true in a unique way in 1946 when I met a wandering stranger.

It was busy in our home in IJmuiden, Holland. The war had just ended and the devastation of property and displacement of people were evident and painful. By God's grace, my family and our home had all survived. Then one day, just after lunch, a neighbor came to the door and said excitedly, "Mrs. Jeeninga, there stands an American at the corner of the Good Shepherd Church. He cannot speak Dutch, but he is repeating the name "Jeeninga, Jeeninga."

"Oh, thank you, Mrs. Pile," mother said. She rushed to the back of the house, shouting, "Fedde, Fedde, come quickly!" Father was busy in the bicycle shed. He left the shed immediately, asking, "Yes, Thea, what's the matter?" Mother replied, "In front of the church stands an American who is asking for us. What do we do?"

I joined my dad as we walked across the street to introduce ourselves to the stranger. The gentleman told us his name was Russell Olt. I should explain that no one in our family spoke English at that time, but we did know some common English words and expressions.

Everyone was curious to learn who this American was, but

especially why he was looking for us Jeeningas. At first the best my father could do was take him into our house and try in some way to solve this mystery. We were unprepared for what we found out. After Mr. Olt was seated in our living room we asked him if he needed something to eat or if he would like to have a cup of tea? He said, "No, thank you, but I would like a cup of cold water, please." We were astonished. In Dutch culture it is expected that the host will offer at least a cup of tea with one or more cookies, certainly not a cup of cold water.

During our feeble attempts to try to understand this heavy and imposing American, my father decided to call a member of our church, Aletta van der Breggen (it was she who a few years later became my wife). Aletta lived in Haarlem seven miles away, near the home of Corrie ten Boom (who later would become well-known through her books, the first being *The Hiding Place* published in 1971). Aletta spoke English rather well. Dad asked her to come quickly to help us and Mr. Olt communicate. Through Aletta we learned that Mr. Olt was the Academic Dean of Anderson College in Anderson, Indiana. In Anderson he had learned from the Missions Board of the Church of God about Pastor Fedde Jeeninga. Apparently he thought that the Church of God in IJmuiden, of which my father was the minister, might be able to assist him in his humanitarian mission of resettling displaced church people in the United States. Aletta started assisting him by being the Dean's translator and guide around the area.

This new relationship with Dean Olt proved fortunate and impacted my and Aletta's lives in the years to come. To begin with, before the Dean left our home in IJmuiden, he had learned that I was about to migrate to the United States and that I had decided to study for the Christian ministry at Anderson College. No doubt seeing an excellent opportunity to help bring to the college a post-W.W. II foreign student with strong church identity, he strongly encouraged me in my plan. He said amicably, "Gus, when you arrive in Anderson, come to my office and I will help you find a job and a scholarship, and I will help you to enroll as a student."

After I arrived at Anderson College in 1947, I paid a visit to Dean Olt's office. The Dean had been busy behind the scenes on my behalf and had obtained a small scholarship for me from the Women's Missionary Society. However, he had found it more difficult to find me a job. The idea of a job at Delco Remy fell through because I could not be cleared for employment, not being an American citizen. But fear not, the Dean, always full of ideas and contacts, finally found me employment in a tool and die shop. The irony was that I, from a Dutch pacifist family, worked in that shop on important components needed for U.S. military aircraft.

After a few months had passed, I decided to visit Dean Olt in his office and surprise him. Besides surprising the Dean, I myself made an unexpected discovery in the Dean's office.

My parents had mailed me a complete Dutch Volendam costume, consisting of a red shirt with black vertical stripes and a heavy woolen, baggy pair of trousers. These trousers closed in the front with the help of two large Dutch silver guilders, used as buttons. On my head I put the typical black fisherman's cap and, of course, on my feet I wore the age-old Dutch footwear, "Klompen" (wooden shoes). To complete the dress up, I put a pipe in my mouth. All looked very impressive.

I knocked at the Dean's door in Old Main. I only had to wait a moment. Then I heard the Dean's voice, "Come in." I entered and said quickly, "Good morning Dean." Before I could sit down the Dean, looking over his dark-rimmed glasses, retorted, "Gus, you cannot do that. You cannot smoke here on campus!"

"Sir," I said, "this pipe belongs to the Dutch costume I am wearing." I hurriedly continued. "Besides, this is an empty pipe. In the men's dorm there are rooms where they smoke real tobacco." The Dean did not respond, but pointed to the couch and invited me to sit down. Suddenly I realized that I was now in the very Dean's office where most students feared to enter. Students had told me about the terrible feelings they experienced in this office. I was about to find out what they meant.

It appeared to me that the Dean, who taught a class on psychology, was putting his knowledge of psychology into practice. For instance, the couch in his office was very low. When you sat on it, you sank much lower than the level at which the Dean was sitting. He reclined on an enormous high chair behind his large, glass-plated desk. It was impossible not to get the message. "You there on the couch, sit in front of your superior!" I felt humbled. I tried to relax, but succeeded only partly. Then something on the Dean's desk bolstered my confidence. Fortune was dealing me a good hand.

From left to right: Dr. Russell Olt, Dean of Anderson College, Rev. Fedde Jeeninga, and Rev. Ludwig Bessler, in IJmuiden, Holland, 1946.

Just before I fell down on that low couch, I had seen something beautiful and artistic that had been placed under the large glass plate on top of the desk. I was thrilled when I recognized it. A wonderful omen of good news it was. What I saw was an artistically painted scene of a Dutch landscape. The painting showed a canal, a Dutch windmill, and a typical Dutch country scene. My self-confidence was bouncing back into my veins when I recognized the signature of the painter. Yes, indeed, it was an oil painting by Fedde Jeeninga, whose name was painted in one corner. My father had given Dean Olt the painting when "The American" visited our home in Holland. As one might imagine, the visit with the Dean now went smoothly. I was assured, at least I hoped, that the Dean would treat me with kindness. The Dean must have appreciated my father's gift to have given the painting such a prominent place in his office. But there was still the lingering question—Could it be that the Dean had again used some psychology on me by placing that painting there to make me feel more confident? I couldn't be sure.

## I WANT TO GET IN!

Over time the friendship with Dean Olt grew progressively more friendly. This was primarily due to Aletta's role as interpreter and guide for the Dean while he travelled across Europe. The relaxed relationship between us made possible a funny incident. The happening could have had a dramatic if not fatal ending. The players were the Dean, a staunch pacifist, and myself, a so-called modified pacifist.

Once graduated from Anderson College, Aletta and I had moved in 1956 into student housing near the University of Chicago to be close to the Oriental Institute where I was studying at that time. Aletta worked as a surgical nurse at Billings Hospital nearby. The potentially dangerous event that was about to unfold turned out to be only an innocent stunt. If it would have occurred under different circumstances, it might have been an entertaining and amusing frolic. But the unique circumstances that surrounded the episode put it into a more serious and almost tragic setting.

We did not truly enjoy living so close to the University. At the time the neighborhood experienced many violent crimes. Many an unfortunate person was left at the doors of the hospital having been beaten half to death, stabbed or shot. Often Aletta was accompanied by an armed policeman, revolver in his hand, to take her safely to work at the hospital or home. This insecurity caused me to take a drastic action. I bought an automatic pistol and placed it under my pillow. I explained to Aletta, who did not favor my plan, "Honey, if anyone tries to come into our house without my permission, I will shoot."

After a few weeks of sleeping with a Hungarian pistol under my pillow, I was not too happy. I realized that if ever I shot an intruder, the newspapers probably would report, "Rev. Gustav Jeeninga shot and killed an intruder with a 45-calibre pistol." The more I thought about it, the worse I felt. I was aware that this pistol was a murder weapon. To soften the image of arming myself with a weapon to kill, I replaced it with a hunting 410 shotgun.

In years past, if I would have been confronted with such a predicament, I would not have acquired this pistol because I was a convinced pacifist. However, my experiences during World War II had so influenced me that by this time I had become a "modified" pacifist. Under certain circumstances I would feel it my duty and my responsibility to defend myself, my wife, or any other defenseless individual around me, even if it meant to kill. It was only a matter of time before my convictions would be tested.

It was a dark day in October, 1954. It was raining lightly, the wind was blowing hard, and it was cold outside. Around six p.m. Aletta was about to serve the evening meal, soup out of a can. I had not yet put the chain on the door, which I did every evening. There was a knock. My alarm bells rang loudly and I turned very tense. I quickly ran up to the door and grasped the doorknob. My knuckles turned white. I set my foot solidly on an angle to help me keep the door closed if someone would try to force his way into the house. Carefully, slowly, I let the door inch open. I peered into the dark. A man was standing in the rain and was leaning against the door. I could feel the pressure. He had his hat deep over his head, his overcoat's collar was raised over his ears.

I could barely make a sound, but forced out the question, "Who is there?" He did not give his name but said, "I want to get in!" Again I asked louder, "Who is there?" While the stranger pushed harder against the door, he answered again, "I want to get in!" I feared and expected the worst. I could not reach for my loaded 410 shotgun hanging on the wall next to my bed in another room. In desperation, I shouted back, "That is too bad, but no!" I pushed the door shut with all my might and shoved the chain into place.

A short moment went by without a sound. Then Aletta and I heard a man's loud laughter. I thought I recognized the laughter and carefully opened the door to see. To my utter disbelief, the man standing at the door in the pouring rain and laughing loudly was Russell Olt, the Dean of Anderson College. The Dean came into our humble abode and Aletta asked him to have supper with us. He accepted the invitation and remarked after supper that the Campbell's soup was delicious.

During the supper I explained to the Dean the serious situation at the door. I pointed out that I might have shot him, even might have killed him. The Dean smiled but showed no alarm. No doubt it was another case study for this psychologist.

Before leaving us that evening, the Dean revealed to us that he had seen several doctors at Billings Hospital and had undergone a series of physical tests. None of us knew that day that the Dean soon would be diagnosed as having cancer. Aletta and I never forgot that ominous knock at the door. Our friend died in June, 1958, being replaced in the deanship by Robert Nicholson. We were very sad at losing such a warm and humorous friend. His personal interest in us and his ever-ready helping hands in difficult times had endeared him to us greatly. We always remembered "the Dean" with great affection.

# ADVENTURES
# WITH VAL CLEAR

WE SAT ON THE GRASS, Val Clear and I, near the Rockefeller Church (Chapel) on the campus of the University of Chicago. It was the summer of 1947. How well we communicated, I surely cannot remember. When I arrived in New York as an immigrant in May, 1947, my English was limited to words or phrases like, "Hi, Babe!" I do know that my English vocabulary did not go beyond about six hundred words when I talked with Val. Somehow we did manage to communicate. That afternoon chat was the start of a life-long friendship.

Val Clear was studying for his Ph.D. degree in the sociology of religion at the University. I first met him at the First Church of God congregation on 81st Street in Chicago one Sunday morning. Val served as choir director there. We had agreed to meet at the University campus to discuss some social and religious issues that had caused me some culture shock. I discovered that Val was a good listener and helpful advisor. Neither one of us could have suspected then that I would be a student in one of his classes in sociology in the near future.

In 1949 I enrolled in Dr. Clear's class, Sociology 2a, "The Study of Society." I was now a junior at Anderson College and he was a young faculty member. By the end of the semester I had heard and read a lot about sociology, but what I best remember of my class with him happened at the completion of the first semester's test. The final examination was not a true-or-false type of test. It was a case study in which a short account tells of a teenager who had committed a murder. The assignment was to explain whether or not the teenager should receive the death penalty. Even though I received a fair grade on my test, Dr. Clear, in his notes written on the paper, strongly disagreed with my sanctioning the death penalty. I learned then and there that my good friend and mentor and I would more often than not disagree on many important issues. But friends we remained until his death in 1992. One example will say much about Val and me.

Drs. Val Clear and Gustav Jeeninga, Anderson University, 1989.

In 1960 I too was appointed to the faculty of Anderson College. I began as an Associate Professor in the Department of Bible. I now had become a colleague of Dr. Val Clear. Our daily activities brought us together especially in areas where our academic interests crossed. Val was deeply involved in the sociology of religion and anthropology, and I was developing some expertise in the field of biblical archaeology. The ground was fertile for something unusual and interesting to happen. From his student days Val had been known as a person full of surprises, such as keeping a monkey in his dorm room.

One day I found in my campus mail a letter from Professor Val Clear, addressed to Dr. Gustav Jeeninga. The note inside the envelope was neatly typed on departmental letterhead, all very official. Dr. Clear told me that he had been in South America recently and had obtained, at considerable cost to him, an ancient coin. He asked me to come to his office to receive the coin as a gift from him and his wife Evelyn to the college's Museum of Bible and Near Eastern Studies (of which I was Curator).

With growing curiosity I read the letter again. Then I asked myself, "What kind of ancient coin could it be? Found in South America?" The possibility that an ancient coin from biblical times would have found its way to the New World was conceivable, but highly improbable. Nevertheless, it would be wise to check it out and go to Dr. Clear's office and receive the gift.

"Come in," I heard Val saying after I knocked on his door in Old Main. I entered. "Hi, Val," I said. "Thanks for your note about an ancient coin you wish to donate to the Bible Museum."

Val opened his desk drawer, took out the coin and placed it on his desk in front of me, the obverse side up. I inspected the obverse side carefully, then held my breath. I judged that this coin had some chance of being authentic and valuable. First, the coin had a heavy patina. This was clear proof that the coin was old. A patina on the face of a coin is a green film formed naturally on copper and bronze by long exposure. Secondly, I became even more excited when I recognized the image of a Greek warrior who was wearing the typical Greek bronze helmet. Thus far, all indications pointed to an ancient Greek coin dating to about the second century B.C. I was elated. This coin was going to be the latest and very important acquisition by the slowly growing museum's numismatic collection.

Val sat looking at me with a controlled smile and an expression of satisfaction. After all, he had invested a good sum of money for this coin, so he had told me. However, I suspected a fly in the ointment. I also detected a gleam of humor and mischief in Val's eyes. The feeling of suspicion about the authenticity of the coin again plagued my mind. But the coin looked so real. How could I make certain that it was genuine? There was one more test I could apply. I needed to investigate the reverse. Most ancient coins reveal a great amount of information on the reverse of a coin. Usually there is an inscription or a symbol. These inscriptions and symbols provide the date, period, and the civilization that produced the coin.

A quietness hung over the table. The aura was one of anticipation. What would the reverse reveal? Both of us felt the excitement of the critical moment. However, I suspected that Val already knew the answer. Leisurely I reached for the coin. With care my fingers touched it and I lifted it from the desk. Val watched intently. Then I brought it closer to my eyes and at the same time I turned the coin over so that the reverse was up. Then . . . ?

A loud groan, which surely could be heard offices away, escaped from my lips. Followed by my breaking voice as I burst out in desperation. "No, no, no. This is a joke. No ancient coin ever shows a precise date like it appears on this coin!" Val could no longer control himself. He laughed impetuously as I discovered the evidence that the coin was a clear fake. There, in large numbers and letters, was the inscription "50 B.C." The best I could do was join Val in hearty laughter.

Notwithstanding the fact that the coin was a modern fake, it found a worthy place in the museum's coin collection. The coin served the purpose of teaching the students the science of numismatics. Unwittingly, Dr. Clear had made a worthwhile contribution to the museum's teaching collection, even if he had not made a great financial sacrifice to do it.

# LIFE IN ANDERSON
## 1960 ~ 1989

# NEW HORIZONS:
# DEAN ROBERT A. NICHOLSON

THE FIRST TIME I SAW BOB NICHOLSON in action I was still a relatively new student at Anderson College and in considerable cultural transition. I had come to the United States in 1947 and only about one year had passed. The setting was a youth rally and he was leading us in a period of fellowship singing. Nicholson was a young faculty member, tall and slender, with short, dark, curly hair and a slightly rounded face. He appeared to be in control of what he was doing. At that time I did not imagine that Bob would play an important role in my life for over thirty-five years. In fact, something happened during that group singing that he was directing that did not favor a closer relationship between us.

After dinner I was in for a surprise and a major culture shock in terms of acceptable expressions or activities. When dinner was finished, Bob stood up and led the young people in singing. I did not know the song, but listened closely. I was wondering what this song was going to teach the students through its text. Then I heard the words:

> Hear the lively frog,
> Sings on yonder pond,
> Crichety, Crichety, Crick . . .

It was that last word and the sound of it that made me almost fall from my chair. I listened in utter amazement to what I was hearing. Yes, it was really true. What I was hearing was something unimaginable, something that would not have happened at dinner in my home or elsewhere, surely not in proper Dutch society.

When the group had finished singing "Crichety, Crichety, Crick," the whole crowd, as loud as they could, made the sound "Buuurrep" (a burp or belching sound). I was aghast and embarrassed. I did not trust my ears and sank back deeply into my chair. How could Mr. Nicholson direct a song which ended with a room full of people belching, a most anti-social behaviour? This truly was my first major culture shock in America. I should add that I survived the experience, but never enjoyed participating in it. Most importantly, Mr. Nicholson's influence on my life was to go far beyond the juvenile activi-

Dr. Robert A. Nicholson.

ty displayed that evening. This influence would begin with his key role in my finally managing to join the faculty of Anderson College. I got over my early cultural shocks, graduated in 1951, and in 1960 received my Doctor of Theology degree in Biblical Studies from Northern Baptist Theological Seminary in Chicago. It was then that Robert Nicholson, by then the Dean of Anderson College, was to enter my life again.

## A SWINGING DOOR

One year before I received my Th. D. degree, I applied for a teaching position at Anderson College and also at Warner Pacific

College in Portland, Oregon, and Azusa College in Los Angeles, California (three Church of God schools). The first response to my inquiry was received from Dean Nicholson in Anderson. His letter explained that Anderson College was unable to offer a teaching position now or in the near future because the Department of Religion was already overstaffed. I bit my lip with disappointment. I really wanted to teach at my alma mater. Warner Pacific College also had no immediate opening for an additional Bible person. I was feeling discouraged and held out little hope for a positive reply from the smallest college in the group of three, Azusa.

Counter to my expectation, I received a positive letter from President Herb Joiner. Azusa was glad to offer me a position for the fall of 1960. However, they could not at that time tell me the amount of salary they would be able to pay. Since Aletta and I were committed to teaching in one of the Church of God schools and the amount of salary was not our major concern, we accepted the offer wholeheartedly.

For several years Aletta had worked as a surgical nurse at Billings Hospital in Chicago. But then she was working for Blue Cross/Blue Shield. She resigned from her employment as of July, 1960. I in turn resigned from my part-time teaching position at the Chicago YMCA's adult program, Learning For Living. As the days of planning our move to California went by, our excitement increased. We began to sell household equipment, furniture, as well as some winter clothing that we would not need in warm California.

Then, unexpectedly, a letter arrived from Azusa. It was a tense moment when we opened the letter. I read with dismay. President Joiner informed us, with deep regret, that the financial problems at Azusa had escalated and now it would be impossible for the college to find the funding to pay my salary. The letter advised us not to move to Azusa. This negative news shattered our hopes and left us totally in the dark about our immediate future.

Both of us had given up our jobs. I was about to graduate and receive my doctorate. We spent many hours discussing our predicament and looking at various options. Our dream had come to naught. We found it difficult to be optimistic about our tomorrows. All doors appeared to have been shut.

## AFTER THE RAIN. . .

During those discouraging days, Aletta and I attended the First Church of God in Chicago. The pastor of the church was Rev. Edgar Williams, who had been my Greek instructor at Anderson College several years before. One Sunday morning just before the morning service, after we had received the devastating letter from Azusa College, Rev. Williams asked me to come with him to his office. He invited me to give the invocation that morning. Also, he told me that during the past week he had been in Anderson for a meeting. There he had heard that Azusa had called off my call to teach there, which meant that I was now out of a job.

Looking at me with deep personal concern, Rev. Williams said to me, "Gus, I learned from Dean Nicholson that the Bible Department of Anderson had suddenly lost two of its Bible instructors. This has put the College in a difficult situation for the opening of classes in the fall. Therefore, they need at least one new Bible instructor. Why don't you call Dean Nicholson and tell him you are available?"

For a short moment I was uncertain how to answer him. I was bewildered about how to react. Finally I said to my dear mentor and friend, Rev. Williams, "Not too long ago I requested from Dean Nicholson forms in order to apply for a teaching position at Anderson College. I completed the forms and mailed them to the Dean. I received a letter that stated that no position would be available in the near future. That application is still in his files. I am surprised that I have not heard from him. I do not like the idea of begging him for that position."

We looked at each other. What now? I then added, "However, if you would be willing to call Dean Nicholson and tell him that I am available, I would appreciate that." Rev. Williams smiled warmly and gave a positive nod with his head. We needed to get into the pulpit for the church service.

A day or two after my conversation with Rev. Williams, I received a telephone call from Dean Nicholson, who was vacationing in Alabama. The Dean asked, "Gus, when do you get your Th. D. degree?" I responded happily and with confidence, "On May 23, 1960." Then the Dean asked, "Would you be willing to accept a one-year contract with Anderson College over the phone? If so, I will mail you tomorrow morning a copy of the contract for you to sign and return to me immediately."

Gus Jeeninga as an Anderson College student in 1949, with his father Fedde, at the home of close friend Dr. Charles E. Brown in Anderson, Indiana.

"Yes, I definitely will accept that contract. I am looking forward to hearing from you. Thank you very much!"

After I put the phone back in its place, I sat in my chair and looked at Aletta. Then I said, in Dutch, *"Na regen komt zonneschijn"* ("After rain comes sunshine"). Word for word, I told her about our conversation and said, "You no doubt heard that I accepted a one-year teaching contract with Anderson College. I hope you agree to that?" She surely did.

The tenseness of the moment dissipated. That evening we talked a lot about the vicissitudes of life and about the unexpected outcome of our quest to secure a teaching job at a Church of God institution. We sensed a divine force behind it all. With hearts overflowing with thankfulness, we retired at last.

In spite of the marvellous ending of our search for a teaching position for me, the drama had not yet ended. One more delicate situation emerged. A critical phone call came to test our determination before the matter with Azusa College was terminally settled. Late in the evening, after my contract commitment with Dean Nicholson, I received a phone call from President Herb Joiner. The President of Azusa College explained, "Gus, our financial crisis has been solved and we are ready for you to come to Azusa this Fall. We will be able to pay you a fair salary."

"Oh, I am so glad to hear your financial worries are solved," I said. "However, I cannot come because I signed a contract with Anderson College just two days ago."

He replied, "That poses a real problem for us. We really want you to come. Why can you not break your contract with Anderson College?"

"Herb, you know I cannot do that. I will not do that!"

"OK. But will it be acceptable with you if I call Bob Nicholson and ask him to let you off the hook?"

"Please, don't do that, Herb. I want to honor my contract with Anderson College."

Expressing regrets on both sides, we ended the phone call. The matter never came up again. Aletta and I were ready now to make the exciting move to Anderson, Indiana. That one-year contract would be renewed for twenty-nine consecutive years. Five years of teaching at Anderson College passed quickly and in 1965 a sabbatical year (1966-1967) was looming as a welcome potential for me. I had a great desire to spend that sabbatical leave doing research in Jerusalem. The great problem that faced me was how I would finance such a desirable goal. I did not see a light at the end of the tunnel, so to say. Unexpectedly help was on the way. Dean Nicholson announced to the faculty the availability of a Ford

Foundation faculty grant to a faculty member with a worthy proposal.

Immediately I wrote a proposal for a one-year sabbatical program to do research in Biblical and Near Eastern studies at the American Schools of Oriental Research in Jerusalem. The competition for the grant was strong. However, working with the good offices of Dean Nicholson, I was awarded the grant. This was a major educational opportunity. It was also the beginning of my involvement in field archaeology and the beginning of the long career of my friend Barry Callen, who was secured to replace me for the year.

After I obtained the grant, the American Schools of Oriental Research made me an Honorary Associate of the Jerusalem Institute. While living at the Jerusalem Institute, I participated in two major archaeological excavations in Jordan. The first was at Tell el-Saidiyeh (biblical Zarethan) under Dr. James Pritchard of the University of Pennsylvania as Director; the second was at Tell-er Rumeith (biblical Ramoth) under the directorship of Dr. Paul Lapp of Pittsburgh Thological Seminary.

Throughout my tenure at Anderson University it was Robert Nicholson (whom we often called "Nick") who made my services to A.U. possible and successful. He influenced my academic growth and success by means of quiet leadership and through his support of my sabbatical programs and his encouragement of my later studies of New World archaeology.

# BIRTH OF THE MUSEUM

*"Museum collections grow not because of wealth,*
*but because of people's generosity."*

VISITING MUSEUMS HAS BROUGHT ME much enjoyment and learning. When I discovered that across Europe, in cities like London, Paris, and Berlin, museums exhibit archaeological discoveries related to the Bible, I began to walk their halls and corridors whenever I found the opportunity. These excursions inspired me to collect artifacts and to dream of establishing a Bible museum on the Anderson College campus in the future. The museum would not happen overnight nor could I have done it by myself. A growing group of patrons joined me and in due time brought into reality my fondest hope.

The first artifact I collected in Palestine in 1953 was a small fragment of a first-century Roman pot. More exciting was a piece of pottery from an early Christian oil lamp that I picked up at Caesarea Maritima. While studying in Chicago at the Oriental Institute I was able to buy several reproductions of ancient objects. One was a Babylonian pictographic stone tablet. The second object was a fourteen-inch tall reproduction of a Sumarian priest from about 3000 B.C. In this manner the museum collection grew from the ground up, as slowly as a redwood tree.

In 1966 my office on the third floor of Old Main in Anderson began to look like a small hidden museum. Five bookshelves were filled with original artifacts and reproductions. They were helpful "show and tell" items and created a lot of interest among the students in a range of classes. While I was on sabbatical in 1966-67, Barry Callen, just graduated from the seminary on campus, occupied this office, began his collegiate teaching career teaching my classes, and supervised all of the objects and their showings. After Old Main came down in 1968, my office and the fledgling museum were transferred to Charles E. Wilson Library. There Alumni Hall, a side room, and a hallway were transformed into museum exhibit areas providing much more space for growth and public visibility.

Dr. Gus Jeeninga and Dean Robert Nicholson in the Bible Museum, Anderson University.

About this time I became acquainted with Dr. John D. Crose, a retired Church of God missionary who had spent many years working in the Middle East. Dr. Crose had a fine collection of biblically-related ancient artifacts that he used in his presentations in churches. When Dr. Crose and I met and learned of each other's interest, he insisted that I should see some of his collection. I said that I was very interested and invited him to come to my office. He arrived at my office the following day carrying with him a large and heavy wooden box. He placed it on my desk and opened the lid. I expected to see something shiny or glittering, but instead I looked at a dark grayish object about 18" x 18" x 5" in size. When he lifted it out of the box, I noticed bits of black tar sticking to one side of it. At first I was not impressed. Then Dr. Crose turned the object over and said, "This is a stamped mud brick that belonged to King Nebuchadnezzar." Astonished, I found myself looking at a clear cuneiform inscription, dated in the middle of the seventh century B.C. I blurted

out, "Dr. Crose, how did you get that brick? Is it real or a reproduction?"

The aging missionary was obviously enjoying my surprise
and smiled broadly. Then he whispered, "Let me tell you the
story." I settled down in my chair and listened to a fabulous
account. "In 1929," Dr. Crose started, "I was visiting the ruins of
the city of Babylon with a friend who happened to be an Iraqi government official. At one place I had seen this piece of mud brick
sticking out of a ruined wall. I shook it free and took it with me.
When I met my Iraqi friend again, and he saw what I was carrying, he pointed to the brick and said, "Dr. Crose, you are not
allowed to remove anything from this official archaeological site."

"Oh, I am so sorry. I did not know. I'll put it right back."
He responded, "No, don't do that. Give it to me. I will take it."

Several days later I again met my Iraqi friend. I noticed that
he was carrying a large box. When we met, he said to me, "Hi,
John, glad to see you. I have something to give you. Here is your
Nebuchadnezzar's brick with a government letter which permits
you to take the brick out of the country."

"That is an amazing story," I said. Then I asked Dr. Crose
what the inscription on the brick tells us. Dr. Crose explained, "I
took the brick to the British Museum in London and they translated it for me." The inscription reads,

> "I am Nebuchadnezzar, the King of Babylon, the
> Restorer of the Temple of E-sagi-ili and Zida. The eld-
> est son of Nabopolassar."

Because Dr. Crose and his wife lived about half a block from
our house, Aletta and I would visit the family regularly. On these
visits I saw more of Dr. Crose's collection of objects. It was a very
special moment when Dr. Crose agreed to donate his personal collection of Bible artifacts to the Anderson College Bible Museum.

The museum also became the beneficiary of a generous supporting gift. Dr. James Pierce, a local dentist, attended my "Introduction to Archaeology" class. After a lecture on numismatics, I laid out to Dr. Pierce my plan for a special exhibit of three Roman coins mentioned in the Gospels. Jim asked how much it would cost to buy the coins from an antiquarian and pay for an exhibit case. I gave him my best estimate. Looking around the museum room for a short moment, Jim turned to me and said, "Gus, I will pay for the coins and also for the case and related costs." That day was another banner day for the small museum. The coin exhibit added depth and breadth to the growing exhibits.

The next valuable gift to the museum throws light on the history of writing. The origin and development of writing play a cardinal role in understanding the thousands of clay tablets and the profusion of inscriptions stored in museums. One of the "keys" to Egyptian writings is the famous Rosetta Stone. The Rosetta Stone opened the door to reading Egyptian hieroglyphic texts, such as the *Book of the Dead.* Financial support for securing an exact replica of the Rosetta Stone came from Dr. and Mrs. Jeeninga. The shipping crate was used to build an exhibit case. The carpenter was Roy Troutman, an Anderson College maintenance employee. A significant financial gift was made available by Mrs. Dorothy Sankey, daughter of Dr. and Mrs. Charles E. Brown, for a special exhibit honoring her parents. Dr. Brown had been a prominent theologian and historian of the Church of God movement (Anderson).

The tallest and most impressive museum acquisition was a reproduction cast of the Law Code of King Hammurabi. The eight-foot tall law code was shipped from the Louvre Museum in Paris directly to Anderson College. When it arrived, the entrance door to the School of Theology had to be removed in order to carry the crate into the Museum. The Hammurabi Law Code is significant for the understanding of the systems of justice in Babylon and in Hebrew tradition. Other large objects in the museum include the Shalmaneser Obelisk (six feet tall) and the Moabite Stone (five feet tall).

What I still needed was a collection of various Palestinian pottery types beginning with the Chalcolithic Period (5000 B.C.) and extending through the Byzantine Period (500 A.D.). A knowledge of pottery typology provides the archaeologist with the means of placing archaeological finds in a historical context. A helping hand appeared just before I started on my sabbatical leave in 1966-1967. Dr. Robert Reardon, president of Anderson College, presented me with an envelope containing a check for $1000. When he handed it

Exhibit in the Anderson Bible Museum, Tomb of Bhabadrah (time of Abraham, ca. 1800 B.C.).

to me, he said, "Gus, use this money for the museum as you see fit." I then left for Jerusalem.

Nearly a year later, the 1967 war erupted between Israel and the Arabs. The day before the Israelis invaded East Jerusalem, Aletta and I drove our V.W. Camper out of the city. That same day we crossed into Syria and by the end of the day we drove into Turkey. This was an important escape for us. In the back of the V.W. Camper was a large footlocker filled with a quality collection of Palestinian pottery. This pottery was acquired with the help of the $1000 made available to me by President Reardon. The manner in which I negotiated with local traders is a story by itself.

A few days after I had arrived at the American Schools of Oriental Research in Jerusalem in 1966, I took a stroll through the Old City, also known as East Jerusalem, and saw an antique shop. I decided to enter. The owner saw me coming and stepped out and said, "Please, come in. How are you? Sit down and have a cup of tea." This type of greeting I would hear over and over again until the merchants knew me well.

"Hi, Dr. Gus. Please sit down. I have something for you, my friend. I only will sell it to you—not to anyone else. Please hold it in your hand and get the feel of it."

"How much does it cost?" I inquired.

"Dr. Gus, from you I only ask $120 dollars. That's a real bargain."

I picked up the vessel, which I recognized as a fine example of a Cyprian milk bowl. It was a beautiful bowl with reddish-brown bands painted against a milk-colored background. Most distinctive of these bowls is a single triangular, horizontally attached handle. I felt a tingling in my chest. I was so excited. This was one of the pottery types I had to have for the museum's Palestinian pottery collection. I went into the usual spin to try to get the price lowered. I softly mumbled, "You must be kidding when you say $120 dollars. This is a very common bowl and available everywhere." A little more audibly, I continued. "Look at this worn spot. Here a chip of paint is missing. This bowl is defective. But I'll give you thirty dollars for it."

"Dr. Gus, believe me, you and I know that this is a rare buy. Only you and your friends have come into my shop and ask about this piece. No tourist ever pays attention to it. It is an odd piece, a type hardly known."

I asked, "Where does it come from and how old is it?"

"Well, let me see what I can do to answer your questions," he replied. The youthful dealer stooped behind the counter and when he reappeared he placed a large book in front of me and said, "You did not know, did you, that I am well informed? A while ago I did business with a German archaeologist who also was buying objects from me for his teaching and a museum. I made a deal with him. I offered him a very good price for the objects he wanted if he gave me one or two books with scholarly reports on archaeological excavations. You see, I have the same resources that you have."

We looked at each other. He smirked and I smiled sheepishly. We haggled some more over other objects. In the end we settled with a warm handshake. I walked out of his shop with the milk bowl ($60.00) and some other trophies. I was greatly pleased with my bargains.

Today when I walk through the Museum on the Anderson University campus in Indiana, I can stop at numerous items and remember how this or that person contributed to the growth of the Museum. There is a host of unnamed individuals to whom I owe an unpayable debt of gratitude for their trust in me and their support in making this Museum possible. I could never have done it by myself. I hope that future generations will come to appreciate the value of what is there.

# PRESIDENT ROBERT REARDON: "I'LL GET YOU A TORAH SCROLL!"

*"Teacher, which commandment in the law is the greatest?" He [Jesus] said to him, "You shall love the Lord your God with all your heart, and with all your soul, and with all your mind.... You shall love your neighbor as yourself. On these two commandments hang all the law and the prophets." (Matt. 22:36-40)*

RINGING LOUDLY ON MY OFFICE DESK, the telephone sounded like a warning. I grasped the handle and lifted it quickly to my ear. I said the usual, "Doctor Jeeninga speaking."

"Hi, Gus, and good morning. How are you doing this day?" I immediately recognized the voice of Shirell Fox, Public Relations Director of Anderson College. "What can I do for you, Shirell," I asked him.

"Gus, I would like for you and Aletta to help me out. We will have Rabbi Steinberg coming from Chicago to campus for a chapel talk and to speak to some of the classes. He will stay over for the night at a motel in town. Would you and Aletta be so kind as to take the Rabbi to supper? Take him to a fancy restaurant and feed him a quality T-bone steak!"

"Wait a minute, Shirell," I replied. "That is going to cost me dearly."

"Hold it Gus," Shirell quipped. "I want you and Aletta to have a fine meal also. Afterwards you will give me the bill and I will refund you."

"Oh, well, that is different," I happily answered. "Thanks for calling and send me the details. We will be glad to do it."

On the By-pass (Route 9) near the campus in Anderson we knew of an attractive steak house, so we decided that we would take the Rabbi there for supper. The conversation we three had over the excellent meal was about things in general, but especially about his thoughts on visiting the Anderson College campus. He told us of his interesting dialogue with the students in a sociology class.

During our visit I realized that here was my opportunity to achieve one of my long-time hopes. I always imagined that it would be exciting and highly educational for my students if I could show them a real Hebrew Torah and then explain to them the significance of the Torah (Genesis through Deuteronomy) in our religious life as Christians.

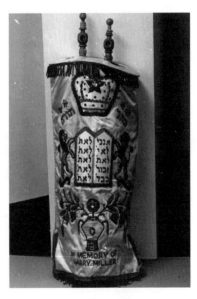

Torah Scroll,
Jeeninga Bible Museum.

However, I never had seen a Hebrew Torah Scroll for sale. Maybe the Rabbi could help me. I found the courage to ask him.

"Rabbi Steinberg, every year I teach my students about the Hebrew Torah and wish that I could actually show one to them when we study Holy Scripture. Could you possibly help me obtain a copy of a Torah Scroll?"

"Mr. Jeeninga," the Rabbi replied deliberately, "you know that it is very difficult to locate a true Hebrew Torah Scroll that would be for sale. Also, even if I should locate one, a used one, it would cost at least $1000 dollars."

Before I could figure out where I would get that kind of money, I said convincingly, "Rabbi Steinberg, that will be no problem. I'll get the money."

The Rabbi looked at me doubtfully. Did he think that I did not realize how much $1000 really was? Anyway, he did not react, but continued. "In case I cannot find a Torah for you, I might find a used Esther Scroll instead. It should not cost more than $50." I appreciated his thoughtful attempt to be helpful.

We parted that evening like good old friends. I had his promise clearly in mind. There was at least some hope. Several months passed, but I did not hear from Rabbi Steinberg. So, I

wrote him a friendly letter and lightly reminded him of the wonderful meal we had enjoyed together. I carefully recalled his promise to try to secure a Torah Scroll or at least an Esther Scroll for us. Soon I received a letter from the Rabbi in which he explained that he was still looking for an Esther

Gustav and Aletta Jeeninga with the scroll, 1989.

Scroll. The Torah Scroll apparently was no longer being considered as a viable possibility. As soon as he had found one, he said, he would let me know. It seems that he never located an Esther Scroll because we lost contact after that last reply.

I gave up my fervent hope of obtaining a Torah or Esther Scroll. I now could not envision a situation that would bring to life my now dormant dream. Then President Robert Reardon and I fell into a conversation one day concerning teaching Bible and how we might find ways to go beyond the same class notes from year to year. I explained to him my efforts to obtain a true Hebrew Torah Scroll as one way to bring greater meaning and reality to my teaching. I also recounted my disappointment when my efforts to acquire a Hebrew Torah through Rabbi Steinberg had turned out to be a dead end.

"Don't you worry any longer, Gus," the President said as he put his hand on my arm to give words of encouragement. "I will get you a Torah Scroll!" We separated. As I walked away I said to myself, softly so that the President would not hear me, "That is Bob for you. He thinks he can take care of everything."

Six weeks later my telephone stirred me from my reading. I heard a lady's voice. "Dr. Jeeninga, President Reardon is on the phone and wishes to speak with you."

"Yes, President," I said, wondering what he was up to now.

"Gus, could you call all of your Bible 101 sections in Old Testament to meet together in Decker Hall 133 the next class session? The Rabbi of Bethel Zaddik Hebrew Congregation of Indianapolis will be on campus to speak to the students on the Hebrew Torah. After his lecture he will present a copy of the Torah for the Anderson College Bible Museum."

I said that I could and then hung up. After I replaced the phone, I shouted out loud, "Terrific! I cannot believe it! He did it! He did it!"

The students were in their places when I guided the Rabbi to his seat on the platform of Decker 133. There was a subdued murmur in the lecture hall as I walked to the lectern. Then there was complete silence. I introduced the Rabbi to the students. He wore a business suit and looked very much like any other teacher. However, in his manner he projected both seriousness and a discernable lightness. He obviously was a man who loved life and enjoyed what he was doing. His address was simple but to the point. He stressed the sacredness of the Torah and emphasized that its life-guiding message was abundantly clear. He concluded with a homily on the cardinal message of the Bible which, he said, is found in Micah 6:8. These ancient words were read aloud:

"He has told you, O mortal, what is good;
and what does the Lord require of you
but to do justice, and to love kindness,
and to walk humbly with your God?"

After the Rabbi had finished his lecture, he turned to his assistant to bring the Hebrew Torah Scroll. He asked me to join him at the lectern and made this declaration: "The Indianapolis Hebrew Bethel Zaddik Congregation is pleased to present this Hebrew Torah Scroll to the Anderson College Museum of the Bible. We hope the students will learn about the Torah and adopt its supreme lesson of faith, "to walk humbly with your God."

After the students were dismissed from class, the Rabbi turned to me and said, "Dr. Jeeninga, you must promise that you will never put the Torah Scroll on exhibit in the Museum or elsewhere. The Torah is not an item to be exhibited, but to be read and studied by you and your students. With a firm handshake, I promised the Rabbi that I would honor his request. I always did. Here is my opportunity again to encourage awareness of and appreciation for this special scroll.

This Hebrew Torah is one of the last Hebrew Torahs written in Germany while the Nazis rose to power. The scroll is made of velum, animal skin; it is 97 feet long, 14 inches high and consists of many leather sections sewn together. The text is handwritten in Hebrew square letters using a quill. There are two, three or four columns of writing on each sheet. Reading starts from the right and goes to the left. The Scroll is covered with a decorated mantle. Embroidered on the front of the mantle is a jewelled crown, with a star; below it are two lions of Judah who hold the two tablets of the Ten Commandments; at the bottom of the mantle is a pot with a tree. These symbols can be interpreted to mean:

> The Torah is the Crown of Life.
> The Torah holds the Ten Commandments.
> The Torah is the Tree of Life.

# TEAM TEACHING WITH
# JAMES EARL MASSEY

ACROSS THE UNITED STATES the horn was blowing in support of a new, innovative style of teaching. It was labelled "team teaching." The new approach was promoted actively by the Anderson College academic administrators and by a number of senior faculty members. This new instructional method of teaching appealed to me, so I decided to visit my colleague James Earl Massey.

Before I had approached Jim and asked him to team teach with me, I had written down for myself several points about both of us to see if we were a good match. Here are some of the characteristics I considered: Jim was handsome, but I was younger looking; Jim spoke English fluently and with excellent diction—people loved to hear him speak, I had a foreign accent that many of the students liked, so they told me; Jim was a master teacher and preacher, my speech was simple and often tinted by my Dutch accent and my teaching was filled with anecdotes related to my experiences during World War II and included many visual presentations; Jim had majored in New Testament studies and theology, and I in Old Testament, biblical archaeology, and church history. One might conclude that we were both well qualified to team-teach and make a success of it. The only thing left to do now was to eat the cake and really taste it. So to Dr. Massey's office I went.

"Jim," I said, "would you be interested in joining me to teach Bible 101-102? You know that team teaching is being encouraged by the administration and I would love to try it out. But only with you."

Sitting behind his desk, Jim, in his usual gentle manner, responded, "Please explain a little more about how you perceive us proceeding. What are the rules and responsibilities that each one of us would have?"

"We will take turns teaching the class," I explained. "After a 35-minute lecture, the other teacher will respond for five minutes. The last ten minutes will be for the students to interact with the instructors."

Jim responded with his usual, "I understand," then added, "Who will be responsible for putting together the syllabus and for writing the examinations?" I explained: "We will take turns. Furthermore, in my opinion, we will avoid trying to outsmart each other in front of the students. Our

Drs. Gustav Jeeninga and James Earl Massey.

primary purpose will be to supplement each other's contribution and to bring to the daily class experience more depth as well as some delight. Do you agree?" He was obviously interested and the plan was put in motion. From the many incidents that happened during the three years we team-taught, I have chosen two occasions to illustrate the value and success, as well as the funny things that took place in such an approach to teaching with this very special colleague.

One day it was my turn to lecture. I do not remember the precise subject I was discussing, but I found it necessary to explain to the students the difference between Hebrew and Aramaic. Both languages occur in the Hebrew Bible. I went to the blackboard to illustrate the problem and wrote down one Hebrew word and one Aramaic word. After I returned to the lectern, Dr. Massey walked up to the blackboard and made a minor correction of my spelling of the Aramaic term. I watched him and was ready to defend myself, but realized that the correction was proper. We were really team teaching and Dr. Massey was putting it into practice. What could have been made embarrassing for me he skilfully made an addition to the learning experience of the class. It was one of his fine characteristics never to be confrontational in any demeaning way, but he looked for ways to improve matters for the good of all.

The second happening that resulted while we team-taught was appreciated by the students and by me also. I was discussing the importance of the Book of Psalms in biblical times and the church today. The presentation included a brief history of the role of Psalms that had been put to music. These Psalms were being sung during worship services. In days gone by, some Protestant Christians were recognized and identified by "those who sing the Psalms." When I was a teenager back in Holland, we sang the Psalms in my father's Church of God congregation. Personally, I did not enjoy this because they were sung with a slow meter. To illustrate this experience for the students, I sang a Dutch Psalm. Based on Psalm 23, the title was *De Heer is Mijn Herder*. My singing received an appreciative response from the students, not because I had a fine voice, but because of my intentions and effort.

It was probably the week following my singing for the students that Dr. Massey was lecturing on somewhat the same material. Then, unexpectedly, he too launched into singing the 23rd Psalm. The class was spellbound, and so was I. He sang with a beautiful voice and with great clarity the well-known and beloved

Scottish rendition of Psalm 23. Of all the years of team teaching, the highlight and best memory I have of what we did for the students and for ourselves was listening to Dr. James Earl Massey pour out his heart in this lovely hymn of praise. That was real teaching!

# BATTLE OVER THE BIBLE

THE MOST DIFFICULT AND CRITICAL STRUGGLE I dealt with in my years as Chair of the Department of Religious Studies at Anderson University (1974-1983) was a move by some of the faculty against mandatory Bible courses for all students in the liberal arts curriculum.

Among a few of the teachers a plan had been growing in the 1970s to submit a proposal during an upcoming faculty meeting to remove the requirement that each student must take a minimum of six hours in Bible study in order to graduate. The week prior to that fateful meeting, Barry Callen and I met for several evenings and drafted a counter proposal. Then we waited to see what would happen during the following Monday's faculty meeting.

Sunday, the day before the faculty meeting, Aletta and I attended the worship service of Park Place Church of God where we attended regularly. On our way out, we met President Robert Reardon and his wife Geraldine in the church's narthex. Aletta and I were delighted when Bob invited us to join them as their guests for dinner at the Anderson Country Club.

The dinner was delicious and the fellowship warm and pleasant. However, my mind was on Monday's meeting. I had told myself not to talk about school matters while we enjoyed a wonderful time together. In spite of feeling uneasy about bringing up a business concern on such an occasion, I had a sudden urge to talk to Bob Reardon about what was about to take place the next day in the faculty meeting. "Bob," I said somewhat timidly, "are you aware of what is going to be presented tomorrow in the faculty meeting?"

"Well, no, but tell me about it," was his curious reply.

I proceeded to explain to him that several faculty members were bringing to the floor for a likely faculty vote a proposal to drop the requirement that all students must complete at least six hours of Bible study in order to graduate. There was a long silence. When Bob spoke again, the subject had changed. We did not return to the matter I had spoken about—but I knew that he had heard me and shared my deep concern.

President Robert H. Reardon.

Monday afternoon, as the faculty meeting was just about to start, President Reardon walked into the meeting place and sat down in the front row. When Dean Robert Nicholson rose to start the meeting, President Reardon also stood up and asked the Dean if he could address the faculty with a short statement. The Dean respectfully agreed. Then turning to the surprised and waiting faculty members, President Reardon said: "Ladies and gentlemen, I want you to know that as long as I am President of this institution, the requirement that each student must take a minimum number of hours of Bible study will stay in effect."

After that short, but clear and final statement, no proposal to the contrary was brought to the floor. There was no need for the counter proposal that Barry Callen and I had developed. Some faculty members were offended by what they saw as administrative arrogance on the part of the President. Even so, in a very courageous and convincing manner the President had led the way in personally protecting one of the original reasons why Anderson College had been founded originally as Anderson Bible Training School, namely, that the young people of the church should be informed about the Bible, the Word of God, and its message of salvation as an essential part of their education. The vision of our forefathers had been preserved, although the struggle to remain biblically distinctive is perennial.

President Reardon led his administration in 1979 to develop a set of campus intentions for the 1980s, with the Church of God movement about to celebrate its centennial in 1980. Campus intention number one read:

> As an institution of the Church of God, we shall seek to broaden and deepen our involvement in its mission. New and serious efforts will be made to exalt the Word in our common life, to understand it more fully, and to live more freely in its light as a practicing community of love, obedience, discipline, and concern.

This encouraged me, my colleague Barry Callen, and many others.

# DIGGING UP THE CAMPUS

SOMEONE IN THE CLASS SUGGESTED, "Let's search for the baptismal pool and then dig it up!" Dr. John W. V. Smith and I were team teaching the course "Church of God History" at Anderson University and on this day the discussion had centered around the probable location of the old baptismal pool which had been in use during the early days of the Church of God Camp Meeting convened annually in Anderson, Indiana. Originally the pool (8' x 12') had been located somewhere on what today is the campus of Anderson University. It had not been visible for decades and its original location was now questionable. This gave rise to the suggestion that we search for it and actually dig it up. Why not mix education and actual archaeology?

Even though interest about the pool was high, nothing came of the suggestion to excavate it. Several years later, in 1989, the idea was again suggested. Could I not organize an archaeological excavation and bring the old baptismal pool back to life? At first I was dubious about getting permission from the University administration to tear up some parts of the campus. Maybe even more critical was the question about what if anything might be learned from such a dig. What could we expect to find? Certainly there would be no beautiful artifacts, no gold and silver. What would be the contribution to the history and practices of the Church of God if something could be found? Only an organized excavation could provide any answers, and by now I had become fascinated by the possibilities. I needed no other incentives. The romance of archaeology had again captured me and drawn me into its tantalizing web. Someone once said of archaeology, "You either like it or you hate it." I liked it.

I contacted President Robert Nicholson and was bold enough to ask for permission to excavate on the University campus. Having explained to him in some detail my plans, procedures, and purpose, President Nicholson gave his permission. I agreed that after the excavation was completed, I would return the dug-up area to its original status as closely as possible. There would be no cost to the University. I would be in charge as the director of the excavation, and therefore would be responsible for carrying out the oral agreement.

Based on my experiences of serving as an area supervisor on six major archaeological expeditions in Jordan, Cypress, and Israel, I set out to systematically plan this fascinating project. Of primary importance would be the gathering of information regarding the location of the pool. Several people volunteered to be interviewed. These interviews provided some helpful information and even some photographs. This was a promising beginning. Next we searched for literary resources. With the help of historian Dr. Merle D. Strege, we consulted the Church of God archives housed on campus. A few more photographs were located, as well as some descriptive references, but nothing particularly helpful regarding the pool's exact location. Modern archaeology relies heavily on the use of aerial and infrared photography to locate underground structures. But the high cost for such photos was too burdensome for this out-of-pocket undertaking. We had to rely on the few old photos and fragile memories.

One day, while we were doing a survey to determine where on campus to excavate, an Anderson resident came by to see what we were doing. He carried with him a metal detector and asked if he could be of some help. We showed him the area under consideration. He then scanned the area with his metal detector, walking back and forth systematically. Several times his detector gave a reading and we dug up the spot immediately. Several of these searches proved negative. A few produced a number of copper coins, like pennies. We also found iron nails and bottle caps.

Baptismal Pool, Anderson Camp Meeting, 1930s.

However, no major find turned up. With the help of the metal detector we had hoped to locate the pool by means of the iron used as reinforcement of its concrete. Only later did we learn that no iron rods were used to reinforce such small structures in those early days. One coin that was discovered, a wheat penny, was of general interest and was dated 1918.

Having failed thus far to find the baptismal pool, I turned to a more promising resource. What better help can one obtain than from eyewitnesses? Such people surely would all agree as to the location and the condition of this historic site. I could count on their detailed descriptions and interesting personal anecdotes connected to the history of the pool. I was more optimistic at this juncture of my investigation than I had been previously. With the passion of a committed archaeologist, I contacted a cadre of persons to take me to the exact spot. Dr. Russell Renz remembered the times he and his buddies had played ball on the campus. He told me that he knew the precise location of the pool. In those early years the upper parts of the structure were easily visible, but the pool had been filled with sand to prevent people from falling into it. It was no longer used, but had not been forgotten by at least a few people.

One day Russ walked with me to the Anderson University campus and pointed to an area where he was certain the pool had been. I marked the spot on my area map. However, when we dug a small probe, the evidence was negative. Then Dr. T. Franklin Miller told me that he had seen the pool for many years and would have no trouble walking right to the location where it used to be. I was delighted and convinced that now we would pinpoint the site's exact location. I asked him if he were willing to meet me in the morning. With certainty in his voice, he replied, "Naturally, Gus, I will be happy to help you. I'll see you tomorrow." The next morning at 10:00 a.m. we met on the campus, walked here and there, and I soon realized that he was having difficulty finding the precise place. "Well now," he started, "the situation has changed radically at A.U. These new buildings that have gone up over the last years are throwing off my orientation." We both were disappointed at not being able to pinpoint the pool. We agreed that it is very difficult to recall precise geographical areas after many years have passed. This search turned out to be another dead end.

I was given the name of a local senior citizen who had been born in Anderson. She was greatly advanced in years, but quite alert mentally. I went to see her and asked her about the baptismal pool. She told me that she could never forget that pool for she herself had been baptized in it. I asked her if she could show me where the pool was located. She smiled kindly and pointed with her finger in the direction we should go. While we walked to the site, we talked about her past. When we arrived at the designated location, she walked up to a large tree. I guessed the tree to be close to one hundred years old. My guide said, "Look at this here, where this faucet sticks out of the ground. The pool was just east of this tree. It was filled with water from this faucet." I became excited. "This is it!" "However," she continued," it could have

172

been next to that old tree over there." I marked both places on my survey map and crossed my fingers.

At this point in my investigation I was beginning to lose confidence in my eyewitnesses. How accurate were their memories? The changes on the University campus over the decades had been substantial and confused them all. I realized the necessity of finding a more precise source of information if I were ever to be successful. Remarkably, that help came suddenly and from an unexpected source. It did offer a new possibility of success. Among my friends was a gentleman who had been born on an Indiana farm. During a visit with him to find out what he knew about the location of the baptismal pool, I told him about the up-coming excavation. But I also told him about my frustration at not being able to find the pool's exact location, even with the help of several eyewitnesses.

"Maybe I can help you, Gus," my friend suggested. "I have seen the pool often and also witnessed people being baptized in it."

"That would be most kind of you," I responded. I thought that one more eyewitness account could do no harm. I was total-ly unprepared for the next development. I continued to describe to him the difficulties others had in locating the pool with so many changes that had taken place.

"I understand that quite well," he told me, and then explained, "I will not rely on my memory. When I was still living on the farm I looked for and found water sources for our farmer neighbors by using a divining rod."

"Are you telling me that you are a diviner? I had no idea. Are you sure that it really works?" I asked these things with some mis-givings. I then prodded him to explain how that technique worked. Leaning back in his chair, the old-timer had a grin on his face, expressing satisfaction as he began to lay out the facts.

"The divining rod," as he described it, "is usually made from a forked branch of a willow tree. The diviner walks across the field holding the rod horizontally in front of him. The rod will indicate the presence of water by dipping downward when it passes over an underground stream, spring, or lake."

I was greatly intrigued by this search method. Many years ago I had heard about it. Apparently its rate of success was not too high. Nevertheless, I could not pass up this pseudo-scientific approach to locating the pool. A few questions needed yet to be asked and answered. So I inquired, "How do you expect to find a concrete baptismal pool construction with your divining rod, a method that searches for water?"

My friend responded, "That is not difficult to explain. Because the pool was filled with sand and clay, any moisture that seeps into the ground, such as rain, would get trapped. The water sinks to the bottom of the pool and stays there. Therefore, a divining rod detects the more than normal water collected at the concrete floor of the pool. Do you understand?" I thought that I did.

My friend picked up his tool kit to begin the search for the pool. He pulled out his divining rods. Watching him pull out his unique equipment brought a momentary stop to my already irregular heartbeat. What I saw coming out of his tool kit just about dashed my hope of finding the pool's whereabouts. I stared at his hand in utter incredulity. He was removing from his bag two pieces of wire cut from a coat hanger, each about fifteen inches long. Each wire had an end of three inches in length bent down to serve as a handle. Instead of the commonly used willow divining rod, my friend was using metal wires!

"What is going to happen now?" I asked myself. Because I knew very little about the diviner's "art," or the nature of its equipment, I remained silent, but my confidence in any positive result vaporized. With diminished enthusiasm I followed his every move. My diviner walked back and forth over the general area holding the divining wire rods in front of him. Having completed more than half of the area, my friend suddenly stood still. The left hand wire had flipped to the right. Excitedly, the diviner burst out, "This is it! This is the spot we are looking for." I remained speechless as he tapped his foot on the grass. "Here, right here. But wait. Let me try it once more." He backed up a short distance and walked again over the same terrain. When he crossed over the "hot" spot, the lefthand wire rod moved to the right, as it had done earlier. We watched each other, he with a gleam of joy and pride on his face, I with doubt in my heart. "Did it work after all? Have we really discovered the pool?" I marked the spot on my map. A wooden peg was driven into the ground at the precise location.

By this time I had four areas of five meters by five meters marked off to be excavated. The next step was to open one square meter as a test. Only after this probe yielded evidence of archaeological significance would a complete dig be attempted of the entire 5m x 5m locus. Two of my student volunteers helped to set out the pegs and connected the ropes from one peg to the other, carefully delineating the square. First the top layer of grass sod was removed. After one hour of digging we had reached a depth of two feet. Nothing of significance had been encountered. From this probe, a trench was extended across the square. Results here were also negative. No signs of any sort were found that related to the baptismal pool. It was deemed best not to continue this investigation. The use of the divining rod had not produced a positive result.

Over the next few days, with hope still driving us on, the team of about twelve volunteers set to work. The three remaining squares were tested. These also were at locations where eyewitnesses had claimed, "I know exactly were the pool was." As we progressed, the only objects unearthed were rusted tin cans and bottle caps dating back over some thirty years. We also found scattered bricks and fragments of bricks, potsherds from various periods. There were pieces of glass and several large pieces of concrete. The results of the dig thus far had been very discouraging. Only one large slab of concrete, molded and formed, might have been a cap to one of the edges of the pool. Noting the modest results of this dig, I was conscious of the problem. We may not have located the precise site of the pool. Somewhat jokingly, I revealed one day when the question regarding the accurate location of the pool was being discussed, that I knew where the pool really was. I said, "The baptismal pool lies between Martin Hall and the Eisenhower Bridge" [an area that includes most of the campus and far beyond!]. There was a muffled laughter. Everyone understood my frustration.

After the unsuccessfully excavated areas had been put back to their original status, the following conclusions were highlighted. The presumed knowledge and memories of eyewitnesses are often unreliable. The use of a divining rod is of dubious value in scientific archaeological investigation. In surface archaeology, the metal detector is quite useful. The expedition had found no evidence of an existing baptismal pool. Two single slabs of concrete were exposed that might have been parts of the original pool. The apparent absence of the pool's remains might be because of the many trenches that have been dug across the University campus for various purposes over the years. The volunteers testified that the experience of participating in this limited excavation had been profitable to them. They had learned much about archaeological methods, types of tools to be used, and about problems in the field. May the baptismal pool, wherever it is, rest in peace.

# LOOKING SOUTH
# WITH VAL CLEAR

AT LAST MY WIFE ALETTA AND I were on our way to Mexico City with Val and Evelyn Clear. It was December, 1970, and we planned to vacation across the border. The Clears had persuaded us that the Christmas season in Mexico City was lively and very colorful. It also would be delightful to be in Mexico and away from the cold weather in Indiana.

For some time I had tried to get Val to go with me to Egypt and Palestine. I wanted him to see the pyramids of Giza. I never succeeded in convincing him to go with me. Instead, Val persuaded me to go with him to Mexico City and see the Pyramid of the Sun and the Pyramid of the Moon at Teotihuacan, the capital city of the Aztecs. According to Val, these two pyramids were more impressive and larger than those at Giza in Egypt. I doubted his claims but wanted to see it for myself.

Before reaching the Mexican archaeological zone, one can see the pyramids outlined against the distant mountains. The enormous dimensions of the stair-like ceremonial plaza and processional road were proof of the presence of large crowds of worshipers during festivities of the past. Everything directed one's eyes toward the Pyramid of the Sun.

A wide staircase with unusually high steps goes up one side of the pyramid. The total staircase is divided into three different stages. The first one third of the ascent is easy, the second stage unusually steep, and the last section somewhat less so. The total ascent is at times frightening. When we arrived at the top we found a large square area that is about 215 feet above the valley floor. The panoramic view was worth the effort.

I pointed out to Val that the Pyramid of Giza in Egypt is 481 feet high, quite a bit higher than the Pyramid of the Sun. Also, the Aztec pyramids were constructed of rough fieldstones, whereas the Egyptian pyramid had been built from large blocks of limestone each weighing over two tons. I explained a number of other contrasts between the monuments. Especially important, I noted, is the fact that the Pyramid of the Sun was built about 100 A.D., but the Pyramid of Giza is almost 2500 years earlier.

My first visit to Teotihuacan was the beginning of my involvement with Pre-Columbian archaeology. It was at the urging of Val that I promised to develop a course for the Anderson College curriculum in which I would teach Pre-Columbian archaeology. I did and taught it for years. Inspired by this first visit to these famous Aztec ruins, I have returned to visit them three times, as well as extending my research to such outstanding ruins as Monte Alban, Palengue, Bonampak, Copan, Chich'en Itza, and Uxmal. In due time I studied additional Pre-Columbian historic ruins, including Machu Picchu (Peru) and Tiahuanaco (Bolivia).

Visiting and studying these fabulous centers of ancient learning and worship increased my understanding of worldwide cultures. Comparing the information I accumulated to biblical life and thought was both fascinating and enlightening. But most of all, my awakening insight and awareness of the intensity and authenticity of primitive religious beliefs and practices across the millennia grew dramatically. Some of these new perspectives I have attempted to reveal in the report of my visit to Copan, Honduras (chapter 37). Before that, however, I was to be very involved in the archaeology of the Middle East.

# EXPLORING
# THE ANCIENT PAST

## 1963 ~ 1996

# CONCERNING "ARCHAEOLOGY"

ARCHAEOLOGY HAS BEEN A LARGE PART OF MY LIFE. On occasion a little wisdom or humor has arisen concerning what it is all about. Here are a few samples.

"Do you 'dig' these sayings?"

I once asked my five-year-old nephew, "What is archaeology all about?" He answered: "Digging up old things."

From my class notes on archaeology: "People are interested in three things: 'Money, sex, and archaeology.'"

A colleague once introduced me before my talk on archaeology. He said: "The future of Dr. Jeeninga lies in ruins."

Another colleague (Frederick Shoot) introduced me and said, "Dr. Jeeninga teaches at the University a course in 'Cracked Pots.'"

It has been said that the best man any woman could marry is an archaeologist because the older she becomes the better he likes her.

How does one define "archaeology"? Like this: "Human thought objectified and then fossilized becomes archaeological data" (Professor G. Childe). Here is an illustration: The ten command-

Dr. Jeeninga in his office in Decker Hall, Anderson University.

ments of Moses are Moses' thoughts [the commandments] objectified [on two tablets of stone] and then fossilized [in biblical literature] to become archaeological data.

# POTSHERDS AND PRUDENCE

PICKING UP A PIECE OF BROKEN POTTERY in the Holy Land was my introduction to the science of pottery reading. As an archaeologist, I learned that pottery sherds can be made to "speak" and provide information about the life of ancient people. We note first of all that the Hebrew word for potsherd is *cheresh*, "to scratch" or "rough." The translation of the Hebrew phrase *cheresh keli* is "earthen vessel."

Potsherds are so common in the lands of the Bible that a traveler can hardly avoid stepping on them. It comes, therefore, as no surprise that potsherds are mentioned numerous times in the Bible and present us with some interesting lessons. Here are several examples.

> In Psalm 22:15 a "potsherd" is used as a metaphor to express lack of strength. ". . .my strength is dried up like a potsherd...."

> In Isaiah 30:14 a reference to a potsherd is used to express total uselessness. ". . .among its fragments not a sherd is found with which to take fire from the hearth or to dip water out of the cistern." This verse also implies the various uses of a potsherd, including "to carry fire" and "to dip water."

> In Job 2:8 a potsherd was used as a scraping tool ". . . and he [Job] took a potsherd with which to scrape himself, and sat among the ashes."

Dr. Jeeninga's first find and restoration. Israelite cooking pot,
Tell es-Sa'idiyeh, Jordan, 1967.

In Jeremiah 19:2-10 the prophet points to potsherds as symbols of total hopelessness. ". . . at the entry of the Potsherd Gate you shall break the flask, so will I break this people and this city as one breaks a potter's vessel, so that it can never be mended."

From a non-canonical book, Ecclesiasticus 22:7 ("Wisdom of Jesus the Son of Sirah"), comes this humorous but serious instruction: "He who teaches a fool is like one who glues potsherds together."

I have learned much from the leftover pieces of very old earthen vessels. They still can be made to speak. But an archaeologist must learn to listen closely. I learned this from a coin "dealer."

I had first learned to identify ancient biblical coins from books, articles, and museum collections that I had studied. The next step came when I had a hands-on experience with coins of the past while travelling in Turkey in 1963. I was stopped on the road by a man who was hiding behind some bushes and waving me to stop. In his hand he held a small object. Curious, I slowed down and stopped in the hope that he might have some interesting ancient object for sale. The "dealer" acted very secretive, looking to his left and right. Then he took me behind the bushes. He showed me a coin that was for sale and said that it was very old. I recognized the coin as a silver half-shekel, a valuable and important Hebrew coin. I decided to buy the coin. I was paying a fair price for it, I thought, but there was a lingering doubt in my mind.

A few weeks later I visited a well-known antiquarian in Jerusalem. The experienced dealer took one look and said, "That is a cast, but a very fine and accurate reproduction. How much did you pay for it? Not willing to reveal how much money I had squandered, I thanked him and left the shop in a hurry. How I wished I had been more prudent behind the bushes! I had been tricked and had paid for my not knowing how to recognize a true from a fake coin.

Much later I realized that I had gained greatly from this humiliating experience and that I had in fact only paid a modest "tuition fee" for learning something about numismatics, an important science in the field of archaeology.

*"I, wisdom, live with prudence, and*
*I attain knowledge and discretion."*
*(Proverbs 8:12)*

# THE AXE IN THE TOMB

IN 1963 ALETTA AND I DECIDED to travel to Egypt in the hope of visiting the famous temple of Abu Simbel. The temple was to be moved to the top of a mountain some two hundred feet higher up in order to save the temple from being flooded with the completion of the new Nassar Lake. The incident that sparked this story happened when we made a side trip to the pharonic necropolis known as the Valley of the Kings. We stumbled into a very uncommon experience that I delight in telling to my friends.

After visiting the temple of Abu Simbel, we viewed various royal tombs. This journey included a walk down a steep corridor into the tomb of Pharoah Tut-ankh-amon where we admired his beautifully preserved sarcophagus. After we emerged from the grave of Tut-ankh-amon, our guide asked us to wait near a tomb entrance while he arranged for our transportation back to our hotel in Luxor.

It was a very hot day, typical for Upper Egypt, and we looked around for some shade. The entrance to this unmarked and probably insignificant tomb offered us some comfort in its shade. We entered through an iron door that was for some unknown reason left unlocked. While our tour group milled around in the entrance, I walked deeper into this sepulcher. I noted further down the corridor the entryway to a side room. My curiosity aroused, I walked on down the hallway until I reached the side chamber. A bit of daylight penetrated the hall, enough for me to see that the room was completely empty. What a shame and disappointment. I thought, "Don't give up and go on." I barely recognized a small door that gave access to a cella (small room). "Wow!" My mind was working feverishly as several ideas flashed through my head. Might there be a burial in the cella, or maybe even a sarcophagus, or possibly mortuary furniture? Who knows what might lie hidden there! Possibly there were archaeological finds not yet published.

Gus and Aletta Jeeninga in the Valley of the Kings, Egypt, 1967.

I crossed the large chamber and reached the cella door, merely an opening in the wall. By now the daylight was nearly gone. I waited, impatiently, for my eyes to get used to the darkness. When I finally could visually survey the small room, I was quite disappointed and I heard myself say, "Rats, bad luck!" The room was totally empty—but wait. What was that object in the far corner of the cella? I leaned forward to reach the object. I picked it up and rushed back to the corridor where there was enough light to see the artifact I was holding firmly in my hand. The object was heavy and made of iron. At first I could not tell if it was ancient or modern, but soon I was convinced that it was a modern axe, a cutting tool. Now, what do I do with this object?

A funny idea struck my mind. I contrived to have some fun and tell members of the tour group, who were still waiting in the shade of the corridor, that I had made a major discovery of an ancient Egyptian tool. As soon as I showed them what I had found, they formed a circle around me. I put on a serious face and with an air of authority I elaborated on the significance of the development of the iron industry in the ancient world and explained the importance of this discovery to the science of Egyptian archaeology and culture.

At this point my attention was drawn to the entrance of the tomb. An Egyptian fellahin (peasant) had entered the hallway and was walking briskly toward us. The man was wearing the typical Egyptian tunic and I guessed him to be about fifty years old. He did not look like a beggar. I had no idea what he was doing here in the tomb, and deemed it wise to continue my talk and ignore him.

The fellahin—or was he something more than that?—walked up to our circle and stood behind us, listening to what I was "concocting" about the axe I had discovered in the cella. Then this strange man stepped forward and to my utter amazement asked me, in quite good English, "Can I buy that object from you?" I smiled at him incredulously and thought that this must be a joke. He wants to act out a typical Egyptian haggling scene for the entertainment of our tourist group. Maybe the man is an Egyptian tourist guide out to earn "backshish."

Well, I was game and decided to go along with the prank. I asked, "How much do you give me for it?" He answered, "I'll give you one Egyptian pound (ca. $5.00). "No way," I responded and replied, "Give me three pounds for that is a fair price for such a well crafted axe." The fellahin threw up both of his arms to heaven and declared, "Let Allah be a witness between you and me. No, but I will give you two pounds." I continued the demonstration, still thinking that this was a plot, and I responded to him, picking up the local mannerism. "In the presence of my friends I will give this axe to you as my friend. Give me three pounds. What are three pounds between you and me? Blessed be Allah."

The Arab made a sad face but pulled a wad of money from below his tunic and counted out three pounds and said to me, with sorrow in his voice, "Let Allah be a witness between you and me. No, I will give you three pounds. I will give them to you because your are my friend. Here, take it." Still convinced we were playing a game, I took the money and he took the axe. Then he turned around and quickly walked out of the tomb. Everyone around me looked at me, waiting for me to explain what had happened and what this all meant. I expected the fellahin to return, give me the axe back, and receive his returned money so that we all could have a laugh. However, I have never seen the man again.

The whole episode took only a few minutes and I was dumbfounded. "What happened?" I asked myself. A few people in the group wanted to know and queried, "You really found that axe in this tomb and sold it for three pounds to this Egyptian farmer?" I looked at my hand, still perplexed, and yes, there were three pounds. Then I started to laugh and my friends joined me.

Now, let me tell you the rest of the story. Someone insisted on knowing what I thought had happened. Could I explain the "show." Then I told them my theory. During the day, and while visiting the Royal Tombs in the Valley of the Kings, I had bought a flake of limestone that had carved and painted on it an Egyptian Pharaoh and hieroglyphic writings. The local dealer told me that it had come off a wall of a tomb, and many like it were sold to tourists, which is illegal, of course. I am convinced that our fellahin had been involved in flaking such fragments from the tomb walls and selling them to tourists. When not working his illegal trade, he had hidden his iron axe in the cella where I found it and wanted it back so badly that he bought it from me. Think how funny that was. The man bought his own tool, then disappeared quickly so as not to be arrested by the tourist police. The eagerness with which the fellahin tried to get back his axe shows that the iron axe was difficult to obtain, expensive, and provided him with a good income to support his family by selling flakes cut from decorated walls of the Royal Tombs.

At the end of this episode I was left with the predicament of whether or not I had broken an Egyptian law and was now myself a robber and thief. Then I remembered Moses' law, "Thou shalt not steal" (Exodus 20:25). But in spite of it all, my Exodus from Egypt went smoothly.

# WILD BEAST OF THE FIELD

ON MAY 5, 1953, A TAXI DELIVERED ME at the iron gate of the American Schools of Oriental Research (ASOR) in East Jerusalem. I had arrived in the Holy Land! It had been my dream since I was fifteen. I was in high spirits.

After checking into my small bedroom, I learned that tea was being served in the courtyard of the Institute. How surprised and delighted I was when I arrived at the social hour and saw my professor from Union Theological Seminary in New York, Dr. James Muilenburg. Dr. Muilenburg had been appointed the Annual Director of ASOR. Fortune was on my side. I was sure of that because Dr. Muilenburg was the Director of the Institute. Some dramatic and meaningful happenings surely lay ahead for me.

Soon I was rubbing shoulders, so to say, with several important Bible scholars with worldwide reputations. At the time I could not guess how many of these scholars would influence my academic pursuits then and there, and for many years to come. To point out just a few of these individuals, there were: Dr. Frank Cross from Harvard University, a brilliant linguist of biblical and related Semitic languages and leader in the publication of many of the significant Qumran Scrolls; Dr. John Allegro, famed for his controversial books on the Dead Sea Scrolls and their meaning; and Dr. Lucas H. Grollenberg who is best known for his book *Atlas of the Bible*.

After introductions and while still sipping on sweet tea and munching on locally baked cookies, Dr. Muilenberg announced that in a few days there would be a field trip of several days into Trans Jordan, including a visit to Petra and to Aqabah via the

King's Highway. I sensed that I had arrived at a propitious time. I was anxious to explore the Holy Land, to visit its ancient sites and get the feel of the geography and topography. A rare experience awaited me on this anticipated field trip, more than I could have hoped for. It would have an especially unique biblical aura.

Early in the morning of the day on which our small group was leaving for the five-day field trip, there was a knock on my door. I heard a voice say, "Mr. Gus, are you ready?" It was our driver, Ahmed.

"Wait! I am coming right now," I shouted back. Picking up my rucksack, I rushed down stairs to find my seat in the waiting van. Soon Dr. Muilenburg arrived, then John Allegro and Frank Cross. Dr. Grollenberg had another appointment and could not join the party. Shortly we were on our way.

I watched with great interest as we passed Herod's Gate, located in the north wall of the Old City. Rapidly we lost sight of El Quds (the Holy City) as we drove down the Judean hills toward Jericho. In the next twenty miles we descended from 2200 feet above sea level at Jerusalem to Jericho at nearly 1200 feet below sea level. It is quite a descent. We stopped at an excellent Jordan Valley overlook and scanned the Jordan Rift. Right opposite from where we stood it was possible to see the vague outlines of the lands of Moab, Ammon, and Gilead. The three territories appeared to be floating in the haze covering the land.

Pointing with his somewhat arthritic index finger, Dr. Muilenburg said, "That is our first destination, the land of Gilead. There we will find the remnants of many of the hoary Dolmen. These Dolmen served Neolithic man (ca. 6000-3000 B.C.) as burial sites."

Fascinated, I asked Dr. Muilenburg, "May we explore the Dolmen graves. Will we find ancient burial gifts there?" The professor gingerly explained, "For many years archaeologists have studied these burials. However, even they have not found contemporary pottery in them. Over millennia, curious boys and men have rummaged through these sacred necropoleis and removed anything of interest or value. We walked back to the parked van to continue our journey. With a false optimism I hoped that there might yet be something lying around these old tombs that might be of some significance to me.

Continuing down the Jericho road, the highway meandered through the clay hills of the Jordan Rift until we reached the Jordan River. We crossed over the modern steel bridge and were now officially in Trans Jordan (the Hashemite Kingdom). A silence fell over our party. "Was it due to the isolation and emptiness of the land we had entered?" I wondered. For miles toward the north, east, and south the land before us rose gradually to the

Dolmen (gravesite) from about 7,000 B.C., photo by Dr. Jeeninga, Jordan, 1966.

height of nearly 2300 feet. As far as I could see there were only sporadic patches of bushes and trees. Wondering why the land was so barren of what the Bible describes as "a land of milk and honey" (Ex. 3:8), I gathered my courage, broke the silence, and asked no one in particular, "Why is this land so barren?" Someone explained, "In early Hebrew times, Canaan was covered with thick forests. However, conquering armies swept over the land again and again, scorching enemy possessions and cutting down timber for use in burning down city gates and walls. The land was left devastated."

Parking the van at the foot of the Jordanian plateau, we began to scramble up the hillside. Progress was slow because the surface was cluttered with rock and loosened stones. We were warned to watch out for scorpions and poisonous snakes. The group broke up. Some went on alone; a few stayed together. I was glad to be alone with Dr. Muilenburg. This professor had been my favorite lecturer and teacher. I had observed him closely when he lectured. He realistically dramatized the stories of the Old Testament. In fact, I saw in him one of my captivating heroes, none other than Abraham. When Dr. Muilenburg and I arrived at our first close-up look at one of the better preserved Dolmen, he remarked, "Gus, it has been suggested that the presence of these huge stone structures gave rise to the legends of the 'mighty men that were of old, (Gen. 6:7) and the 'Anakim' (giants, Deut. 1:28) who built these graves. Maybe they did, maybe not. Nevertheless, it must have been an enormous task to lift these stones into their present positions."

I watched my professor as he inspected the burials. I noticed something interesting about his physical features. Even though Dr. Muilenburg was close to retirement, he was very energetic. But it was his personal appearance that caught my imagination. His hairline had somewhat receded. His hair was white and a simple wave lay across his forehead. His nose had a slight downward bend that one might interpret as semitic in shape. His eyebrows were well manicured. Across his face were wrinkles of aging that enhanced the impression of a strong and healthy person. I mused. In my mind's eye I saw old Abraham standing before me on the mountain. We were only about twenty-five miles from where Abraham and Lot had once stood and viewed the land of Canaan (Gen. 13:9-12).

Time passed. We explored several Dolmen, but then we needed to return to the station wagon. Most of the others had already reached the van and were waiting for us and watching us. Dr. Muilenburg and I looked for the easiest way down the slope, but the many loose rocks made it treacherous. There were also many outcroppings of rocks that were natural ledges, making it very difficult to go down. Often we had to make short jumps down to a lower ledge. We moved on slowly and cautiously, not knowing what problem would come next. We had no idea that something dangerous was right in our path. No, it was neither a large snake nor a cluster of scorpions. Then came the next ledge.

I said, "Why don't I jump down to the next ledge and from there I can help you to come down?" I knew that I could do it. I leaned forward and jumped down. All was going fine. I landed beautifully just where I had aimed. As I straightened out, in an instant my eyes focused on something that made my blood stand still. I stared into the eyes of a gigantic creature—no, it was a beast. "What is that?" was the question that raced through my mind. I realized that my life was in danger. It flashed through my mind that I had no gun, rifle, not even a good-sized hunting knife to defend myself. Besides, the events unfolded so rapidly that, even if I had been in possession of a gun or knife, it might not have helped me. While the seconds ticked away the wild beast dashed by me so closely that it rubbed along my hip bone as it leaped from its lair down the mountain slope. Soon it was out of sight. I breathed easier.

To my surprise, I heard someone from our party, way down in the valley and standing near the van, shouting, "Gus, watch out, there is a hyena next to you!" But by the time I heard that warning, the episode already was history. After Dr. Muilenburg and I reached the van, I explained the event.

When I jumped on the ledge below me, I did not think that it might be the favorite lair of a Palestinian hyena. When my feet reached the ground, I was astonished to see what I first thought was a huge German shepherd dog. Then I recognized the square shape of the beast's head, its broad shoulders, and its very narrow hind. In a glance, I recognized the black and yellowish color of the animal's skin. But only after the wild brute had touched me and was out of sight did I realize that it had been, no doubt, a hungry hyena. This was not a daily encounter, to say the least. Since I was not a carcass or dying creature, I escaped being meat for the brute.

For a while we did discuss the subject of "Wild Beasts of the Field" (Mark 1:13). Our Palestine guide was a great help in explaining some of the particulars of the wild animals of Palestine, with special emphasis on hyenas. He told us: "The hyena is a large and strong nocturnal carnivorous scavenger. I have encountered them several times during my travels here. They do attack human beings, but rarely. They have such strong jaws that they can easily crack the bones of an ox. In biblical times they were numerous in this land. The KJV calls them 'doleful creatures' and Isaiah 13:21 refers to hyenas as 'beasts of the field.'"

I was a bit shaken up, but slowly I settled down. We had just started our day's survey and were yet to visit various other sites and haunts in this wilderness. Another dangerous encounter was a well-grounded possibility. It did not help me that Ahmed, our driver, told us that he had forgotten to bring his rifle. Not knowing what might jump up in front of me suddenly, I looked around hoping to find something that would make a reasonably worthwhile weapon to defend myself if I should be attacked. God forbid. I now knew that that was a distinct prospect.

Soon my eyes roamed the vicinity and chanced upon something white. It caught my attention. I nonchalantly walked up to inspect it. It was a large animal bone. I lifted it from the ground to consider it more closely. The one end of the bone was narrow and the other end gradually broadened into almost a sharp edge. Between pursed lips I told myself, "This looks like the jawbone of an ass." Taking the bone in my right hand, I play acted. I was fighting off a wild beast with vigorous blows and the animal dropped to the ground with a roar of pain. I was convinced that this jawbone was my weapon to ward off any ferocious creature. I was even more assured when a biblical passage crossed my mind about Samson: "And he found a fresh jawbone of an ass and put out his hand and seized it, and with it he slew a thousand men" (Judg. 15:15). When I returned to the van with my Samsonian jawbone, there was some laughter and teasing. However, I was confident that I had at least something to count on to help spare my life if I would face another encounter with a "beast of the field."

I could not have anticipated what happened to me at the end of the day. The sun was setting fast over the lands of Moab and Ammon. Leaving the ruins of one of the several so-called Desert Castles, Dr. Muilenburg announced, "This is it for the day. We will head for our hotel for the night." I stood near the van with my unused jawbone in my right hand. I hated to part with my security blanket, but knew that I had to leave it behind. With some feeling of pride, I told everyone, "Look what a fine piece of ancient bone weaponry I possessed." Then, with all my power, I struck the jawbone on a large rock. Bewildered and confused, I looked at the result of my powerful stroke. The jawbone had totally disintegrated into a puff of white dust. What had happened?

That day I learned an important lesson about reading and interpreting the Bible correctly. Turning to Judges 15:15, I reread the account and found the answer.

> "And he found a new [*fresh*] jawbone of an ass, and put forth his hand . . . and seized it, and with it he slew a thousand men."

# ONE OF SIXTY-ONE

BREATHING WITH DIFFICULTY, I finally reached my goal, the High Place. For a long time I had wanted to stand on top of the summit of Petra, the Red-Rose City in Jordan and the former capital of the ancient Nabateans (ca. 400 B.C.-A.D. 400). With my colleagues from the American Schools of Oriental Research in Jerusalem, I now had traveled by van across the Judean plateau to visit the archaeological ruins of Petra, the city of mystery. I was not another Indiana Jones in search of the Ark of Moses. My objectives were more modest and realistic.

I had dreamed of walking among the hidden ruins of this famed lost city to take in the majesty and grandeur of these silent wonders of the distant past. The dream justified the cost and hardship of this journey. Best of all were the unexpected human encounters possible in the heart of this hoary metropolis. Of course, I could not ignore any opportunity of making a significant discovery. I was in the land of dreams. In fact, not too far from Petra, the Joseph of long ago had dreamed unusual dreams. His night visions had become realities. Yes, I had enough reasons to be optimistic and imagine that soon my dreams would become very real.

Viewing the High Place, I could easily identify the ancient cistern for ritual baths, the sacred obelisks, and the circular altar cut out of the rock. Magnificent! The panorama of the city below overwhelmed my sense of distance and proportion. Was what I was surveying really real? The immense rock-cut buildings below me begged to be explored. Looking up from my panoramic gaze, I noticed a movement out of the corner of my left eye. Something black rose up beyond the edge of the rocky High Place's sacred boundary. I thought, "It is a wild goat." I was wrong. The black movement came into full view. Only then did I recognize it for what it was, a Bedouin woman who had come to the summit.

The woman slowly approached me. I was aware that she, like myself, stood only five feet five inches. However, here the similarity ended. As she came closer, I studied her appearance. Her hair was braided in one long pigtail that hung down her back to just below her waist. The dress she wore was typical of the desert inhabitants of this region. It had long sleeves and reached the ground. Her shoes or sandals were invisible. In her world no man is allowed to see her ankles, not even her feet. Flowing down from her shoulders like a waterfall, there were narrow bands of embroidered purple streamers woven into the

Entrance (Siq) to Petra, Jordan.
Dr. Jeeninga in foreground.

fabric of her dress. Much labor had gone into embroidering the apparel with a wide band of intricate, colorful designs at the bottom of the garment.

When we came face to face, I realized that she was an elderly woman, maybe even an old one. Her face was deeply wrinkled. The skin of her face and hands had been darkened to a deep olive color because of the heat of the Arabian desert sun. Her eyes were dark brown, but lively. They sparkled like a recently cut piece of black obsidian. The woman appeared to be an accurate portrait of a typical desert dweller. She surely was that in spite of or maybe because of the fact that when she smiled, her opened mouth showed the lack of several front teeth. The marred mouth was softened by the four well-crafted, golden teeth prominently displayed. But the best of my encounter with this "mother of all mothers" was yet to come.

The matriarch carried with her an old leather satchel. She placed it in front of me and opened it. From the container she lifted out a large pottery sherd (fragment) and handed it to me. Experience must have taught her to know that I was interested in broken pots. Besides, I held in my hand a few small potsherds I had just picked up from the surface. After she handed me the large fragment, she did not speak, but watched me closely while I studied the object. It was a fragment of a Nabatean vase. The Nabateans had ruled these lands between four hundred B.C. and A.D. four hundred. During these centuries the Nabateans reached their peak of artistic creativity. Their pottery was unique and is best known for its egg-shell thinness. The pottery was well fired and beautifully decorated. I offered her some money for it. She made a disapproving face and shook her hand, "No." I offered her a little more, and we had a deal.

I looked in her satchel while she watched me intently. I opened the carrying case more widely. Only then did I see the nearly complete small Nabatean vase, measuring 5 inches high by 3 inches wide. The vase had an unusually wide, flaring rim and was decorated with Nabatean red-floral designs. I whispered, "Eureka!" I did not want the Bedouin to know my excitement at finding this vase. So the bargaining started and continued unabated for a while. Offer after offer she rejected, with great emotion. Obviously she knew what she had. When rejecting my counter offers, she would throw both of her hands in the air and cry, "No, no, no, in the name of Allah, no!"

For a few minutes I slackened my obvious interest in the vase and acted as though I had given up and was ready to leave. I handed her the vase and nonchalantly offered her a slightly higher amount than before, adding, "What are a few dollars between you and me?" The experienced woman squinted and looked at me sternly with her penetrating dark eyes. Then I noticed a careful smile on her face. In a much warmer and softer voice she said, "Let Allah be my witness. I will give you this precious vase as a friend." She pushed the vase into my hand and quickly took my money, which I had ready for her. My money disappeared smoothly under her garment. I was about to leave her when a new episode with her unfolded.

She proved herself to be an extremely successful business lady. It was fun to bargain with her. But was she getting the better deal? Smoothly and swiftly she pulled out from under her garment a small bundle. I expected to see some precious object of gold, alabaster, obsidian, or silver. Maybe there would be a piece of royal jewelry that she had kept hidden until she found a generous buyer. I waited excitedly for her to reveal what was in the bundle, about the size of a baseball. Instead of some precious piece of jewelry, however, she produced an ancient coin that was the size of a dime. I was astonished. My dream of obtaining a major archaeological object melted like a piece of ice in the desert sun.

She extended the coin toward me and said, "Two dolla." The "r" in "dollar" is never pronounced. I took the coin from her hand with a sinking hope of its historical significance and value. I studied both sides of the coin. The bronze coin was heavily corroded. I was unable to recognize anything on either side. I gave the coin back to her and asked, "May I look in the bundle?" She handed me the hoard of coins. I spread the coins out on the cloth in which she kept them. Curiously, I checked them, but could not find even one coin that might be promising. Then I got an idea. I knew that she was a clever trader. I was also convinced that she knew what she had. She very well knew what was the going value of these coins on the open market. These coins had very little value. Because I liked the old woman and realized that a few dollars would mean so much to her, I took an unorthodox business approach and made her this offer: "These coins are all in very poor condition, almost worthless. However, I'll give you $5.00 for all of them." Her immediate reaction was negative. She again tried to sell me one coin at a time. I repeated my offer, somewhat more briskly. When she showed no interest, I grinned and turned to leave her."

"*Shalam,*" I said ("Goodbye"). Not unexpectedly, she ran after me and soon caught up. I turned around and acted uninterested. She showed me the bundle with coins in her left hand, and with her right hand she waited to receive the five dollars. She snatched the money from my hand at the same time that I took the bundle of coins from her hand. When we parted, I sensed that she was happy. I saw her four golden teeth for the last time. No doubt she had done well with me. This day she had earned close to $10.00 and had become a "rich" lady in her tribe. But what had I received for my precious dollars?

It was not until I returned to the Anderson University Museum office that I uncovered the secret hidden in the bundle of sixty-one pieces of corroded coins. In the museum laboratory two months later, I began the arduous task of cleaning the coins, using plenty of elbow grease. With a toothbrush, some water, and a little baking soda, I brushed and rubbed each coin. None of the coins so cleaned yielded anything worth reporting. In desperation I attacked the remaining coins with gusto. Five coins to go, then three, then two. My hand was shaking and my mind numb. I had given up the dream of finding that one, unusual coin. Almost unconsciously I rubbed and brushed. Only when the next to the last coin disintegrated did I realize that there was now only one coin left, one of sixty-one.

I stared at the unpromising, tiny, thumb-sized, black-greenish, corroded and brittle coin with disgust and despair. Whatever inscribed legend this coin might have had, I was sure it had disintegrated just like the other sixty coins. At this sober moment I remembered the $5 I had paid the old woman. I decided to give this last coin one more desperate work-over. While I was scrubbing and brushing I noticed that the coin did not disintegrate. After a while I rinsed the coin clean. Tilting the coin back and forth under a strong lamp, I talked myself into seeing a few ridges on the obverse side of the coin. After repeated periods of polishing, I grew more certain. I was seeing something, but what? I convinced myself that I recognized a few archaic Hebrew alphabetic letters. From my lips dropped the words, "Ridiculous. You only imagine seeing these letters because you want to see them." I continued the cleaning process with a renewed energy.

The conviction grew more certain that there were several lines of archaic Hebrew. I was thrilled. This might turn out to be a wonderful and significant discovery after all. Might it be something totally new or another additional authentication of Hebrew (Jewish) history? It frustrated me greatly that I could not read the inscription. Obviously, I was not as capable of translating ancient Hebrew script as I thought I was. However, I told myself, "Don't worry. Walter can do it." Walter Rast, professor of Semitic Languages at Valparaiso University, and I had studied together at the American Schools of Oriental Research in Jerusalem. I invited him to come to Anderson University to help me decipher the coin's legend. Slowly, but confidently, Walter transcribed the coin's inscription. Neither of us said a word. My eyes were glued to his pencil as he reproduced each Hebrew letter.

Beginning at the top right side of the coin, then moving down, line by line, Walter managed to copy five lines of script. When he was finished, he shoved the hand-written note in front of me, and said, "You give me the translation!" Eagerly I took the note and glanced over it. I mumbled, hardly audible, "Wow, terrific. You see a lot more letters than I do. But still I cannot translate it." I pushed the paper back to him. "Come on, Walter," I pleaded. "What is the translation of this text?" Skillfully, Walter began to translate. I was fascinated. My muscles were tense. I sharpened my ears so as not to miss a word as Walter read out loud the translation to me. He read: "Johanan the high priest and the community of the Jews."

I was elated with the content of this inscription. It was so unexpected. The coin might or might not have great monetary value, but it was important historically. "Tell me more about this coin," I prompted Walter. "What date do you give it?" "This bronze coin was struck during the early part of the second century B.C.," Walter explained, adding, "This coin was issued to celebrate the reign of Johanan, a Jewish High priest during the reign of the Maccabees." Walter turned over the coin and continued, "Look, here on the reverse side, there is no legend but it shows two typical Hebrew symbols."

A Hebrew coin minted during the Maccabean period. Used in chapter headings in this book.

I tested Walter and asked, "What are we looking at and what does it mean?" "Note," Walter pointed out, "this symbol shows a pomegranate between two cornucopias. The pomegranate and the cornucopia are both symbols of fertility and abundance." "Absolutely fabulous, Walter. Thanks a lot for all this information!"

The dream I dreamed when standing on the High Place in Petra had come true. From the bargain for a Nabatean vase until the decipherment of a Nabatean archaic Hebrew legend, the experience had been an adventure full of emotion, excitement, and discovery. The conclusion of this episode reads like a final report of many archaeological expeditions, namely, "At the end of an unsuccessful season of digging, we made the most exciting discovery on the last day and in the last hour." My final archaeological report for Petra might well read, "one of sixty-one was a winner!"

# THE SILOAM INSCRIPTION

## I

## A ROYAL MESSAGE

FIVE OF THE SIX STUDENTS ENROLLED in the course were already seated when I breathlessly hurried into the classroom. The course, "Palestine Archaeology" taught at the Oriental Institute of the University of Chicago, promised to be an exciting and challenging one. Dr. Raymond E. Bowman's class started at 9:00 a.m. sharp. Only once did I receive a speeding ticket trying to get from my early morning job to my class on time. The professor, who had entered the classroom right behind me, handed each one of the students a black and white photo and announced, "Today we will start a study of ancient Canaanite inscriptions."

The class was on its way. I listened closely to the new and fascinating information that the hour brought. It clarified and confirmed the historicity and accurateness of many biblical accounts. At the end of the lecture Dr. Bowman held up his copy of the black and white photo and reminded us, "Please, tomorrow morning bring to class your understanding of the origin, nature, and translation of the inscription. Class is dismissed." We all left the class apprehensive about the difficult assignment. At a minimum we knew that the stone with the markings in the photo was an inscription. But in which language or dialect, or from which century it dated was a total mystery to us.

That evening I sat at my desk and gazed at the photograph. The roughly textured stone in the picture appeared to be of limestone. Its jagged edges and deeply cut incisions indicated that the slab had been in pieces at one time but had been glued together. On the surface of the obscure plaque were numerous engravings

Aletta Jeeninga and Dr. Robert Bull, Caesarea, Israel, 1978.

going in every direction. At first I did not recognize anything and felt desperate. Fortunately, I had taken a course earlier in Hebrew palaeography—the study of script styles used in ancient Palestine. After intensely examining the scratches, I succeeded in recognizing a few Hebrew archaic letters, but not enough of them to attempt to date or give even a tentative translation of the text.

The next morning Dr. Bowman invited us to explain the engraving on the slab. His invitation was met with silence by the six students. I was anxious to hear the professor's explanation. To my delight, that was exactly what Dr. Bowman proceeded to do. In brief, he set forth the facts as follows.

In June, 1880, a teenager was playing at the exit of a well-known water tunnel under the ancient city of Jerusalem. His foot slipped and he fell into the water. When he got to his feet, he noticed a section of the tunnel wall that had a small area with deep grooves. He mumbled to himself, "Wow, that is interesting. I wonder how they got there and what they mean?" As the word about this unusual ancient rock carving spread, a Herman Guthe had a gypsum cast made of it. However, in that same year thieves removed the inscription, now referred to as the Siloam Tunnel Inscription after the spring of Siloam nearby. During the removal the slab broke into six pieces. After that a Greek businessman bought the stone slab from an unknown Arab. Fortunately, the Turkish government acquired the pieces and took them to the Museum of the Ancient Orient in Istanbul, Turkey. Here the inscription was restored and put on exhibit.

Dr. Bowman paused. That student from the Netherlands raised his hand and asked, "Why is this ancient inscription so important that we study it so intently?" Dr. Bowman replied, "Let me give you a few more details. The inscription is two and a half feet long and the text is spread out over about the size of a modern newspaper page. As one can see from the photograph, it is written in archaic Hebrew script. Paleographists all agree on that. Based on the style of the letters, they have dated this inscription to the end of the 8th century B.C., and I agree with their findings." It is now generally accepted that King Hezekiah of Judah ordered this tunnel to be cut and the inscription to be chiselled into the wall of the tunnel (cf. 2 Kings 20:20; 2 Chron. 32: 3, 5, 11, 30). This discovery is a most dramatic illustration of the veracity of the biblical record.

In the distance the class bell rang. With a grin on his face, the professor said, "Saved by the bell. Class is dismissed." On the way out of the classroom a thought ran through my mind. How exciting it would be to see the original inscription. Someday, maybe, I might even see the original inscription in the Istanbul Archaeological Museum. A dream was born and in my sub-consciousness I decided that someday I would do it all. Some day.

# II

# ANCIENT WHISPERS

IT WAS 1953. I WAS ON A TRIP "Around The World In Twelve Months." I had settled in at the American Schools of Oriental Research (ASOR) in Jerusalem. After many years of waiting to visit the Holy Land, my dream to do so had come true. During the evening supper, shared with other members of the Institute, the Director of ASOR announced, "Tomorrow afternoon there will be a walk through the Hezekiah Water Tunnel." Right on target. The tunnel walk was one of my major objectives on my Holy Land visit.

The next day, guided by an official from the Jordanian Department of Antiquity, a few professors and two students started on the exploration of the old water course. The entrance to the passage is a short distance from the ruins of the so-called Tower of David in the Kidron Valley, and just below the Eastern Wall of the Jerusalem temple mound. At this point a steep stairway leads to the "Virgin's Spring," where the famous tunnel begins.

Carefully we walked down the twenty or more stone steps leading to the spring. We reached the cave where the spring gushes up from several fissures at the bottom of the grotto. At the far end of the recess, some eight feet away from the cavern's stairway, is a four-foot high by about three-foot wide opening where the water tunnel starts. It ends at the Siloam pool some 1700 feet farther down.

We entered the dark chasm and inched forward carefully. The water was nearly three feet deep. Progress was very slow in the darkness of this ancient passage. Our flashlights dimly showed the path ahead of us. I let my light play on the walls of the channel. Suddenly I recognized what I was looking for. I saw the tool marks of the ancient stonecutters still visible on the rocks. Tapping on the shoulder of our leader, who was just in front of me, I whispered—I do not know why I whispered—"Look here, Mr. Melik, there are tool marks everywhere!" The guide turned around and threw his light on the walls and said, "Gus, you are right. I missed seeing them. Notice, you can even feel the incisions made by the primitive axe."

As we studied the craftsman's work we noticed that the cuts were made by a four-pronged tool. To

A replica of the Siloam Inscription (top) with detail shown in bottom photo.

cut this limestone with such primitive iron tools must have been arduous, but as we could see, very successful. According to earlier explorers and archaeolgists, the Hezekiah Tunnel showed evidence that the engineers had difficulty in going in the right direction. Every so often a section of the tunnel turns into a dead end, even visible today.

As we progressed the water reached our waist level. Other times we walked stooped because the tunnel was very low. It was at those times that I was afraid. I was worried we might drown.

My fear was based on the story told to us that one of the early excavators of the conduit had drowned. The spring's flow is unpredictable. There was a sudden surge of water from the spring that quickly filled up the tunnel. The archaeologist was unable to get out fast enough and consequently drowned.

I pushed these morbid thoughts out of my mind. I did not wish to miss seeing every nook of interest on this adventure. We continued pushing on through the 1750 foot long corridor to reach the Pool of Siloam. It was there that Jesus had healed the man born blind (John 9:7) and it was near the exit of the tunnel that the student had seen the inscription. I expected we would arrive at this exit shortly. Finally, just ahead of us, I saw some daylight. Mr. Melik, who was a short distance ahead of me, motioned and said, "Come here, Gus. I have found the original." I moved quickly towards him, and commented, "Mr. Melik, how can you say you have found the original? Original of what?" He said, "What I mean is, I have found the original location of the Siloam Inscription. Look here, the marks of where the inscription was cut out of the rock are quite clear."

"No doubt about it," I agreed, as I was looking at the chisel marks and felt with my fingers the grooves left behind when the inscription was hammered out of its location. I was enchanted to be so near, and in "touch" with the royal inscription. I wondered if King Hezekiah himself had stood at this spot to inspect his royal commemorative inscription.

We waded through the Pool of Siloam and climbed up the long staircase, some forty or more steps. We left behind us a location pivotal in the history of Judah. I was sure I would return to this location and repeat the walk through the Hezekiah Water Tunnel. It had tantalized my curiosity. More than ever before, I now wanted to see the Siloam Inscription itself. I had to go to Istanbul. "I will go soon," I promised myself.

# III

## SHE MADE A DIFFERENCE

I was awake by six in the morning. It was the fall of 1963. Aletta and I were anxious to get to the Istanbul Museum of the Orient in Turkey. Today we hoped to fulfill our long desired wish to see and study the Siloam Inscription on exhibit in the Istanbul Museum. I had learned about this archaeological discovery while I was a student at the Oriental Institute in Chicago.

Slowly we ascended the many steps that led us to the Museum entrance. The architecture of the building, expressing the intentions of this museum, was Greek and Roman, with features of other cultural influences from the ancient world. The porch was supported by stone columns thirty feet tall, each carrying Corinthian capitals. Passing these pillars, we entered the vestibule of the museum. It was rather dark inside the building and there was total silence, partly because of the early hour. There were only a few people meandering through the halls and corridors.

Because of my eagerness to locate the inscription, I had left Aletta far behind as I nervously hurried around like a bird trying to catch a bug or spider. I crisscrossed the numerous dusty and overstocked rooms and was totally ineffective in locating the inscription. When I was at the point of giving up the search, I heard a faint voice at the other end of the hall. Was that Aletta's voice? I listened more closely. Then my ear picked up my name. Surely, it was Aletta calling me. I quickly returned to find her.

"Why are you calling me?" Aletta looked pleased and happy and asked me, "Are you not looking for the Siloam Inscription?"

"Oh, yes, for sure, but why ask?" I replied and continued, "It is not here. I have looked everywhere."

"Honey," Aletta said with an innocent smile, "I am sorry, but you are mistaken. In fact, you have walked by the stone inscription several times. It is just right of the door in Hall B. It rests on a wooden stand. Go and see it for yourself."

"Tell me," I asked Aletta, "how did you find it so fast and easily, but I could not locate it?"

Aletta showed me a pamphlet in her hand and answered, "While you were running around like a rabbit, I went to the front desk and bought this museum guide. In the guide I found the reference to the Siloam Inscription, its registration number, and floor location, and 'bang,' I walked right up to it."

I looked at Aletta and was a little dismayed. Softly I said, "Thanks. Please take me to the inscription or I might run past it again!" Without making it too obvious, I was extremely thankful to her for locating it. It would have been such a pity if we had not found it after travelling all the way from Anderson College in Indiana.

I must admit that on several other occasions during our many travels together, it was Aletta who saved the day. Not only other museum objects, but also geographical and topographical locations were found or discovered for me by my talented and intelligent wife. A well-known Bible passage has passed in front of my eyes more than once:

> Then the Lord said, "It is not good that man should
> be alone. I will make him a helper fit for him."
> (Gen. 2: 18. RSV)

While the Muezzin chanted his evening prayer, Aletta and I enjoyed a delicious supper at a restaurant overlooking the Bosporus. It had been an exciting day. In silence we thanked the city of Istanbul for giving us the opportunity of seeing and admiring the Siloam Inscription. It was the end of the special saga. The moon hid behind the clouds and it was night.

# A FRIGHTFUL JOURNEY

WHEN ABRAHAM LEFT UR OF THE CHALDEANS, a city located in southern Mesopotamia (now modern Iraq) to go to an unknown land, he had to cross high mountains, an uncharted wilderness, and unmarked deserts. Aletta and I wished to travel in Abraham's footsteps and beyond.

So it happened that we consulted with a waiter in a small restaurant at Ur-Station, a railroad stop, inquiring how to drive to Basra on the Persian Gulf. With a grin on his face the local "know it all" gave us his wisdom, which was, "After you leave Ur-Station you will cross a railroad just outside of the village. There you turn left and follow a desert track, for there is no paved road to Basra. The track runs parallel to the railroad. Make sure that you always keep sight of the tall electric poles that run alongside of the railroad."

Early at dawn the next morning we crossed the railroad and found the desert track leading south. After some five miles the track began turning away from the railroad and the electric poles. That worried us much. Then suddenly the track circled back and brought us to the point we had left earlier, but a short distance further to the south. After driving two hours, the desert no longer appeared benign but had become a frightening land to travel. Our apprehension increased after we encountered the existence of many desert tracks crisscrossing each other and going in every direction of the compass. This situation made it extremely difficult to know which track to follow.

Even more problematic was what to do when, all of a sudden, the sandy road disappeared and we were driving on the bottom of a recently dried out, shallow swamp. Tire marks had disappeared and with them the road we were following. With nothing to go by, we plunged straight ahead—very recklessly—hoping to pick up the track on the other side of the parched lake. After driving a mile or two, we reached the other edge of the swamp bed and stared bewildered at the multiple car and truck tire marks that turned hither and thither.

Our plight had not changed for the better. We determined to follow what appeared to us neophytes as the most often used ruts. We continued. Was fate pushing us onward? Luck had it that at the moment we were wondering if we were lost we sighted a camel rider far away on the horizon. The desert dweller was moving in our direction. When the lonely bedu was close to us and about to cross just ahead of us, I got out of the V.W. Camper to speak to him in the hope that he could give us information about how to get to Basra. As the bedu reigned in his objecting camel, I quickly walked up to him while he remained in his saddle. I asked him, of course in English, if we were going in the right direction towards Basra. I was delighted that the man replied, but alas, I did not understand him, nor, I am sure, did he grasp what I was asking. When it was obvious that we could not communicate, he spurred on his beast and soon was lost from our sight.

What a blow! I never felt so forsaken or lost in my whole life. The sand whirled around me as the noon wind swept over the sand dunes and barren rocks. Except for the lightly blowing wind there was no sound and this stillness depressed me even more. We tried to shake off the feeling of lostness and abandonment and continued our meandering. Aletta asked if we were lost and suggested we turn back. We knew that Ur-Station to Basra, as the crow flies, was a distance of about 150 miles. But we were no birds and the desert tracks were many. I pondered our location and studied the general geography, using only the most general travel map of the territory. I began to grasp that, if we were lost, we could be traveling in circles or be going hundreds of miles to nowhere. With a limited food and gas supply and less than six gallons of water, our chances for survival were slim at best. However, I was confident that we were going toward our goal. I therefore insisted that we continue our wilderness adventure.

How mistaken I was to believe that the desert was merely a flat, dry stretch of sandy territory through which people journeyed along well-beaten caravan routes. We discovered that we were facing a wilderness. I do not know what better word to use to describe it. In addition to the stretches of shifting sands and dunes, we found rocky outcroppings blocking our way, and, due to recent local storms, swamps or sun-dried bottoms of shallow lakes so hard that they did not show any tracks that we could follow. Adding to our dismay at the sinister nature of the desert wilderness were the automobile tracks zigzagging through the wasteland like snakes fleeing before a fire. The lost or discarded human products had turned into low, sandy hills. These sandy hills seen from one direction appeared to be a pile of barbed wire; but looking at them from the opposite side, they appeared as small sand dunes.

Intermittently the wind howled across the land and created micro sand storms or small tornados called "sand devils." The horizon's air shimmered as the heat rose at noon and the low bushes, scattered across the land, looked like dancing dervishes. Extremely unsettling was the absolute loneliness and silence that encompassed us every mile. We penetrated deeper into what Lawrence of Arabia might have called the "Empty Quarter," a land of sunburnt earth and flash floods.

Looking nervous and unhappy, Aletta again suggested that we might be "wandering" and we should turn back. Once more I argued that I was certain that we were on course. The mood in the V.W. cabin dropped to zero and communication ceased. We traveled several more miles in total silence. It was about lunch time and we stopped to eat and drink a bit, in monk-like silence. Staring through the front window, we both saw in the distance to our right tall poles carrying electric wires. This was our first indication of civilized life and the vindication of my view that we were heading for Basra on the Persian Gulf. Sadly enough, within the next half hour I was proven totally wrong.

Quietly we downed slices of bread with cheese and British jam until Aletta broke the impasse and in desperation begged me to turn around and attempt to go back to Ur-Station. Studying the promising poles just ahead of us, I proposed that we follow those electric wires only as long as they were visible to us. If we could not follow them we would immediately go back to Ur-Station. Aletta looked at me with a frown and hesitantly agreed to my plan. The simple lunch completed, I started the engine and turned the car in the direction of the electric poles. I could not believe our good fortune, coming upon such a clear road sign to direct us to Basra. The possibility of running into a deadly trap just ahead of us never entered my mind.

With a grin on my face we continued our incredible journey. The country just ahead of us appeared flat, consisting mainly of loose sand with low bushes scattered everywhere. We had barely driven half a mile when I suddenly felt the tires were driving heavily, as though they were sticking in mud. I saw to my terror that immediately ahead of me and as far as I could see in the distance we were driving into a desert swamp! I turned the steering wheel hard to the left and drove away from the terrifying crisis. While we were inching away from the trap, I could hear the suction of the tires as the car, with difficulty, crept back to solid earth.

Only after we were a safe distance away from the swamp did I stop the car. I was shaking. Then I realized the seriousness of this unfolding episode. Had we gotten stuck in the swamp we most surely would have perished. In my mind I saw the headlines in the newspaper reading, "Dr. and Mrs. Gustav Jeeninga found dead in the Iraqi desert not too far from Ur of the Chaldees." I felt sick in my stomach.

As I had promised Aletta, we started back to Ur-Station. However, as we soon discovered, we were not yet out of trouble.

A truly disturbing new fact became clear. The wasteland before us looked quite different now. It was like riding a train or bus sitting backwards. The landscape that passes you looks similar to what you saw when you were riding forward, but now you see a different landscape. However, I was certain that the many piles of wasted oil barrels which we had seen earlier lying scattered across the land, and the sand dunes and rock outcroppings, of which I had made mental notes earlier in the day, would serve us as road markers. These road markers would take us back to Ur-Station with ease.

With complete confidence I was driving, so I thought, on the same track we had traveled hours earlier. Nobody would blame me for the problem that suddenly faced us. Visibility had been declining gradually due to the drifting sand. Presently we were in a dust storm. In a short while we could no longer see the track I had been following and I was compelled to stop. When you cannot see where you are going, the most logical thing to do is find out where the road is. Consequently, I got out of the car and did what only an inexperienced desert traveler would do. I began to circle the V.W. in ever larger circles to find the track again. With fear in her voice, Aletta shouted, "Please do not go any further than your ability to see our car." I understood the significance of that desperate cry and kept the vehicle in view.

How lucky we were for I soon found the track—although I did not know whether or not it was our track or another. However, the rut I was now trailing was crisscrossed by many other tracks. Nevertheless, I had a hunch we were home bound. My optimism was again rudely shaken when, looming ahead of us, the sandy spoor forked clearly to the left and to the right and both ways had been well traveled. I halted abruptly and stared at this nasty problem. Should I go left or right, and why? There was no one anywhere to tell me. All day long we had seen only one human being. We might well be on the moon. Since I was satisfied with my sense of direction, we went left because I just knew that this was the right track. Then again I said to myself, "It could well be that the right turn would be the correct road." My heart was beating fast and audibly and I felt sick in my stomach as I admitted to myself for the first time that day that I did not know where to go. I was truly lost and my next act proved it.

Being anxious to get back to Ur-Station before nightfall, I followed my instinct and took the left turn. After a short while doubt swept through my mind and in a husky voice I whispered to Aletta ever so reluctantly, "I am sure I made the wrong turn. We will go back and try the other track." I slowed down and began a shallow turn. Suddenly Aletta cried out, "Hold it, I see two small poles on the horizon and they look like they might be the electric poles we followed when we left Ur this morning!" Personally, I could see nothing, but I knew that Aletta's eyesight was superior to mine. I stopped the V.W. to better concentrate on the distant scene. Just then the visibility was improving and I was able to make out the poles. Most eagerly we traveled on and after one more hour we crawled out of the camper and stumbled exhausted and relieved into the "Hotel Ur-Junction."

One hour later Aletta and I were sitting at the counter of the hotel bar and were asked to explain why we had returned to the hotel. We were surrounded by a group of locals who were eager to get some evening entertainment. When we told them of our day's journey and misadventures, there was a lot of sympathy but also a lot of laughter. A handsome local bard recited a tale about lost desert travelers and said, "You Americans think you can do anything. You drive into the 'Empty Quarter' where there are no paved roads, but only an uninhabited wasteland. Then, when you get stuck in the drifting sand, you do not know that wolves have been watching and following you. Then when you are stuck in the forbidding desert they sneak up to you and bite through your tires so you cannot leave, and calmly they wait for you to attempt to walk out of your predicament and right into a pack of wolves."

With this story ringing in our ears, and a few well wishes for a peaceful sleep, we left the curious crowd and happily retired.

*"As a bird that strays from its nest is one who strays from his home."*
*(Proverbs 27:8)*

*"Some wandered in desert wastes,*
*finding no way to an inhabited town;*
*Hungry and thirsty, their soul fainted within them.*
*Then they cried to the Lord in their trouble,*
*And he delivered them from their distress."*
*(Psalms 107: 4-6)*

# IN SEARCH OF ERASTUS

STANDING AT THE RAILING OF OUR OCEAN LINER, Aletta and I watched excitedly as we entered the harbour of Rotterdam, the Netherlands. It was on June 25, 1963, when the Harbour Police stamped our passports. Our ninety-day car tour (June, July, and August) of Europe and the Middle East had started. It was to be an adventure with many anxieties and pleasant surprises.

One of our principle destinations was to explore the city of Corinth, Greece. The reason for going there was to locate a specific inscription and to photograph it. I had only a vague idea about where we might find the relic and this made the challenge even more appealing to me. It would be like discovering an archaeological object for the first time.

The ruins of ancient Corinth had been excavated over many years. The size of the city was immense. It had been one of the great seaports of ancient Greece and Rome. The drawings and photographs of its marvelous temples, government edifices and plazas were most helpful in my search for a first-century A.D. artifact. But I suspected that to pinpoint an inscription among the vast area of excavated ruins might be difficult if not impossible. Nevertheless, the tug of the quest spurred me on.

The most I knew about the commemorative plaque was that it had been discovered near a theater. In front of the theater was a sixty-foot plaza paved with blocks of limestone. On several of these blocks the inscription was laid bare. The writing has been dated to about the middle of the first century A.D. Furthermore, it was written in Latin, *Erastus—Pro-Aed/S-P-Stravit.* Translated it reads: "Erastus, in return for the aedile-ship laid the pavement at his own expense." This stone tablet was the objective of my search.

I hoped to locate and verify its existence. I did find it, but in a most unusual way.

This saga begins with our arrival at modern Corinth. Because of the famous Corinthian ruins, much of the new town is a commercial center and serves hundreds of tourists. So we too were at first caught up in the frenzy of shopping for souvenirs and soon packed away our trophy of a replica of a Corinthian decorated ceramic bottle. Then we turned away from tourist interest to focus on our pursuit for Erastus.

Immediately we faced our first dilemma. Wherever we looked we saw excavated structures. There were no written signs or descriptions of what these ruins represented. I became uneasy and apprehensive about our search. "Aletta," I said, "we have a problem. If we do not find some indication of where to start looking for the inscription, this journey will be a bust."

"You are right," Aletta responded. "Why don't we drive around a bit and get a better oversight of the various excavated areas?" So, without knowing where we were going, we drove down the main street of the shopping center and followed the road away from the hub of the city.

"Dead end," I murmured. The road ended in a large open field. "What do we do now?" I complained. As had happened before, Aletta helped by saying, "Time out. Let's have lunch, I am starving, and you get dangerous when you get hungry."

We drove on several hundred feet down the field. Fortunately I did see it in time and pushed hard on the brakes. The field had ended and straight ahead of us there was a sharp drop of some thirty feet. The field we had been driving on was nothing more than a thick layer of debris covering the ruins of the ancient city. I got out of the car and cautiously walked to the edge of the drop-off. From this vantagepoint I could view, about thirty feet below, a large section of the ancient city. Aletta had followed me and we gazed in silence while we absorbed the spectacular vista of stone upon stone.

Borrowing a Greek expression, I whispered, "Eureka!" and said to Aletta, "I think we may have stumbled upon ancient Corinth. I am now certain we will find Erastus' inscription." I spoke rapidly and emotionally and continued, "Aletta, look, there in the distance you can see the ruins of a theater. That must be the one mentioned in the archaeological report which reads, 'Near the theater at Corinth was a sixty-foot plaza paved with limestone. On one of the blocks is an inscription . . . .'"

Aletta responded, "How lucky we are. But, Gus, you remember there was also a reference to a second, but smaller the-

The Erastus Inscription in ancient Corinth.

ater. We do not know whether it was the theater we now see where the inscription is located or elsewhere. Anyhow, let's eat first and then we will go down to look. It is too steep for me to go down and up and not to forget that the blasting hot sun might surely kill me. I'll stay with the van." So I drove the V. W. Bug as close to the edge of the plateau as I dared, and parked it. Munching away at our lunch, I impatiently ate my food and scanned the area below.

"You know, honey," I said, "wouldn't it be a miracle if we should find that small inscription in this enormous archaeological field? It is going to take a lot of time to locate the memorial text. We do not know where to look for it. Do I expect it to be high or low on the standing walls? Do I concentrate on the corners of the buildings? Maybe it is on the pavement of the street. But that, I guess, is unlikely. That certainly is not the place where one would place an important public memorial."

Aletta did not respond, but gave me an encouraging smile. I really needed that. She handed me a second cup of coffee. When I opened the door to start on my search for Erastus, she said, "Good luck, honey. Take your time. I will sit here and watch you."

While I struggled down the steep slope of debris, I muttered, "You wish me well while you sit there at ease and watch me struggling to find a small inscription in this labyrinth!" I felt a pit in my stomach. Entering this maze of ruins was like wandering through a bombed-out city. What I now feared most was the distinct possibility of not finding anything in spite of my earlier optimism. I began my search.

Scrutinizing every scratch, groove, or indentation as a possible remains of an inscription, I combed the streets and the walls with the best of my archaeological skills. One hour later I began to feel the physical and emotional strain of the unfruitful search. Also, the sun's heat was wearing me down. But I continued the quest, even though my hope of succeeding began to decline and replaced my earlier certainty of success. Finally, despairing and defeated, as well as physically exhausted, I found myself standing at the exact location where I had, several hours ago, waved good-bye to Aletta and started the investigation. There was no shout of victory. There was no loud "Eureka!" There was only a bowed, sweaty head and a sense of utter defeat. My eyelids twitched nervously and I had a bouncing headache. Even miracles were not possible at this hour and I knew it. I looked up the embankment to our car and waved to Aletta. Then I gave her a negative sign and shouted, "I quit. I am coming up."

Then, a miracle happened. Suddenly, Aletta jumped out of the car and excitedly waved her arms and shouted, "No, no, don't come up. You have found the inscription!"

"What are you talking about?" I shouted back, "I did not find anything."

Aletta, now reeling at the edge of the drop-off, shouted back, even more strongly, "Yes, you did find it. In fact, you are standing on it." I thought she must be kidding me. Again I hollered back to her, "What do you mean that I am standing on it?"

"Honey, just look at your feet. Believe me, and you will see the letters of the inscription which are chiseled in the limestones of the pavement. From up here I have a perfect perspective of the text and can see the whole inscription in one glance."

I looked down at my feet and moved away a few steps. *Ongelofelijk!* ("unbelievable") I said in Dutch. I was dumbfounded and dazed. A miracle happened right in front of me. Now I stared at the clearly visible eight-inch-tall letters etched into stone. The two-line inscription had survived the centuries. I dropped to my knees to get a closer look and noticed that each letter was partly damaged. Obviously the grooves of the letters had been filled with precious metal in the past. The metal had been forcibly removed in subsequent years. I stood up and with a sigh of relief walked around the inscription. Next, I took my camera, my faithful Leice MII, and shot my best slides of the trip. For many years the slides of the Erastus inscription enlivened my lectures at Anderson College (University) describing the journeys of Paul to the city of Corinth.

Aletta and I reread Romans 16:23 where Paul mentions Erastus, "The City Treasurer," probably of Corinth from which the Apostle Paul was writing. This Erastus might have been known to Paul and might even have been one of his friends. "Erastus, the city Treasurer, and our brother Quartus, greet you."

We felt greatly privileged to have been in touch with the members of "The Church of God which is at Corinth" (1 Cor. 1:2) of nearly two thousand years ago. The New Testament history was again authenticated.

Before I left, I took a final and thoughtful look at the memorial inscription and pondered, "It is possible that the Apostle Paul had looked at this inscription as we had done this day."

# CUP OF TEA
# WITH AMOS

Dr. James Muilenberg was a dramatic teacher, so much so that often I thought he was like an Old Testament prophet. During his lively, almost theatrical portrayals of Old Testament personalities, he inspired me forever. His personification of biblical men awoke in me the desire to meet one of these unique personalities. Accordingly, later meandering through the Holy Land, I unexpectedly ran into—as later I interpreted it—Amos, the Old Testament prophet. It happened in this manner.

It was during the summer of 1966. My wife, Aletta, and I were trying to locate the village of Tekoa, the hometown or region only five miles south of Jerusalem where the prophet Amos once lived (Amos 1:1). We had bought a detailed map of Judea, but had not been successful in identifying any specific "tell" (archaeological mound) or "khirbet" (visible ruins above ground) which might have been biblical Tekoa. The area where we were searching consisted of barren, rock-strewn hills and valleys. We did not see a hare, scorpion, or bird, nor did we hear the bray of a donkey. In mid-winter there would have been green grass visible across these hills, but now in mid-summer the grass had turned brown under the sun's scorching heat.

Discouraged at being unable to locate Tekoa, we parked our camper on the side of the gravel road and decided to survey the surroundings carefully. Overhead a single sparrow hawk rode the thermal updraft. While scanning the territory, we saw a lonely Bedouin tent high up on the opposite hillside. It was a typical Arab shelter made of dark brown camel's hair and supported by several slanted wooden poles. In the tent we observed a Bedouin moving about.

"Aletta," I said, "I think I will walk over to that tent and ask the Bedouin where we should look for Tekoa. Maybe he can tell us."

It was a strenuous descent into the valley below and up again to the other side. The heat made this climb a warm and thirsty adventure. Slowly I approached the desert dweller's abode. When he saw me, he came out and encouraged me to come to him. He greeted me and lifted up his right hand as a welcome, saying, *Shalam Aleichem* ("peace to you").

On my way up the hill I had been trying to put together a few questions for me to ask in a simple and quite imperfect Arabic. With some confidence I asked him, "Where can I find Tekoa?" What happened next was unexpected, to say the least. The Bedouin answered me in English, "Yes, this is it, right here!" He waved his hand in a broad arch.

I was elated, but also still in the dark about the physical evidence of the Tekoa of Amos. Furthermore, I doubted that this isolated wasteland could tell me much of anything of the prophet Amos. Nevertheless, it did. Before I could express my thanks to the man, he said, "Today is my birthday. Please, you must stay awhile and celebrate it with me. We will drink tea together."

I could not refuse his request. It would have been most impolite in Bedouin culture to refuse to accept an invitation to enter this man's "home" (tent) and have tea with him. So, raising my hands, I said, "Thank you so much, but my wife is waiting for me in our car."

"Oh," the desert dweller responded immediately, "Ask her to come and join us." In Arab desert culture this invitation was most unusual. While Aletta came up the hill, the Bedouin lit his primus (stove) and boiled the water. I looked around the dwelling. There was an iron bedstead and underneath the bed was a large trunk. I speculated what might be in it. Possibly there was an old-fashioned rifle, a precious stone decorated dagger, and an antique revolver. Well, who knows what else. I continued glancing around. There were two wooden stools. A small round table made up the rest of the furniture.

The Bedouin offered Aletta one of the stools. I already was seated. When the water boiled the bedouin added the tea and waited for it to steep. Then he washed out two small glasses. The cups were slightly larger than a liqueur glass. He filled a glass and handed it to me, but stopped half way and said, with jest in his voice, "In your country you say, 'Ladies first.'" He turned to Aletta and gave her the glass.

Surroundings of the Tekoa of the prophet Amos.

The tea was very sweet, with a tiny mint leaf floating on top. Enjoying the hot beverage and Arab hospitality, I dared to ask, "What are you doing here all alone?"

Sitting on the edge of his bed, the man shifted to a more comfortable position and explained, "I am a sheep farmer." I stared at him in disbelief and queried, "But where are your flocks. I don't see sheep or goats anywhere around here?"

"Right you are," he said and continued, "I can explain that. My flocks are with my servants. They are grazing further to the north."

Now I was even more curious to know about this individual. Here I meet an Arab farmer who lives in a tent, has sheep and servants, and speaks English very well. So I went on to probe, "But what do you do when your flocks are far away?"

He rose and walked to the entrance of the tent. He looked across the valley with dreamy eyes. Then he spoke softly. "Well, I write poetry."

There was silence for a few moments, after which I pressed on. "You are a poet, you say. What do you mean?"

The Bedouin chuckled and seem pleased to elaborate. "Yes, I write poetry in Arabic and in English. Would you like to hear some of my poetry?" "Very much so, yes," I said hurriedly.

The sheepherder poet pulled out the footlocker from underneath the bed, opened it, and

An unidentified Arab similar to the biblical Amos.

lifted out a large, oblong volume. He opened the book of poems and leafed through the pages until he found the page he wanted. The poem reading began, in English, a piece that he had composed, probably one day when his sheep were being cared for elsewhere. If someone would ask me today what I thought of his poetic ability, I would have to say with sorrow that I have no memory of the kind of poem it was. During the conversation that followed, however, I learned much. He was quite a well-informed person. He had travelled far and wide and his opinions of the countries he had visited were also broad. He had visited England and travelled in the United States where he had a brother living on the East Coast.

This modern Judean sheepherder was obviously wealthy, hardly just a farmer who daily walked his flocks of sheep up and down the Judean pastures. Instead, he visited nearby centers of commerce, crossed borders to visit neighboring nations, and listened to international news in the marketplaces wherever he did business. After about an hour of tea and conversation, we thanked our new friend profusely for his hospitality. We left with the local departing greeting, *Shalam* ("peace be to you") and added, "We hope to see you again." The bedouin nodded and replied, "*In Shallah*" ("if God wills it").

Aletta and I returned to our own small and simple "home," the V.W. Camper, and reluctantly waved goodbye to our surprising new friend. As the coming days passed, I began to reflect on this unique encounter in the hills of Judea. One day this thought hit me: "Gus, you had tea with Amos, the prophet of the Old Testament." What I realized was that, like this contemporary Bedouin, Amos was not merely a simple sheepherder or a tender of sycamore fruit trees (7:14).

The Bible tells us that Amos was not a professional prophet (7:14). Then who and what was he? Amos was a herdsman and farmer. When we read the book of Amos, we are astounded by his knowledge of other nations. He was aware of the world at large. No doubt he had visited Damascus, Tyre, Bethel (chapters 1, 2, 3, etc.) on his business trips to sell or buy sheep. While in those cities and countries he became aware of the political, social, and religious developments—especially the idolatry in Judah and Israel. After he returned from these business journeys, we can imagine Amos sitting down on a wooden stool in his sheep farmer's tent and creatively composing the words he "must" speak to the people about what he "saw" (7:1, 7; 8:1).

Searching for the best expressions, Amos would wax poetic as an inspired servant of the Lord. In this way he left us beautiful, descriptive literature. His technique included puns, plays on words, and numerical parallelisms. All this he did while his servants were tending his sheep. Amos reflected about the state of the world, Israel and Judah in particular. His zeal and emotions were deeply stirred and caused his literary craftsmanship to soar. His message to the nations burst forth across his world in the finest poetry, something like a divine hurricane.

Our visit with this modern Judean sheepherder, who was also a world traveller, opened the door to us for sharing a few intimate moments, at least in our imaginations, with the Old Testament prophet, Amos of Tekoa.

# I FOUND THE
# TEN COMMANDMENTS!

IT WAS SEPTEMBER OF 1967, just before the first semester started. The Anderson College faculty had finished eating a fine dinner in the Olt Center dining room. President Robert Reardon got up and asked, "Gus, can you tell us something interesting that happened on your trip to the Middle East this summer?"

I had not been prepared for this request and stood up with some apprehension. I swallowed twice and coughed once. I was worried about what kind of response that the story I was about to spin would receive. Of course, it was a true story—in the main, but it had some apocryphal elements to it. Dr. Reardon had asked me for an interesting account and not for a scientific treatise. I was going to give him both. This is what I told the faculty.

Last spring I was talking with Dr. Fred Shoot and told him that during the summer I would be traveling to the Sinai Peninsula to visit the fourth-century monastery of St. Catherine at the foot of Mt. Sinai. I told him that I was going to reach the top of Mt. Sinai, a difficult two-hour climb from the monastery, to visit the traditional site where Moses had received the two tablets of stone on which were the Ten Commandments, direct from the hand of God.

"You know," I told Fred, "that while I am making that climb I will be keeping my eyes open to see if I, by chance, might finally be the one to find a piece of those original broken tablets."

"You must be kidding," Fred said with a funny look on his face. "You don't really believe that you might find such a fragment.

Surely you don't accept that story of Moses going up a mountain and writing laws on two tablets of stone."

"Well now, Fred," I said trying to sound convincing, "yes, I do believe the biblical account. There is no compelling reason not to accept it as historical. There is, in fact, good archaeological evidence that the story of Moses is historical. Let me tell you something very interesting and clearly factual. Archaeological evidence tells us that the Amorite king Lipit-Ishtar, who reigned ca. 1864-1854 B.C. (the time of Abraham), produced a law code consisting of a clay tablet (8" x 9") that had writing on both sides. This law code precedes the Mosaic Law Code (Ex. 32: 15-16) by about four hundred years. In light of this evidence, Moses surely could have written a similar law code. The Bible also records that Moses, on his return to the Hebrew camp from the mountain, broke the two tablets out of anger when he found the Israelites worshipping other gods. Therefore, on the lower level of Mt. Sinai there could be one or more fragments lying around. I shall be looking for them."

Later that summer I left Tel-Aviv, Israel, on a bus that soon was laboring its way up to Mt. Sinai. The bus, as old as Methuselah, finally came to a halt at the foot of the monastery. We were guided to the dining room. It was already late in the day. The evening meal was spartan, to say the least. The night was terrible. Bugs and mosquitoes were hunting for blood. With virtually no covers and the heat, the insects feasted on our bare parts. At four in the morning the group of about thirty travelers met for breakfast. I cannot, or will not, remember what we got to eat. I do remember that we could not get out of the monastery because the monk who had the only key to the outside door did not arrive. While we waited unhappily, a search party roamed through the ancient building and finally located the monk. The door screeched open. The long and difficult climb to the summit began.

I found the demanding experience exhausting. Little sleep, little food and not much to drink joined forces to sap my strength.

The path was terribly rocky and many patches consisted of loose gravel. We climbed over large boulders and crept up steep slopes. My mind was not on the fragments of the Ten Commandments. Instead, I was seriously considering the possibility of giving up the scramble.

I continued the ascent, but not because I was brave, strong, or determined. What kept me going was an old pastor aged 83 who was right ahead of me. He was not going to give up, he had told us, even though he had to sit down quite often to rest. He was going to the top. "When I get there," he said, "I will stand on my head!"

My legs buckled and my body told me to quit the climb. Ahead of me the old man stood up, straightened out, and continued with a grin on his face. He looked back at me. What could I do but follow him?

When we reached the summit, the sun had just cleared the mountain range in the far distance. We had arrived at the small chapel which marks the spot where tradition reports that Moses received the famous commandments. The old man stood on his head—with some help. I dropped to my knees and clung to a rock of granite, then quickly mailed a personal "thank you" to heaven. This was truly a Mt. Sinai experience. We were high up above most other mountaintops around us. Nothing could better show us the impressiveness of this location. We were there! This was an unforgettable moment. I rested a long time and gave my mind the freedom to roam.

The thought flashed through my mind, "Look for the Ten Commandments!" I had almost forgotten this key objective. I whistled softly. This was my secret mission. This might be my lucky day. I just might put Anderson University on the international map.

Gradually a few individuals from the group started on the long descent, returning to the monastery. The way back was easy to find because the monastery was always visible, serving as a beacon. I too started on my walk down, but I picked my own route back. The trail was not easy but, it seemed to me, a very interesting path and little used.

Fortunately, I was alone and could concentrate on my special search. I wondered how many people had done the same before me, looking for the physical remains of the ancient Ten Commandments. Certainly there had not been many—and they all had failed.

Every so often I stopped and looked around or bent down to take a closer look at something that caught my eye. A few times I picked up a fragment of granite or some piece of mixed rock and investigated it. A few rocks showed black markings. Having examined each of them closely, they all turned out to be petrified ferns inside the rocks. I tested these rock fragments with my fingers to locate ridges caused by incising the stones. But I had no luck.

While eyeing the various promising chips of stone, I remembered my classes in paleography at the Oriental Institute at the University of Chicago. Under the able guidance of Dr. Raymond Bowman, we had studied ancient styles of writing dating from 2000 years before Christ. He had taught us how to read inscriptions. I was confident that I would be able to identify the old writings. Of course, that was only if I actually found them. But what were the chances of doing that? Probably not very good.

Sauntering along while watching the ground in front of me, a thin piece of stone about 3" x 6" caught my eye. "There, you found it," I mumbled to myself. But in the next moment I continued, "Your imagination is getting the best of you, Gus. Don't be silly." Even so, I was bending down on the rough ground and reaching out to pick up the tiny piece of stone. I stood up and turned the stone over to look at it more closely. What had caught my interest were several visible scratches. Often ancient script looked like the imprints in the sand of many chickens that had criss-crossed a yard.

Happily, no person was near to watch me and chide me for

looking at chicken-feet imprints. I continued my study. Turning the stone over, I found that the scratches were on that side also. "Shucks" I mumbled. "I cannot recognize any archaic Hebrew letters on this stone."

Next, I slanted the object in such a way that the early sunlight fell across the face of what I hoped was a tablet. Yes, it left a shadow in the depressions formed by each letter.

"Ahah," I whispered. "This looks more like it. This stroke here could be the Hebrew letter "L." I sat down and looked more closely at each scratch. The longer I looked the more it appeared that these were archaic Hebrew man-made letters. But what were these letters saying?

Suddenly it came to me. I was looking for the Ten Commandments. Here then was my clue. Any one of the fragments of the Moses Law Code must say something about a law. With that in mind, I began to read. The first letter on the stone fragment in my hand was an "L" and the second was an "O." Here was the Hebrew word for "not." I read out loud the stunning "Not" and then shouted, "I got it, I got it!"

After a few more attempts I was able to read the rest of the line. Here is what I read. "Thou shalt not steal."

I stood affixed on Mt. Sinai. My mind reeled. Then it happened. I awakened from my dream.

# ON THE WAY TO
# THE ACROPOLIS

IT SEEMS THAT ON MOST JOURNEYS I HAD TAKEN, something happened that was not anticipated. But what could go wrong when two Anderson College professors, Barry Callen and myself, were on our way to the Acropolis in Athens? It was the summer of 1972. Barry and I were guiding a group of A.C. students and colleagues on a January tour of Rome, Greece, and Palestine. The tour group had arrived in Athens and spent one full day exploring the historic city. In the evening, Barry and I discussed the program for the following day. "Well, Barry," I asked, "what do we do tomorrow for the students?"

Barry suggested, "Would you not agree, Gus, that the students would now enjoy exploring the city on their own?"

"That is not a bad idea," I responded. "I am sure they would agree. Also, this is our chance to do some sightseeing on our own."

As expected, the students agreed readily and we separated. Small groups went in every direction. We admonished them to stay together and act wisely. "Come back with some interesting information to share this evening after supper," we encouraged them.

With a small map of Athens in hand, Barry and I set out to find our own enlightenment. "Where shall we go first?" Barry wanted to know. I pointed to the temple of Athena high up on top of a steep and rocky outcropping. "What about going up to the Temple of Athena on the Acropolis?" I suggested. Then I explained to him, "It is a short walk up there; it is easy to find because the 'Highplace' is visible in Athens from about anywhere."

We were excited. The sun shone brightly. To be in the center of ancient Greece lifted our spirits. We did not have the slightest notion that our intellectual pursuit would soon turn into a moral dilemma that could have been dangerous. For quite awhile we walked, but had not been able to find the road that would put us at the foot of the Acropolis.

"Sorry, Barry, but I think I am lost," I said. "Let me take another look at the map." Barry handed me the city map he was carrying. Looking around, I saw that we had entered a main city square. The Acropolis was not too far away. Opening the map, I showed Barry and said, "Look, here is where we are and this is the road that leads to the Acropolis."

At that moment a young Greek man, wearing a neat, dark suit, white shirt, and necktie, stopped and asked us, "Are you lost? May I help you?"

"Thank you so much," I promptly answered, "but we just found the road we are looking for."

"Oh, I can hear that you are Americans. Have you ever been in Chicago? My sister lives there."

"Oh, yes," I said. But I was not interested in continuing the conversation with this stranger. Who knows what he was up to? The young Greek looked at me with a smile and continued undisturbed. "That is marvelous. I also have visited Chicago and I like it there." Then hurriedly he added, "Please come to my shop. I will serve you some coffee and we will visit for a short while."

My warning signals went up. From prior experiences, I remembered the few times I had been lured in this manner into a shop. Rarely did I leave without having bought one or more objects that surely I did not need.

I turned to Barry and said, "I am not interested. However, it might be a new experience for you. If you would like to go to his shop, of course I will go with you." Barry smiled with some interest. The Greek merchant appeared to be pleased. He led the way to the other side of the square, but did not say much. Later on I

Anderson College trip through the Holy Land, January 1975. David's Tower, Jerusalem, is in the background. Dr. Jeeninga is on the far left.

realized why the Greek was so happy. It was because he had snatched two gullible Americans and talked them into entering his shop. We had no idea what was about to happen to us.

Having arrived at his business, the Greek, who had never given us his name, led us down a wide staircase that took us below street level. "Holy mackerel," I forced out between my lips. "Where is he taking us?" Then our eyes began to adjust to the dim light. The photos on the wall showed dancing girls, almost in the nude, inviting the adventurous to come down and meet them. Before I could react to this embarrassing situation, our friendly Greek ushered us into a barely lit room. A few soft lights danced over a bar and in a wink the Greek had us sitting at the counter for a free drink, we supposed. He had suddenly disappeared (probably back up on the street looking for two more suckers).

Barry and I faced the bartender alone—but not for long. Suddenly I felt something against my right knee and a warm body touched my shoulders. I slowly turned my head to the right to see who or what it was that was touching me. I was alarmed when I looked into a smiling face of a woman. I studied her for a brief moment. I was not impressed by the intent of her look. At the same instant, I was curious to know what had happened to Barry. I casually turned my face to the left.

"Good gracious," I mumbled. "Poor Barry!" He also had been joined closely by what was supposed to be a glamorous, but not so virtuous local lady. I was sure he too was feeling his own uninvited contacts. The voice of the bartender called me back from my wandering mind. I heard him ask, "What drink can I serve you, sir?"

"I would like a Coke, please."

"What did you say? A Coke?"

"Yes, please."

Then the bartender turned to Barry and asked him, "What can I serve you, sir?"

"Please give me a Coke also," Barry said. The man gave the girls a puzzled glance, uncapped two bottles of Coke, and served us the drinks. The caps came off behind the bar and out of our sight, raising concern that some drug could have been added.

It is difficult to report on the conversation we carried on with the Athenian beauties for neither Barry nor I were in control of the Greek language—or of the situation in general. The English the pin-up girls spoke appeared to have been limited to asking our names. Time had barely passed when the bartender turned to me and asked, "Would you like to buy the girls a drink?" Barry looked at me. He appeared anxious and looking for a way out. I replied, "No, I don't think so."

"And why not?" replied the surprised and irritated bartender.

Before I could think of a proper reply, I answered, "Because that is not my lifestyle." The expression "my lifestyle" was widely discussed on the Anderson College campus those days. Barry couldn't help but smile. The bartender forced his face into an irritated grim, but the two girls looked blank at best. They did not understand what was said. They preferred the language of touch. We trapped Americans were anxious not to offend and not to stay much longer, if possible.

"Barry," I said urgently but quietly, "we don't belong here. Let's get out of this clip joint!" Turning to the bartender, I asked how much we owed him. He waved his hand and said, "Nothing, nothing at all."

We swiftly left the place of temptation, relieved to escape successfully to the sunshine above ground. We knew that we had been fortunate to get out of that den of wickedness. It could have been an expensive experience for us that day in more than one way. Barry carried in his pocket some $800.00 in cash to pay for a bus trip to Delphi and Corinth for the whole tour group the next day. Had we been drugged down below, we would no doubt have been $800.00 poorer—and maybe worse.

That evening we had a worship and sharing session with our students back at the hotel. They told of their adventures during the day. Based on our own personal experience, which they insisted we share, we warned them about the dangers of travelling in foreign countries. The students were amused to hear of the embarrassing incident of their leaders.

# THE MIDDLE EAST SEMINAR
## SUMMER, 1968

A GENEROUS GRANT FROM the Lilly Endowment, Inc., provided a significant opportunity in the summer of 1968 for the firsthand learning of six members of the faculty of Anderson College (University) and its graduate School of Theology. For some years campus leaders had been studying new ways to become more effective in the offering of its programs of religious education. One way already accomplished was the establishment in 1963 of the Jeeninga Museum of Bible and Near Eastern Studies. Now had come this special opportunity for the enhanced education of select faculty members. Being made possible was a traveling seminar to a range of key locations in the Middle East that were often involved in campus instruction (see the map).

The objectives of this seminar were geographical, archaeological, topographical, socio-political, and religious. My colleagues and I would be visiting Lebanon, Jordan, Cyprus, and Israel. Participants were Boyce W. Blackwelder, Barry L. Callen, George Kufeldt, Gene W. Newberry, Marie Strong, and myself. Dr. Newberry, then Dean of the School of Theology, was responsible for all financial matters. My roles included planning the five-week itinerary and providing a series of learning resources and appropriate lectures along the way. My lectures were based in part on personal experience gained during visits to the Holy Land in 1953, 1963, and on my sabbatical leave in 1966-67 when I participated as area supervisor in two major archaeological excavations.

On June 21, 1968, our highly motivated group boarded a plane in Indianapolis, Indiana, and flew to Beirut, Lebanon, via

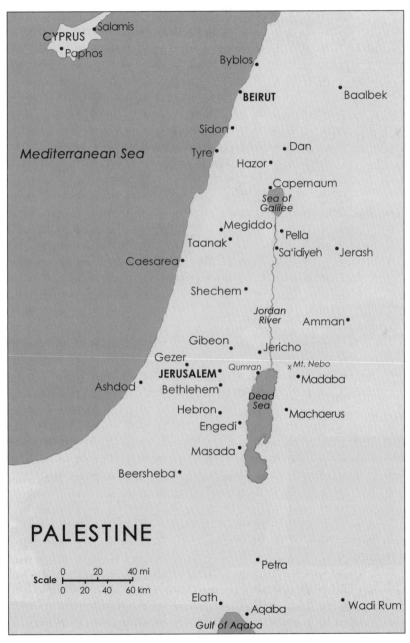

Select sites visited by the seminar group.

New York City. The big educational adventure had finally begun. These very special weeks together included viewing "Mighty Cedars and Huge Stones" (ancient Lebanon), traveling "Along the King's Highway" (Jordan), and making the pilgrimage "From Dan To Beersheba" (a study of Palestine). Following is a brief record of seminar highlights. The numbers inserted into the text identify key locations on the map provided.

## MIGHTY CEDARS AND HUGE STONES
### A STUDY OF ANCIENT LEBANON

### The Sarcophagus of Hiram

A few pigeons alighted and sailed away from Pigeon's Grottoes near Ras-Beirut. Pigeon's Grottoes is presently the oldest historic site in Beirut. The cliff formation is interesting and has a cave some 50 ft. wide, 131 ft. long, and 65 ft. high. Of historic value, however, is the Roman necropolis on the heights that has yielded many sarcophagi. Nearby, along the shore, evidence still abounds that here ancient Neolithic man made flint tools.

The Archaeological Museum of Beirut is especially worthwhile to those who wish to study ancient Lebanon, the country that in earlier years was inhabited by the daring, seafaring people known to us as the Phoenicians. Among the most exciting objects in the Beirut Museum is the famous sarcophagus of Ahiram, King of Jeball (Byblos, 11th century B.C.). Particularly important is the Phoenician inscription, using the ancient alphabet, carved around the edge of the lid. The depiction of winged creatures on the sarcophagus helps the imagination when reading 1 Kings 6, 2 Chronicles 3, and Psalm 99:1.

### The Lord Breaks the Cedars

Beginning with Sargon of Akkad, imperial rulers of the ancient East marched toward the Lebanon mountains to subject the peoples of these regions and to make themselves masters of the cedar trees. The list of these rulers includes Babylonians, Assyrians, Egyptians, Phoenicians, Hebrews, and Persians. With the help of the kings of Phoenicia, King David and King Solomon obtained the coveted cedar beams to build the House of the Forest of Lebanon and the Hall of Pillars and the Hall of Thrones (1 Kings 5:8-12, 7:1-7). The remnants of the famous ancient trees at Becharre grow at an altitude of 6,000 ft. About 400 trees ranging from 200-1000 years old are growing there now. The biggest trees measure as much as 82 feet high and have a 40-foot circumfer-

The Cedars of Lebanon.

ence at the base. As our seminar group stood among these giants of the past, Psalm 29 was read and one can really appreciate and understand the mood and force of the words:

"The voice of the Lord is powerful;
the voice of the Lord is full of majesty.
The voice of the Lord breaks the cedars;
the Lord breaks the cedars of Lebanon." (Psalm 29:4-5)

South of Beirut on the coast lies the city of Sidon. Moses spoke of the land of Sidon as the northern border of Canaan. The town has an impressive history as recorded in the Bible and by historians. The city is of interest to Bible students also because the Apostle Paul embarked here on his way from Caesarea to Rome (Acts 27:1-4). During the Byzantine domination Sidon became a bishopric and in 1200 A.D. the city was bought by the Templars. A visit to the well-preserved Qalaat-el-Bahr, the Castle of the Sea, reaffirms the significance of this castle in Crusader times.

Standing (l to r): Gene Newberry, George Ramsey, George Kufeldt. Seated (l to r): Fred Shoot, Marie Strong, Gustav Jeeninga, Boyce Blackwelder. Replacing Ramsey in the seminar was Barry Callen.

## Jezebel of Tyre

South of Sidon on the coast lies the city of Tyre. The city dates back to as early as 3000 B.C., but the origin of the city is lost in the darkness of time. The now visible ruins date for the most part to Crusader times, but recent excavations are beginning to bring to light Roman remains as well.

Tyre played an important role in the history of Egypt and the early Hebrews. It was in the days of David and Solomon that Hiram of Tyre had friendly commercial relations with the Israelites (2 Sam. 5:11, 1 Kings 5:1, 1 Chron. 14:1). Hiram provided the building materials for the Jerusalem Temple (2 Chron. 2:3-16). The ties between Israel and Tyre became even stronger when in the ninth century Jezebel, a daughter of Ethbaal the Tyrian king-priest, married Ahab of Israel. This marriage greatly affected the life and thought of the Hebrew people and was primarily responsible for the religious crisis in Israel during the time of the prophet Elijah. While sitting in the shade in a small garden in Tyre, the seminar was led in a study of Mark 7:24-31, the story of Jesus and the Syrophoenician woman. The contrast of religious feelings and loyalties of the Syrophoenician woman and Jezebel of Tyre came to life.

# ALONG THE KINGS HIGHWAY
## A STUDY OF TRANS-JORDAN

### The Place was a Place for Cattle

Visitors to the Holy Land usually limit their journey to the territory west of the Jordan River, thinking that biblical events occurred basically there. Scripture gives abundant evidence that East Palestine, now known as Trans-Jordan (West Bank), was coveted land in the eyes of the ancient Hebrews. The sons of Reuben and the sons of Gad insisted that Moses permit them to stay on the east side of the Jordan because the land they had just conquered was a land for cattle. They said to Moses, "Your servants have cattle" (Numbers 32:1-5).

### War Victims

Members of the seminar group were war victims to the degree that several important archaeological sites which were on the original itinerary had to be dropped because they now lay in the firing line between the Israeli and Arab military emplacements (the 1967 war had delayed the seminar's departure until 1968). These sites included Teleilat Ghassul (a chalcolithic city), Tell es-Saidiyeh (biblical Zarethan), and Pella that appears in the story of Christians fleeing from Jerusalem during the Roman attack on the Holy City in 69 A.D.

**Byzantine Christians Lived Here**

Entering the environs of what was at one time Byzantine Christian territory, the student goes through an unforgettable experience. Mr. Hazboun of the Tourist Resthouse in Madaba served as the guide for the seminar, showing us the famous Madaba Map and the mosaics found in some of the private homes. The story of the Madaba mosaics has many ramifications for Christian historians. Some of the mosaics in the private homes in Madaba (mosaics which were discovered when these houses were built in 1880) date back to before 325 A.D. It was at that time that the Roman world turned Christian.

The Madaba Map is a large mosaic found in a sixth-century Byzantine church. The map was laid in 560 A.D. and is only partially preserved. The original map was 75 feet long and 25 feet wide and covered the geographical area from the Nile Delta in the south to Sidon in the north, and from the Great Sea (Mediterranean) in the west to the Great Desert in the east. Of special interest is the Jerusalem cartouche that shows the city of Jerusalem in the sixth century. The main outline of the city is still to be seen in the present-day Old City of Jerusalem.

With the many other remains of Christian churches that are found east of the Jordan River (as is evident from excavations and surveys done by Dr. Martin Noth and Dr. Ute Lux) and the frequent references to Christian sites indicated on the Madaba map, one comes to the conclusion that before 900 A.D. both East and West Palestine were a "Christian" Palestine.

**Rose-Red City: "Sela"**

After Madaba, the Kings Highway took the seminar to biblical Dhibon. Crossing Wadi Arnon was an impressive experience. The ruggedness and steepness of the Wadi show clearly the reason why this became the natural boundary between the territories of Reuben and Moab.

The famed capital of the Nabateans was Petra or Sela, located in a fertile, well-watered basin of the Wadi Musa at an elevation of 2700 feet. This romantic city carved mainly out of living rock can only be reached through a colorful, narrow, twisting cleft known as "the Siq." Rising to a height of 950 feet is a huge, rocky acropolis called Umm el-Biyarah (Mother of Cisterns). This mountain appears to have served as a fortress in Edomite and Nabatean times. Umm el-Biyarah has been tentatively identified as the "Rock" or Sela of the Old Testament (cf. 2 Kings 14:7-10; Jer. 49:16-17; Psalms 60:90). Indirect references to Petra also appear in 2 Corinthians 11: 32-33 when Paul mentions Aretas who was King of Petra (9 B.C.-40 A.D).

Mr. Khair Yassine had given the seminar a letter of introduction to Mr. Mohammed Mujahed Khadiya who was then excavating in Petra. Mr. Khadiya showed Petra first in a general way, including climbing up to the High Place of sacrifices, and then explained the excavations that were in progress. A fine staircase built of masonry with painted plaster was just being uncovered. No conclusions as to date had as yet been decided. The enthusiasm for his archaeological work at Petra and the courtesy shown to the seminar by Mr. Khadiya will long be remembered.

## Arabia Deserta

Skirting the northern regions of Arabia Deserta the seminar group braved the heat and dry dust of the desert traveling towards the Gulf of Aqaba. Through this waste and barren but beautiful desert wilderness the Hebrew tribes made their way northward in search of a land that would be good for cattle and flowing with milk and honey. According to Prof. Nelson Glueck, Solomon built his copper refineries at Eziongeber (Aqaba) and obtained copper from the hills to the west. Several later kings of Israel tried to develop a commercial fleet based at Aqaba. From Aqaba, now the Jordanian seaport, the seminar drove to the fabulous Wadi Rum, the "Grand Canyon of Jordan." After a social visit with the

Visiting with the Jordanian Border Patrol.

Jordanian desert police and after sipping several cups of tea and coffee a visit was made to the ruins of a Nabatean temple. With a new appreciation of oriental social customs and niceties the group returned to Amman.

**The City of Brotherly Love**

In Old Testament times the city of Rabat (Amman) was an insignificant desert city. The first biblical reference to this city known as "Rabat of the Ammonites" is in Deuteronomy 3:11. Here one reads that the great iron bed of Og, the King of Bashan, was in Rabbah. The famed bedstead was likely carried off as a trophy of war and kept in the Ammonite capital. During the Roman period the city was renamed Philadelphia and was probably one of the larger Roman towns since it has Roman baths and a large amphitheatre. Mr. Khair Yassine and his American wife had invited the seminar members to their home for an Arab dinner. A delicious meal called "chicken makhluba" was served. Again Arab hospitality was greatly enjoyed by the whole group.

## Herodian Strength

Choosing trustworthy allies was a virtue of the Romans. They accepted the Jewish king Herod's oath and never regretted it. In order to control his people Herod built Herodium, Masada, and Alexandrium west of the Jordan River and Machaerus east of the Jordan River. It was at the latter, according to tradition, that John the Baptist was beheaded at the instigation of Herodias. During the summer of 1968 Dr. Jerry Vardaman of Southern Baptist Theological Seminary had excavated Machaerus and Mr. Khair Yassine had been the representative for the Jordan Department of Antiquities at the excavation. Since the excavation had been concluded at the time the seminar arrived in Amman, Mr. Yassin invited the group again to his home where he gave an interesting and informative illustrated lecture on the result of the first archaeological season at the Herodian stronghold.

## Search for a City

The Jordanian police refused to give the seminar the needed travel permits to drive via Mafraq and Umm el-Jemal, with its Nabatean and Christian ruins, to Tell er-Rumeith. However, when the group visited the Amman Archaeological Museum, I met Mr. Ahmed Odeh, the assistant curator, whom I knew from the Rumeith excavation where we had worked together for six weeks. Mr. Odeh was introduced to the seminar and took them on a special tour of the museum. Having Mr. Odeh with the group, all military check points were cleared without any difficulty.

The black basalt ruins of Umm el-Jemal impressed everyone, as did the many signs of Christian occupation of the first centuries A.D. After arriving at Tell er-Rumeith, I, having previously excavated there with Dr. Paul Lapp, explained the significance of this city and the work that had been accomplished in trying to identify this tell with biblical Ramoth-gilead (1 Kings 22:1-4; 2 Kings 9:1-6). From the summit of the tell the surrounding terri-

Main street of Petra, Jordan.

tory can be viewed. The fields surrounding Ramoth-gilead were fertile and much farming was carried out, as was proven by the many stone implements for grinding grain found during the excavation. In these same fields many important battles were fought for the control of this border city. From Ramoth-gilead one can see the vague outlines of the snow-covered Mt. Hermon some sixty miles away.

## FROM DAN TO BEERSHEBA
### A STUDY OF PALESTINE

### The Center of the World

Joining millions of people across the centuries, the seminar members arrived in Jerusalem, in more than one way the center of the world. The American Schools of Oriental Research served as headquarters for the seminar while in the Holy City. The School was significant because of its academic resources, its personal contacts, and its central location.

## The Sons of Light

Descending at a rather fast speed from Jerusalem, the Jordan Valley was reached quickly. Stopping at a vantagepoint overlooking the valley, I gave the seminar members and President and Mrs. Robert Reardon of Anderson College (University), who had joined the group for this one-day tour, a thorough geographic orientation of the area with the help of a large National Geographic map of Palestine pasted on a stiff cardboard. Leaving the observation post and after a ten-minute drive, the group arrived at the ruins of Qumran. Sitting in the shade of a tourist pavilion, I presented an introduction to the history and meaning of the Dead Sea Scroll community. Several maps and the reading from the *Manual of Discipline* and the *Book of Hymns* proved very helpful.

Dead Sea Scrolls Caves, Qumran.

After a visit to the ruins of Qumran the group drove on to Jericho and climbed up the dusty sides of the ruins of the oldest known city in the world. After a brief introduction to the background of the archaeological history of the site, the group was led to the most exciting discovery made by Miss Kathleen Kenyon. It was the great tower. The tall stone structure with a center staircase was one of the defense towers belonging to the pre-pottery neolithic city. To the disappointment of most Bible students, Miss Kenyon did not find any remains of Late Bronze Jericho. No remains have been found dating to the 13th century that was the period when Joshua invaded Canaan. It is therefore highly

251

improbable that any evidence will be found of the fallen walls of the Jericho of Joshua's attack.

## By the Waters of Megiddo

Traveling from Jerusalem to Taanak "by the waters of Megiddo" (Judg. 5:19), one obtains an excellent view of the country of Benjamin, Ephraim, and Manasseh. In the New Testament period these regions were Judea and Samaria. Dr. Paul

Dr. Jeeninga (center) and archaeological colleagues bargaining for antiquities.

Lapp was excavating at Taanak and received the seminar cordially. He led the group to the main trenches and explained the work in progress. During this visit the seminar members witnessed several just-discovered child burials and the opening of what was thought to be a Middle Bronze tomb. A number of beautiful pieces of pottery were lifted out and everyone was elated to be present at this exact moment of discovery.

## Another Herodian Masterpiece

Climbing up to the top of Herodium, another Herodian masterpiece of fortification building, is best done on the back of a donkey. These formidable remains of Herod's four-towered fortress, built on an artificial hill, are well worth the steep climb. I lectured on the history and archaeological significance of the position of Herodium. Of all four fortresses Herod built, Herodium appears to have been the one he visited most—and tradition claims that his body was buried here.

Traveling further south, Hebron, the city of the patriarch

Abraham, was an important visit. The Oak of Mamre, though a traditional site, does recall that nearly 3800 years ago Abraham settled here for some time. It was noted that the Oak of Mamre appears on the Madaba map of the sixth century in nearly the precise location of the present tree. Among the highlights of the visit to Hebron was the visit to the mosque with the tombs of Abraham and Sarah, Isaac and Rebekkah, and Jacob and Leah. Informative and delightful was a visit to the Hebron potter.

A Hebron potter fashioning a Dead Sea Scroll replica for the Jeeninga Bible Museum at Anderson University.

## The Pool of Gibeon

One day on a trek north of Jerusalem, a stop was made at Gibeon where Dr. James Pritchard had discovered wine jar handles with Hebrew stamps reading "Gibeon." These handles were found in the debris filling the famous Gibeon stairway that was part of the "pool of Gibeon" (2 Sam. 2:12-17).

## The Navel of the Land

When Abraham came to Palestine, he settled for a short while at Shechem. The centrally located Canaanite city lay between Mt. Gerizim and Mt. Ebal and has been called "the navel of the land." One of the Shechem excavation staff members showed the seminar group the Hyksos gate and temple and some of the more important and recently discovered objects.

Next, the excavation of Tell er-Ras on top of Mt. Gerizim was visited and Dr. Robert Bull of Drew Theological Seminary explained the history of the site and the work accomplished. He showed the spot where the archaeological team believed they had found the foundation of the Samaritan temple. Taking the group from one excavated field to the next, one could easily comprehend Dr. Bull's descriptive and enthusiastic explanation. The group left Tell er-Ras with the feeling that here we had learned more about archaeological methodology and what it can accomplish than on any other site visited.

Before leaving this archeological and historically pregnant region, the seminar stopped at the traditional site of Jacob's well. During lunch, just a few feet from this life-giving fresh water well, a lively discussion developed about Tell er-Ras, Jesus' dialogue with the woman at the well, and his words "whoever drinks of the water that I shall give him will never thirst" (John 4:1-15).

## The Old City

A walking trip was planned through and around the walled Old City of Jerusalem. Most of the city gates were visited, also the Wailing Wall and the so-called Horse Stables of King Solomon. Before visiting the Dome of the Rock, I gave an historical resume of the Temple area, beginning with the Abraham-Isaac offering episode, the building of the Temple of Solomon, and the discovery and meaning of the Hezekiah Tunnel. After visiting the Dome of the Rock, the group went into the Kidron Valley and waded through the Hezekiah Tunnel. Even though the tunnel inscription had been taken out and is now in a museum in Istanbul, we could still see the location where it had been removed.

At 8:30 a.m. the next morning, Sunday, the seminar visited Gordon's Garden Tomb. In the silence and beauty of this traditional place of Jesus' burial, Dean Gene Newberry gave a devotion based on several selected passages from the Gospel of Luke. The guide of the garden took the group on a short excursion before entering the tomb itself. In the afternoon Dr. Paul Lapp met with the seminar at the American School and gave a comprehensive address on "The Conquest Story." His thorough knowledge of the region and his archaeological knowledge helped greatly in understanding this knotty problem.

A rare privilege came to the seminar when Father Roland de  Vaux agreed to address the group during an informal meeting. Father de Vaux spoke on a subject of his special interest, "The Exodus Tradition." The meeting was held at the Ecole Biblique at Jerusalem and the presentation was animated as only Father de Vaux is able to do. The scholarly presentation, rounded out with

A street in East Jerusalem.

much human interest, impressed us all. For those who had never met Father de Vaux personally but knew his writings in the field of Bible and archaeology, this was a unique opportunity to become acquainted with the man behind the printed pages.

At 5:30 a.m. one morning the seminar group started on a walk from Bethany across the Mount of Olives to Bethpage and down the other side to Gethsemane. With the help of a planned program of Scripture readings and selected hymns, this devotional walk retraced the walk Jesus made on his last journey to Jerusalem before his crucifixion.

## Towards Galilee

At the Gezer excavation site Dr. William Dever gave the seminar group a detailed explanation of the organization of the excavation and the recent successes of the campaign. Besides the enormous Early Bronze city walls, the most exciting discovery was the unearthing of a Solomonic gate. After the tour of the wall there followed a lecture on the object finds that were stored and exhibited in the registration building. All evidence points to the fact that Gezer must have played a very important role throughout the history of Palestine.

At Megiddo the well-posted descriptions near archaeological remains made a tour of the site a unique experience. A special event was the descent into the huge stairway and rock-cut tunnel of the Megiddo water supply. The small Megiddo museum exhibits a few artifacts and several well-done ground plans which

The Jordan River.

were helpful in understanding the water and defense systems of Megiddo. Then followed visits to Nazareth and Cana, and the ruins of Capernaum and Chorazin. The volcanic nature of this region was clearly visible in the black basalt stone structures of what once had been the city of Chorazin (Matt. 11:21).

**The Source of Life**

Cutting across the war-torn Golan Heights, the seminar group arrived at the main source of the Jordan River called Panias. Here fresh water spouts out of the ground from subterranean caverns and rivers that are supplied with water from the melting snow of the Ante-Lebanon range. Panias, better known to the New Testament reader as Caesarea Philippi, was the place where Jesus asked his disciples, "But who do you say that I am?" Peter answered him with the significant confession: "You are the Christ" (Mark 8:27-30).

Between Dor and Joppa, Herod the Great built a seaport and called it Caesarea in honor of Caesar Augustus. The city was a showplace of Roman culture and even today the ruins give evidence of that. In New Testament times the city was the home of Philip the Deacon (Acts 21:8) and Cornelius the Centurion whom Peter converted to Christianity (Acts 10:1). Paul departed from here on his way to Tarsus (Act 9:30) and returned here after his second and third missionary journeys (Acts 18:22; 21:8). Paul stood trial here before Felix (Acts 23:23-33).

The student of the Bible who now visits Caesarea has the added excitement of seeing and photographing the recently (1961) discovered inscription of a slab of stone with the name "Pontius Pilate prefect of the Judea." This discovery is another find which strengthens our assurance of the accuracy and authenticity of the Bible.

### The Negev

The Southlands of ancient Palestine have always been a wilderness. However, Dr. Nelson Glueck has proven that the Negev was inhabited as early as the Bronze Age. On the way to the Negev the seminar group visited Ashdod, a Philistine city. Archaeologists Dr. Howard Kee and Dr. James Swauger of the Carnegie Museum took turns as guides through the excavated areas. A new method had been put into practice. A bulldozer had been used to cut a deep and wide trench through part of the mound. It was hoped that a better understanding of the stratigraphy of the tell would be obtained and, based on this knowledge, more meaningful digging at a slower pace could begin. This was the first full-scale excavation of a Philistine city. Dr. Kee, who is an expert on Hellenistic pottery, explained new types of ceramic findings.

Turning east from Ashdod, the seminar group headed for Abraham's wells at Beer-sheba. The present city is of little historical importance. However, the weekly livestock market at the edge of the desert had some fascination for all. Early in the morning the

Bedouin drive their goats, sheep, and camels to the market and the haggling begins.

Continuing eastward, the seminar group joined another group going to visit the excavations of the Jewish stronghold called Masada. This tour was worth all the effort of climbing up and down the dusty, rugged path in a scorching heat. A well-trained guide gave a vivid explanation of the history and drama that occurred on the top of Masada. Going from room to room and building to building, one can see the architectural achievements of Herod the Great. Then followed the story of the last days of Masada that climaxed in the suicide tragedy of nearly one thousand men, women, and children. In 73 A.D. the Roman engineers had succeeded in reaching the walls of Masada, a feat never thought possible by the Jewish defenders. After the Roman soldiers scaled the walls they were met by utter silence and 960 dead bodies strewn across the site. Masada had fallen. The archaeological evidence of the last terrifying hours was abundant and stared at the young twentieth-century volunteer excavators of the site.

## Strongholds of Engedi

Looking southeast from Masada it is possible to see the oasis of Engedi. It takes less than thirty minutes to arrive at the freshwater spring, but to reach its main source one has to climb over some mighty rocks and through a thick growth of various plants. At the end of the gorge the water pours down from high up in the rocks, making a strong waterfall. One can well imagine why David sought out this spring among the rugged mountains as his hiding place from Saul. "And David went up from there, and dwelt in the strongholds of Engedi" (1 Sam. 23:29; 24:1-2). Leaving behind this oasis of Engedi, one finds a great contrast on the salty coast of the Dead Sea. This area is truly dead. It smells sulphurous and the silence is oppressive. Any one of the strangely formed rocks could be the salt pillar of Lot's wife. Somewhere here lies buried under the bitter and stinking waters of the "sea of all that is dead" the cities of Sodom and Gomorrah.

# EVALUATION

Long ago the German Bible scholar J. G. Herder said that geography shapes the character of a people. This truism fits the biblical people in more than one way. The geography of Palestine was responsible for tribal loyalty and disloyalty among the early Hebrews. It also made the land of Canaan both a buffer state between Egypt and its eastern neighbors and the corridor for the Egyptian conquest of the East or the Mesopotamian conquest of Egypt.

These words of Mark Twain apply to a visit to the lands of the Bible: "You are not wood, you are not stone, but men." Fortunately, much of the ancient customs and folkways are still present in these countries. Donkeys, camels, and cows are used for travel, plowing the fields, and food. Families still live in tents with goats, sheep, chickens, and dogs. Those not in tents live in simple mudbrick dwellings. Many continue to wander up and down the land, as the Habiru did in Abraham's day. Those who live in villages still "tell on the housetops" the gossip of the neighborhood. Grain is harvested and winnowed by hand. Water is drawn from wells in water jugs and carried on heads. Sheep are still carried on shoulders and the Bedouin women continue to sell their products using stones as weights. Social ways and mannerisms still highlight non-western ways of living, as the following experience illustrates.

Having finished our social tea and coffee at the Wadi Rum police post, we seminar members walked toward the Nabatean temple less than a mile away. Between the police post and the temple stood a Bedouin tent. As we were about to pass this tent, the Bedouin of this simple desert dwelling came out to meet us and invited us to have tea with him. With our western eagerness to complete our visit to Wadi Rum, we politely thanked him and continued. However, he would not let us pass. Standing in front of us, he insisted that we should have tea with him before going on our journey. We were literally forced to oblige and did have tea with him. Stronger than ever before did we begin to understand Abraham's behavior when he insisted that the three strangers passing his tent had to rest and eat a meal in his tent before he would permit them to continue their journey. This adventure characterizes well the wonderful learning experience the seminar members were fortunate to have.

Seminar group in front of the American Schools of Oriental Research, Jerusalem.
(l to r) George Kufeldt, Gustav Jeeninga, Barry Callen, Boyce Blackwelder, Gene Newberry, and Marie Strong.

This Middle East seminar was a great success. The words of Mortimer Wheeler (*Archaeology from the Earth*, 241-242) express well our whole seminar experience and the hope we had for our students once we were home and back in the classrooms of Anderson University:

> I am firmly of the opinion that our young men and women will lose nothing by a little real adventuring, and their search as archaeologists for the footsteps of civilized man in Asian or African tracks will add an incidental stimulus of a kind which is otherwise increasingly hard to find. I am commending firsthand adventure as a necessary medicine to the character of the young, and archaeology of the kind which I have been trailing before the reader is fraught with the right sort of adventure.

# THE TEMPLE OF MEDITATION

As a teenager I watched a movie in which an airplane crash-landed in the Honduran jungle. I was spellbound to see how eleven people would survive the jungle and the Indians, probably descendants of the ancient Mayas.

Today I am interested in knowing about the history, life, and thought of the Mayan Indians who lived in Copán. So, with my friend Jimmy Usher behind the wheel, we left San Pedro Sula in Honduras on May 16, 1996, and drove to Copán. Early the next morning we viewed the ruins of the city, sometimes called "The Athens of the Mayan World." What a fantastic sight! Numerous stelae — free standing, sandstone, carved pillars — show portraits of kings, while hieroglyphic texts give dates and names of rulers, such as "18 Rabbit," A.D. 736. With growing excitement and fascination we walked along the ball court with its six stone-carved heads of the macaw until we stood in amazement before the "Hieroglyphic Stairway" with its sixty-three carved steps and 1250 individual glyph blocks, which scholars say is the longest Mayan inscription in existence, covering some 200 years of Mayan history and listing thirty specific dates between A.D. 700 and 900.

Recently archaeologists have discovered tombs deep inside the pyramids. These tombs hold royal or priestly skeletons and burial gifts of jade, gold, and pottery. Of special meaning to me was Temple 22. This temple illustrates the religious beliefs of the Copán Mayas. The temple builders used cyclopean masonry for the staircase and the temple. The monumental doorway symbolizes the arch of heaven. Two large stone skulls on the floor on each side of the doorway signify death and the all-sustaining earth. On top of the skulls are seated human figures that symbolize life and

Copán, Honduras, 1993. The "Athens" of the Mayan world.

death of both gods and humans. Temple 22 was completed in about A.D. 750. While I stood among these majestic and fantastic ruins of more than 1500 years ago, I realized that the inhabitants of Copán had developed a high culture that is difficult to imagine until one walks among these impressive remains.

Through their art, architecture, and written texts, these Mayas left us to ponder their history and their religious life and thought. Mayan wanderers settled in the Copán Valley around 1800 B.C. At that time Abraham left Ur of the Chaldees, and when the ancient Hebrews lived in slavery in Egypt from about 1600 to 1280 B.C., the Mayas of Copán laid the foundation for a high culture. Then, when under Roman Emperor Constantine (A.D. 350) Christianity became the state religion in the Roman Empire, in faraway Honduras, in the valley of Copán, priestly rulers founded a dynasty of Mayan kings. This dynasty dominated the valley from about A.D. 300 to 900.

On the flight back to the United States I meditated on the fate and meaning of the Copán civilization. When one asks a Honduran Indian, "Where are the Mayas?" he or she will grin and reply, "You are looking at them all around you." When I looked at the Copán ruins, I concluded that the Mayas, like so many other peoples, expressed their religious concepts in monumental architecture, art, and writing. Even now they share with us their search for spiritual answers to life's perennial questions. I found in the ancient monuments of Copán, but especially in the symbols of the "Temple of Meditation," something that links my spirit with the ancient Mayas of Copán.

> "All who have sinned apart from the law will also perish apart from the law, and all who have sinned under the law will be judged by the law. For it is not the hearers of the law who are righteous in God's sight, but the doers of the law who will be justified. When Gentiles, who do not possess the law, do instinctively what the law requires, these, though not having the law, are a law to themselves. They show that what the law requires is written on their hearts, to which their own conscience also bears witness; and their conflicting thoughts will accuse or perhaps excuse them on the day when, according to my gospel, God, through Jesus Christ, will judge the secret thoughts of all."

> *Romans 2:14-16 (NRSV)*

# IT'S A JUNGLE OUT THERE!

COUNTING THE SECONDS between the lightning strike and the next thunderclap, I was listening to the howling wind and the groaning trees outside my attic window. I was nine years old and imagined myself in the depth of a faraway forest. I was dreaming of the day I would be wandering through a true jungle.

The dream of my youth came true on October 11, 1995, when Bob Lowndes and I boarded an American Eagle in Jacksonville, Florida, and started on our eight-day adventure to Belize. After one night at Colton House in Belize City, Bob and I drove to the municipal airport where our six-seater, one-engine plane waited for us on the runway. One hour later we landed at the Gallon Jug (Bowen's farm) landing strip and drove the last five miles by van to Chan Chich Lodge, our final destination. At Chan Chich ("Little Bird" in Mayan) we hoped to birdwatch and study wildlife and archaeology.

Our first full day of activities began at 6:00 a.m. Our native guide was pleased to see that we were dressed to meet the jungle challenge—long pants, proper footwear, hat, and repellent. The first bird for our "bird list" was the melodious blackbird; then we saw the bat-hawk and two species of hummingbirds, all within a few feet of the lodge. The jungle was full with the sounds of birds and insects. But what made these morning walks so memorable was the sudden sound of howler monkeys nearby and far away. The various groups of beasts made known their territorial claims.

Our guide, Gilberto, fifty-five years old, is alert. He first listens for a song, then identifies the bird, and then looks for it. We creep silently behind him. As soon as he has located the bird, he helps us find it through our binoculars. Suddenly Gilberto signals and whispers, "Keel-billed toucans." We focus our binoculars where his finger points. "Yes, I see it," I answered softly. Bob was enthralled as he caught sight of the toucans feeding on fruits fifty feet high up in the trees—a large bird measuring about forty-eight centimeters from the tip of the bill to the end of the tail. The long canoe-shaped, colorful bill is structurally porous and very light in weight and its function is mysterious. Its field marks are a bright yellow cheek and chest and a huge, brightly painted bill (green, blue, red, and orange); the rump is white and parts under the tail are scarlet. Fantastic!

Abruptly, between the higher branches, we get a glimpse of a mother spider monkey moving through the trees, followed by her baby. To our right we hear, "cow, cow, cow." Once again our guide points his finger and following it we see the slaty-tailed trogon, fourteen inches long with green head, red chest and belly, and slaty tail.

Bob and I had discussed the fate of the ivory-billed woodpecker in Florida, now presumed extinct. What a thrill we experienced when we heard the "ka ka ka ka ka kay" of the Belize Pale-billed woodpecker (Guatemalan Ivorybill), and observed two of them hammering into the same tree on opposite sides. This bird, with its fiery red head and cheeks and barred underparts, appears like a flash of fire crisscrossing from tree to tree.

One day our trail crossed some grassland. To my utter amazement a beautiful and healthy-looking buck with a fine rack stood at the edge of the forest and watched us with curiosity. When we came too close, he nimbly walked into the jungle.

On the last day of our birdwatching excursion we were rewarded with a most impressive view of the king vulture, about seventy centimeters. This magnificent bird was perched on a dead branch, providing us with a clear view. Then it flew upward and circled over our heads. What a royal creature with its creamy white back, head, knob and neck bare, bright orange and white underparts, and black flight feathers—a master of the sky and on the ground.

By this time our bird list over six days had climbed to 120 sightings, of which some eighty species were new for both Bob and myself. However, our interest at Chan Chich was also in its archaeological history. The lodge is surrounded by Mayan ceremonial buildings and tombs. Several of these tombs had been plundered. The ruins date to the classic period, about A.D. 250-800. Bob and I investigated several "robber" trenches and studied the now empty tombs.

In contrast to the silent tombs, the jungle is vibrant, alive, and noisy with the songs of melodious blackbirds and the thunder of howling monkeys, while ocelot, the jaguar, the puma, and the fer de lance imperceptibly creep through the bush. This is the world we left behind when we winged low over the green sea of trees looking so peaceful below us. Now we knew by experience that "it's a jungle out there!"

*"O Lord, our Lord*
*How excellent is Your name in all the earth,*
*You who set Your glory above the heavens! . . .*
*When I consider Your heavens, the work of Your fingers. . . .*
*All sheep and oxen—even the beasts of the field,*
*The birds of the air, and the fish of the sea. . . .*
*How excellent is Your name in all the earth."*
*(Psalms 8:1, 3)*

# LACANDÓN INDIANS

MY FRIEND VAL CLEAR AND I drove one afternoon to a small airport outside Villahermosa, Mexico, in the State of Chiapas. At the small airport we arranged to hire a pilot and his three-seater Cessna airplane to fly us from Villahermosa to a landing strip on the Mexican-Guatamalan border callen Yaxchilan. We planned to visit there some Mayan archaeological ruins and make a visit to a small group of Lacandón Indians who lived nearby. We had learned that these Lacandóns belonged to a larger group of Indians totaling about three hundred who were considered to be the remaining direct descendants of the early Mayan tribes.

The next morning at 9:00 a.m. we arrived at the airport and walked toward the plane that was parked on the tarmac. The pilot arrived shortly after, a person barely four feet tall, carrying with him under his right arm three pillows that he used to put on his seat so that he could sit high enough to see out the window!

I climbed on board on the left side of the plane and the pilot slammed the door shut. Then Val climbed on board on the right side and sat next to me while the pilot closed the door. However, that door did not lock. After slamming the door three times, without success, the pilot looked around and found a piece of rope that he used to tie the door closed. While the plane taxied down the runway, rapidly gathering speed, I noticed an old plane wreck near the runway. It looked like some other small plane had nose-dived into the ground at take-off. As we gained momentum I had a close look at yet another plane that had burned out totally. It was lying a short distance from the runway on my left side. I was beginning to feel dubious about leaving the ground at all. Just then our airplane left solid earth and while we climbed rapidly I spotted the

Dr. Jeeninga with Lacandón Indians, on the
border of Mexico and Guatemala, 1974.

broken-up frame of another Cessna airplane lying right below us
at the end of the runway.

Our plane, rather than joining the wrecks, rose and then
swept over the jungle, flying just above the treetops while I listened to the rudder chains rattling loudly below our feet whenever the pilot corrected the flight path. Small holes were visible in
the floor of the plane and it was possible to see the earth passing
below us. It was a beautiful morning and at times a light fog lay
over the lower jungle valleys while we enjoyed looking at the beautiful red, white, and purple flowers of blooming trees that decorated the tree canopy and created a virtual flower garden.

To my surprise, I noted that Val sat rigidly and did not speak
or answer my questions. As I studied his face I realized that it had
turned white. I was worried about his health. Only after we landed did I find out why he had been so quiet, withdrawn, and tense.
I asked him what was going on. Val answered, "Did you not look
at the instruments? Not one of them was functioning!" I therefore

feared that we would not arrive at our destination but would crash in the jungle. I realized the seriousness of what Val told me because I knew that Val had been a licensed pilot years before and knew this type of small airplane.

To my great disappointment, we learned that the Lacandón Indian families whom I had met many years before on my first visit to this tribe had withdrawn into the jungle. According to a local guide, the Lacandóns had become disenchanted and unhappy with the increasing number of tourists that were arriving to see them.

The return flight to Villahermosa was pleasant and smooth, in spite of the lack of functioning instruments. Val appeared to be more relaxed this time. As we landed at Villahermosa, the destroyed airplanes lying along the landing strip did not appear as foreboding as they had been when we departed on this venture.

# LOOKING TO
# THE FUTURE

## 1989 AND BEYOND

# COLLEAGUES WHO CARRY ON

FINISHING A SCHOOL YEAR can cause several different emotions to swell up. First, the academic year has been completed and an exciting summer of relaxation, travel, and new encounters is awaiting. Secondly, when one is looking over the class of students, one gladly says goodbye to a few of them, but feels sadness at having to say goodbye to most of them. They have been so wonderful and eager. Now they are leaving and one might never see them again.

Looking back over forty years, the reality turned out to be quite different than I had expected. Several of my former students came back into my life unexpectedly and marvelously. Let me mention a few of them.

My star student years ago was James Edwards, who is now the President of Anderson University. He earned a very decent grade in my class, Bible 401. A pupil I enjoyed talking with was Spencer Spaulding whom years later I recruited to teach in the Department of Religious Studies. Another bright and eager former student of mine was Fred Burnett, now a scholar in Anderson with excellent credentials in New Testament. Searching for a new instructor in New Testament studies, I chose one other of my former students, Fred Shively, who is now a fine photographer, linguist, and teacher on the Anderson campus. My former student Merle Strege is now chair of the Department of Religious Studies, the role I fulfilled from 1974 to 1983. Barry Callen taught my classes and fulfilled my Museum duties while I was on sabbatical in 1966-67 and later became my valued colleague, special friend, and editor of this book, my autobiography.

For several years prior to my retirement I searched for someone to fill my place as Director and Curator of the Bible Museum.

The likelihood of finding someone to fill the coming vacancy was bleak. I was forced to abandon my search and just hope, trust, and pray. A spark of optimism came my way when a former student of mine, who had majored in Biblical Studies but was then working for the College in a staff position, came to see me. He told me of his interest in the Bible Museum and was volunteering to help and give some of his time and skills if I had any needs. This offer I took seriously and soon David Neidert was involved in the activities of the Museum. Shortly before my retirement I was able to arrange for David to teach my course, "Introduction to Archaeology." Having been a highly motivated and academically successful

Dr. Jeeninga and his successor as Director of the Jeeninga Bible Museum, David Neidert.

student in my archaeology course, I did not doubt that he would succeed. That he did, and supremely well.

After I left my teaching post, David Neidert was appointed by the Dean of the institution to carry on as the new Director and Curator of the Museum. Under his leadership the Museum program and exhibits have greatly improved. Since David accepted this new and challenging assignment he has intensified his skills in museology and the area of archaeology. He has visited the lands of the Bible several times. It is now very clear that reciprocity has proven itself to be a formidable force in fulfilling the dreams of a faculty member and his students. If life has any real meaning and value, I have found it in life-long friendships and collegiality between peers and elders. One such relationship, which was exceptional, was with Dr. Val Clear. This story is detailed elsewhere. Another key relationship is with Joe Allison.

When I opened my mailbox at Anderson College one morning, I removed the usual handful of letters. Most of the mail was of the throw-away sort, but this day's mail had a letter from a former student that soon opened up a new dimension to my professional life, providing an opportunity to broaden my influence on the discipline of biblical studies far and wide. The letter had come from Joe Allison, by then serving as one of the Editorial Advisors of Thomas Nelson Publishers, Nashville, Tennessee. In this letter Joe recalled that he had been one of my students in Bible classes and there had seen many of my slide presentations of the lands of the Bible. He had found the pictures very meaningful and of excellent quality. He now was asking if I could select ten slides from my collection for possible use in a new publication to be titled *The Bible Almanac.*

The request caused me some anxiety at first. I was eager to help my former student in his important task, but how would I choose only ten slides from the thousands I had made during my many journeys through the Middle East? In desperation, I searched and selected about 200 slides, provided each one with careful identification and, where fitting, a related biblical passage. I sent them off and waited nearly two months. When I did not hear from Joe, I feared that my slides had been lost. Finally, a letter arrived with a sincere apology. The photo committee, Joe explained, had found it difficult to choose which slides to keep because nearly all of them were judged to be appropriate and excellent for the intended publication. The letter made a financial offer to buy most of them, an offer that I could not refuse.

Over the next few years two fine volumes were published, one after the other. The first volume was *The Bible Almanac* (1980) in which the first five full-color pages highlight the book. These pages also introduced the Anderson Museum of Bible and Near Eastern Studies by using and identifying several of my photos that show important archaeological objects exhibited in the Museum. The second volume, the *Illustrated Bible Dictionary* (1986), was enriched with a large number of additional photos chosen from my personal collection of slides. What a rewarding experience this was for both of us. Joe Allison and I were fortunate that our paths had crossed first in a Bible class and then later in the world of publishing biblically related literature. We now share the common task of bringing to the church across the world the Bible as seen through colorful photographs illustrating and depicting the world of the sacred Scriptures. In addition, my autobiography (this present book) was printed for Anderson University Press through the facilities of Evangel Publishing House in Nappanee, Indiana, where Joe Allison now is Publishing Manager.

I once was a young scholar and teacher, just finding my way. Now, many years later, a series of special persons whom I helped mentor over the years have become valued colleagues who are competently carrying on. I opened some doors and they are opening others.

# JOINING MR. PENNEY

DURING MY ANDERSON UNIVERSITY retirement dinner in the spring of 1989, President Robert Nicholson, ably assisted by my friend Dr. Val Clear, presented Aletta and me with a large (18"x18"x14") and artistically constructed bird feeder. Our love for backyard bird watching was widely known among our friends and neighbors. The final major honor "Nick" had planned for me came during the closing minutes of Baccalaureate in 1989. He had asked me to give the benediction. Just prior to that moment, he announced publicly that the Bible museum on campus had been renamed and now would be known as the "Gustav Jeeninga Museum of Bible and Near Eastern Studies." With this announcement, my college friend and neighbor Robert Nicholson once more had brightened my horizon and strengthened for me the ongoing significance of this campus museum. It was a good way to begin retirement.

Nearly three years later, Aletta and I finally made the big move away from Anderson, Indiana. Driving south and admiring the hills of the beautiful state of Georgia, Aletta and I were in high spirits. We were finally moving to Penney Farms, Florida. It was April 24, 1992. Traveling at times at elevations of more than 1500 feet above sea level, we enjoyed the gorgeous scenery surrounding us. I was smiling. In my mind I saw myself riding my bicycle back in Holland when I was fifteen years old. I certainly could not have dreamed early in life that one day we would be living in Florida. Certainly such a possibility could not be in the future of this little Dutch boy who at times wore wooden shoes to work. A dream I had never even dreamed now was coming true.

Our plan to move to the Penney Retirement Community

(P.R.C.) had been made some years earlier (about 1985). Our Anderson friends Milton and Eleanor Buettner had moved there and given us glorious reports. We needed to investigate. Was it too costly to move to such a place? What were the requirements for acceptance? How long was the waiting list? Would we pass the physical examination? A good time for us to explore Florida initially would be in the winter months. We knew that it was no longer the slogan "Go west young man, go west," but

The Jeeninga retirement home at Penney Farms, Florida.

now "Go south, old boy, go south!" We first arrived at P.R.C. on December 20, 1986, and visited until January 8, 1987.

Nestled in the tree-rich town of Penney Farms, located southwest of Jacksonville, Florida, we found the place to be a thriving Christian community. The retirees are men and women whose lives of service represent the United States and the world. We soon discovered that our own international outlook and interests harmonized very well with this inclusive Christian establishment. The people were from more than twenty Christian denominations and geographically from around the whole world.

What attracted us especially on our first visit was the beautiful Penney Memorial Church, a "micro-cathedral" as I like to think of it. From the very beginning it has been located in the heart of the campus, having been the first building that Mr. J. C. Penney constructed on the site. The church is non-denominational. Attendance is not required for P.R.C. members. Preaching is done by various members of the community on a rotating basis.

While first visiting on campus, we were invited to tour the various living accommodations. It was evident in the course of our visit that most of the housing units were constructed many years before. Nevertheless, they were quite attractive. Built in classic French-Norman architecture, Penney Farms looked to us somewhat like a European village of the past. We fell in love with the town and planned to move there after retirement. Before we left P.R.C. on that first visit to drive back to Anderson, Indiana, we had requested that our names be placed on the five-to-ten-year waiting list. We received notice of acceptance on February 2, 1987. Then the waiting began for an actual vacancy.

In 1991 we returned to P.R.C. for a second visit. It would be a good time to get to know life on the campus and to become familiar with the surrounding country. More significantly, we wanted to get a date for our possible move. We were anxious to move and were troubled by the long waiting list. We called ahead and made an appointment with Dr. Noel White, the administrator. He was waiting for us in his office. I explained to him that we were ready to move to P.R.C. anytime that there was an opening. He said that the waiting list was no longer a problem—good news!

The moment had come for me to ask about the status of four new houses that we had seen being built on campus along Studio Road. We wondered if one of those might be available to us. Dr. White explained that those houses were being built by individual future members of P.R.C. I remarked that we had walked through them, liked the layout, and added that we had not known that it was possible to have a house built. We were saddened to learn that there was limited space on campus for putting up new houses. I made clear that Aletta and I would be very interested in building a new house. Was there not just a little piece of land left somewhere for constructing a cute little house for two people?

A fleeting twitch appeared on the administrator's face as he made clear to us that such a possible site might exist. He rose from behind his office desk and we walked across the campus to see the three apartments now available. We viewed the three cottages thoroughly. After we had completed the round, Noel (as we later called him) led the way towards his office. I remarked that we would be most pleased if he could show us the not-yet-visited plot for building a cute little house. I noticed an interesting reaction in his demeanor. He had a big smile and indicated that we should follow him. He then walked us to the southeastern end of the campus on Studio Road. When we arrived there we saw three old and rusted garages. There was also a neglected shuffleboard pavilion sur-rounded by a somewhat over-grown field of weeds. After cleaning up this plot, Noel elaborated, it would be possi-ble to construct a house for us.

Gus and Aletta Jeeninga,
June 1992.

I glanced at Aletta, knowing her feelings about living in a cottage apartment. I had feared we would never come to P.R.C. When our eyes met, I noticed a gleam of excite-ment in her eyes. A feeling of hope filled my heart. My adrenalin was flowing wild. I felt as though a great burden had fallen from my shoulders. We had found the answer to our quest. Aletta would grab this opportunity with a passion. Moving to P.R.C. was now a "done deal." The Dutch proverb "better have one bird in the hand than five in the sky" fit our condition perfectly. Back in his office, Noel suggested that we plan to build a duplex instead of a single house. He thought that the lot was too large for a sin-gle dwelling. A duplex would be more appropriate use of the land. Aletta and I agreed. We made our downpayment for the con-struction of our new house at P.R.C.

In 1992, on April 20, we sold our house in Anderson and left for Penney Farms that same day. On April 24 we moved into our new home and with that move we started a new life. We had become members of a very special retirement community. Never did we feel like strangers after we arrived at P.R.C. There were ten people present on campus with close connections to Anderson University where I had taught for 29 years, and to the Church of God, to which Aletta and I belonged. The other half of our duplex was occupied by Margaret Smith, widow of my Anderson colleague Dr. John W. V. Smith. Very close by on the campus lives my own sister, Trudee Puetter. Also helpful was the philosophy and practice of volunteerism which has characterized the fabric of this community since its beginning. This opens doors for new friendships in a sharing

Gus Jeeninga (right) with his good friend Bob Lowndes, 2001.

environment. Especially important to me was meeting Rev. Robert (Bob) Lowndes, a retired Baptist minister who became a close friend and traveling companion. We would cruise together often on the Holland American Cruise Line.

Once a week Aletta and I volunteered four hours of work at Beyer House, an assisted living facility located on campus. In addition, Aletta assisted patients in the Nursing Home. I drove people to shopping centers where they could buy needed personal supplies. I also volunteered to repair small electrical appliances to be sold in the weekly campus re-sale program. Being an amateur bird watcher, I was interested in the considerable bird population at Penney Farms. Because of particular concern for the Western Bluebird, which was seldom seen on campus, I built several Bluebird boxes that soon were occupied around campus year after year. With the help of friends, six Purple Martin poles with nesting boxes and gourds were also placed in various sites on campus. A favorite "bird" of the people at P.R.C. are the ducks that make their home in Carroll Pond. These ducks entertain us daily and have a good life because many ladies and a few gentlemen love to feed them. These generous friends of the ducks have also brought great prosperity to the pond's catfish—some of them growing to nearly whale size (almost).

Nearly every day when I walk or ride my bicycle across this French Norman village, I feel a thrill. I am so thankful to be able to live on this "Estate" (as I call it). This truly is a fine place to retire for those who love a small town, appreciate spaciousness, love nature, and above all enjoy the fellowship and camaraderie of world-minded Christian people. It was here that both joy and sadness came.

When Aletta and I learned of her terminal illness, we soon discovered in new ways the quality and character of the members of the P.R.C. community. Leaving the hospital after consultations in early December, 1999, Aletta's doctor told me sensitively, "This will be your last Christmas together." During the next months Aletta and I were overwhelmed by the generosity and concern of our friends on the Penney Farms campus. Beautiful and meaningful cards began to arrive. Plants, flowers, and delicious food were among the expressions of love and concern that lifted our hearts. There also were many visits and supporting prayers. Aletta and I privately shared the sadness and also the many pleasant moments as we spoke of the highlights of our many years together.

We were so fortunate that, with the professional help of the Hospice, Aletta could be home for many months. Finally, the time arrived for me to admit her to the P.R.C. Clinic. Here she received the best of care during her last two weeks with us. Aletta, my wonderful companion, passed away quietly on November 10, 2000, at 11:00 p.m. One mile outside of the town of Penney Farms lies the P. R. C. cemetery. Here, surrounded by relatives and many friends from the Penney Retirement Community, Aletta's remains were committed to the earth. I then watched the people drifting away and the cars leaving. A painful quietness came over me. Aletta was now gone, but, as I turned to leave, I knew that she would be in my heart and soul for a long time to come.

# HELPING AT LEAST ONE

WATCHING INTENTLY, I STUDIED STARFISH clinging against the basalt rocks just below the waterline. I was twelve years old and loved the North Sea and its marine life. A short time later I meandered along the sandy beach and saw hundreds of starfish washed ashore, drying up in the blasting sun and dying quickly. At that time I could not imagine that an episode involving starfish might help me some day to understand that my visits to Honduras have been significant.

My retirement years came to involve serving as well as sorrowing. My most recent visit to Honduras was in May, 1996. I had again joined the medical team of Dr. Larry Lilly, the organizer and leader. Three

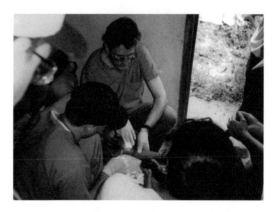

Dr. Larry Lilly, medical team organizer for the needy in Honduras.

other physicians, Drs. Jerry Girarchi, Mike Gittens, and Jennefer White, and fourteen nurses served the team, and I was one of the six translators. Our summer schedule called for setting up clinics in three mountain villages. The first clinic was a two-day affair in the village of Chaguitillo.

Soon after we arrived in Chaguitillo we organized the clinic in a local church. The villagers from near and far were arriving and lining up. I stood a short distance away, observing the people congregating in front of the "clinic" in great numbers. I felt sad and worried, asking myself, "How can we serve all these people? There are too many; why even try?" My monologue came to an abrupt end when Dr. Lilly called for my assistance. Soon I was absorbed in translating for him. First there was a mother with four small children; all had parasites. Then came a farmer who worried about losing his eyesight. Next a mother sat down and complained about head and back pain. She was

Alexander, a local Honduran boy.

followed by a concerned young mother who lacked milk for her baby boy. Especially worrisome was an infected wound on top of the head of a fourteen-year-old girl. Two doctors, assisted by some nurses, operated and cleaned out the festering sore.

During the two days at Chaguitillo the most serious problem we had was the diseased right hand of Alexander, a local boy fifteen years old. His hand was seriously infected, and without immediate help Alexander might have lost one or more fingers or even the hand. Alexander and his father agreed to have the operation right away. Lying on a church bench, Alexander bravely let the doctors and nurses cut into his hand. While many of us watched and prayed for Alexander and the medical team, the operation succeeded. It was then agreed that Alexander would go with us to the team's headquarters for several days so that the physicians could watch the healing process and daily dress Alexander's hand.

After Chaguitillo we held clinics in two other villages. The crowds of people lining up to get into the clinic burdened our hearts. Each day we had to close the door to more patients because there was no more time that day. After four days we had seen some 1200 patients. I was tired and my soul was heavy because we did not help all the people that had come to us in real need. Did we fail in our mission? I asked myself this over and over.

Sitting on the bumper of one of our trucks, I thought of a story I had heard recently. This story provided an answer as to why the Honduran missions had not been in vain. One day a man was walking along the beach. In the distance he saw a man bending down, picking up something, and throwing it into the ocean. After a while the two men met. "What are you picking up and throwing into the sea?" the first man asked. Answered the other, "I pick up starfish that have been washed ashore and I throw them back into the water."

The first man retorted, "What is the use of doing that? Look behind you and in front of you; there are hundreds of starfish. You will not be able to help all of them or do them any good."

Then the second man replied as he bent down again and picked up another starfish and threw it into the sea: "But for that one I did some good!"

When I saw Alexander sitting on some steps, I photographed him, and soon afterwards Matthew 25:36 came to my mind: "I was sick and you visited me. . . ." I rejoiced and said to myself, "but for this one we did some good!"

"I was hungry and you gave me food. . . .
I was naked and you clothed me;
I was sick and you visited me. . . ."
(Matthew 25:35-36)

# AT HOME
# IN SACRED SPACE

ON SEPTEMBER 3, 2001, I flew to the Netherlands to visit relatives and friends. Having nearly finished writing this book, the trip was to be a sentimental journey. I could never have foreseen that this pilgrimage would dovetail with a most dramatic and historic event on the world scene.

On September 11, I was standing, trying to balance myself in an overcrowded train traveling through Rotterdam. A well-dressed gentleman was standing close to me. There was a soft sound of a telephone ringing somewhere nearby. The passenger next to me pulled out his cell phone and discretely carried on a troubled conversation. When he finished he calmly said aloud in Dutch and to no one in particular, "A large Boeing passenger airliner just crashed into one of the World Trade Center Towers in New York City."

There was complete silence in the train. Questioning faces stared at each other. Then someone asked, "How do you know that?" The gentleman replied, "My brother, who is a newsman, just called me on this phone and told me. The event happened just a few minutes ago."

Within seconds my tranquil and highly personal journey had come to an end. In the next few days I listened as President George Bush announced that the United States was at war. KLM announced that in two days all of its passenger planes around the world would be grounded. The stock market was tumbling down, and so did the world around me. The scope of this sinister terrorist attack unfolded slowly over the following days.

Because of the worldwide fears set in motion by this vicious attack on the U.S.A. and its people, my life was drastically affected. I began to plan an immediate return to the States. My visit to Holland was cut short and with it my plans for visiting other friends in Europe. Life chooses its own itinerary and we must constantly revise ours to fit it. My flight back home to Florida left on September 25. During the long hours in the air I reviewed my curtailed journey and concluded that, despite the tragedy, this trip had been a great success. Old friendships had been revitalized and new friendships born. My life was greatly enriched.

St. Bavo Cathedral,
Haarlem, Holland.

Of all the places I had revisited in Holland, my return to the St. Bavo Cathedral in Haarlem, Aletta's hometown, proved to be the Everest experience. It was a deeply emotional and spiritual event. The recalling of the extraordinary moments I spent in that holy precinct will be my final story in this account of my *Doors To Life*.

Wednesday, September 9, at about eleven o'clock in the morning, I entered the great St. Bavo Cathedral in Haarlem, The Netherlands. The oldest reference to St. Bavo (De Grote of St. Bavokerk) comes from a letter written in 1313 by Archbishop Raymandus. The world-famous Christian Muller organ in the Cathedral was built in the years 1735 to 1738. Among the famous organists who have performed on this organ are Georg Friedrich Handel, in 1740 and again in 1750, and Wolfgang Amadeus Mozart who played this organ in 1766 when he was only ten years old.

When I entered this sacred place of worship, the Cathedral was nearly empty. Three persons sauntered ahead of me through the center aisle. I paused half-way down the nave and stopped a short distance from the elevated pulpit. The three other visitors had disappeared behind a pillar. I was now totally alone in what appeared to me to be a sacred grove. The pillars looked like trees whose branches upheld the canopy, the Gothic ceiling. I sensed that I was in the presence of the Eternal. My eyes searched the chairs, all neatly arranged. Soon I located the very chairs where, in 1975, Aletta, her sister Noor, and Noor's husband Hans and I had sat while attending a Christmas Midnight Service. Now all three, Noor, Hans, and Aletta had departed this life. There now was only me.

Slowly I sat down on one of the chairs where we had sat those many years ago. I carefully viewed the details of the celebrated organ. The ornate decorations were the masterwork of Hendrik de Werff and the sculptures of the glorious pipe organ were by Jan van Logteren. Suddenly and unexpectedly, the splendid organ came to life. Solemn and harmonious sacred music filled the arches, and I was deeply stirred. I thought back over the years and remembered. Aletta had lived only four blocks from this Cathedral. On several occasions we had visited this historic church together. Opposite from St. Bavo, Aletta and I had said our wedding vows in the Haarlem City Hall. How painful it was to now be here alone. But how enriching were the wonderful memories that filled my heart, memories of the years we had enjoyed being together.

As the last notes from the mighty organ began to fade, I relaxed. I was now surrounded by tranquility. I was at home in sacred space. I thought of the words of Henry Wadsworth Longfellow from his first sonnet to the *Divine Comedy*. They perfectly described my sentiment in those final moments in God's special house.

> Oft have I seen at some cathedral door
> A laborer, pausing in the dust and heat,
> Lay down his burden, and with reverent feet
> Enter, and cross himself, and on the floor
> Kneel to repeat his paternoster o'er;

Far off the noises of the world retreat;
The loud vociferations of the street
Become an undistinguishable roar.
So, as I enter here from day to day,
And leave my burden at this minster gate,
Kneeling in prayer, and not ashamed to pray,
The tumult of the time disconsolate
To inarticulate murmurs dies away,
While the eternal ages watch and wait.

# INDEX OF PERSONS